BUSH PILOTS DO IT IN FOURS

By

Roy Watson

An autobiography of Roy Watson's flying experiences from his first interest in flying, through his involvement with Tiger Moth, Aeronca, Zlin, Stinson, and Russian aircraft, to his bush experiences flying DC4's and the Boeing 707.

Published 2006 by arima publishing

www.arimapublishing.com

ISBN 1 84549 095 9

© Roy Watson 2006

All rights reserved

This book is copyright. Subject to statutory exception and to provisions of relevant collective licensing agreements, no part of this publication may be reproduced, stored in a retrieval system, or transmitted in any form or by any means, without the prior written permission of
the author.

Printed and bound in the United Kingdom

Typeset in Garamond 11/16

This book is sold subject to the conditions that it shall not, by way of trade or otherwise, be lent, re-sold, hired out, or otherwise circulated without the publisher's prior consent in any form of binding or cover other than that which it is published and without a similar condition including this condition being imposed on the subsequent purchaser.

arima publishing
ASK House, Northgate Avenue
Bury St Edmunds, Suffolk IP32 6BB
t: (+44) 01284 700321

www.arimapublishing.com

This book is dedicated to my wife Jane, and my two wonderful sons Courtney and Patrick, as well as to my brother Tony and the memory of our parents, who were instrumental in my progress all those years ago.

I would also like to mention all the other people who influenced the path of my life. I am sure that they will see themselves in the story even if not individually named. They will know the parts they played. I thank you all.

Introduction

This book is an account of my exploits in the skies of Africa, and the hours of working on the aircraft in an ongoing attempt to break the bond of gravity. I hope that you will find it good, light reading. I have avoided technical descriptions and tried to narrate my flying life in a manner suitable to non-technical readers.

I hope that the reading brings you as much joy as the writing brought me. The book was stimulated by the reply to a letter that I wrote to a good friend Stephen Spencer recounting my first trip up Africa in the DC4. He wrote back to say how much he enjoyed reading the letter and suggested that I write a book. Unfortunately I did not keep my letter, but he had planted a fertile seed.

I started to jot down my thoughts and recollections, never having any thought of a book, and soon I was getting an enormous joy out of writing. As we all know, joy and happiness comes largely out of happy memories, and also from making plans for the future. As I wrote, recollections came back, and the details became clearer. The joy that all the memories brought was wonderfully warming, and in a year I had pages of script all around me.

I had no idea why I was doing it, except that it gave me such a high that I carried on writing. The concept that Steve had planted took root and grew and soon I was planning on how to turn it all into a book, and after some years here it is.

Chapter 1

All little boys (and sometimes even little girls) seem to grow up in similar ways. Because they crawl around on all fours, pushing their little toy cars, trucks and other vehicles around, their first aspiration is to drive a fire truck, bulldozer or something similar to their toy vehicles. As they are able to stand up and walk instead of crawling, their toys progress from push toys to those that they can play with while standing. As they make 'brrm – brrm' noises and propel them around, they start to relate to the huge space of air above them. They gain another axis in their world, which is then fully three-dimensional. With this new awareness, they become aware of birds, aircraft and other objects flying around in the sky. Their toys change to aircraft, and that is when a special transformation takes place in a few of us.

A quest to conquer the world above becomes an absorbing thread in the life of those people undergoing this change. They get involved in an age-old quest and compare the ease of flight of the birds with that of man-made machines. The huge chasm that exists between the two seems to be the fuel that keeps the interest going. At this early stage, a phase of their development starts that will be an ever absorbing quest for flight, particularly if they have a mechanical aptitude. It creates a special bonding among the group, something that will remain a mystery to the outsiders until the end of time. Some will end up flying for a living, others will fly for recreation and yet another section will end up in aircraft design, manufacture or similar vocations. Seldom is the special thread of flight destroyed, it invariably calls the need for a flying interest and keeps the person in the flying world.

I cast my mind back to my own childhood and remember the way that there was always an underlying flying interest, even though I did not come from a flying family. I grew up in the days when Superman was introduced as a comic character, and it obviously had quite an impact on me. I clearly remember having lifelike dreams of flying and waking up with a strong feeling that I had really been transformed from Clark Kent into a body, which, with the gentlest of ease, could sail off balconies and swoop above the mere mortals below. Fortunately the realism was contained within my dreams and it was probably a good thing that I was never tempted to put my feelings to the test.

I grew up in a very unusual family. My father's hobby centred around racing and the restoration of vintage and veteran vehicles. He was a founder member of both the pre-war Junior Car Club and the Sports Car Club. My recollections, as far back as I can go, are that of spending time at local racetracks where Dad was the chief scrutineer. I was always with him while he was checking all the cars entered, for oil leaks, safety, and their overall condition. One track where I spent much of my early childhood was Palmietfontein, just outside the city of Johannesburg.

It had been the first international airport and when it closed down it was used as a racetrack with cars speeding up and down the two runways separated only by straw bales. Each runway had cars tearing along to the sharp hairpin just to return on the other side of the straw bales to the runway intersection. A quick, almost right angle turn then sent them outwards along the other runway turn around its hairpin to return to the intersection again. This time a section of interesting track took them back to the first runway. I can clearly remember sitting in Peter Whitehead's single-seat Ferrari when he was out from the UK for a race. My other memories are of the Bugatti with a Ford V8 engine that I was later to acquire, a host of Bentleys, Talbots, TR2's and also the locally built Protea sports car. The Bentleys used to dwarf many of the other cars as they thundered past each other often in opposite directions separated only by the straw bales.

My mechanical interest started young

If we were not at the track or at home fixing cars we were most likely involved in old car motoring activities, visiting one of our many friends in the middle of a rebuild project, or off on a wild goose chase for some vehicle or other. As a result a love of machinery and "old things" generally became part of me and a focal point of my interests.

Tools, dismantling and re-assembling were all around me both in the house, where all the handyman jobs got done, and in the garage where the true repair work abounded. Components that most people would discard were lovingly transformed back to their original condition and given a new lease of life. I guess that this exposure was what really got me this mechanical bent.

I was about 10 when my brother and I had our bicycles stolen, much to the family's dismay. The insurance paid out and Dad asked what I wanted to do with the money. "I don't know, just keep it, until I find something" was my reply. That day soon came around when I found an Austin 7 for sale for thirty Rand and I presented the advert to Dad with glee. This was to be a turning point in my life as at that moment my destiny of being umbilically tied to machinery was sealed.

We went to see it and by the time we got there the owner had broken a half shaft in the back axle and it could no longer be driven. With apologies he said that he would take only 15 Rand for it. With great aplomb the car was towed home, and I began my first full rebuild, scarcely even a teenager.

A year or so later, with much support from the most loving father in the world, saw a chassis with a home-made seat ready to be test run. I waited for Dad to give it a go once I had started the engine, but he stood back. "You rebuilt her, you hop on and try her out," he announced. Rather surprised at his confidence in me, I got on to the familiar seat that I had made, and drove around the garden. Through the rebuild I learned how it all works and so it seemed natural to put all my theory to practice. It was only years later, having seen how so many people battle, that I realised how different I had been having the knowledge behind me.

In chassis form I used to drive around the garden, possibly a touch too fast. I had a route (dare I call it a circuit?) around the house, one section going between the house and a large, well-established part of Mum's foliage. On one occasion I came driving (tearing?) around the house on my penultimate lap when, to my horror, I saw that one of her friends had parked her car in the gap since my previous lap. I tried to brake but I was already in the middle of the wide, sliding turn on the gravel and so stopping was impossible, all I could do was avoid the impact. I just managed to get the bodiless car under control and to squeeze through the gap under full opposite lock with my left tyre running the full length of her car's body. When it stopped I sheepishly got off and looked at the damage. Fortunately there was no more than a long black line of rubber and I was able to remove it with a bit of polish. When done, neither Mum nor her friend were any the wiser.

Now able to drive, but not permitted on the open road, I took part in a number of Veteran and Vintage Club events such as driving tests and gymkhanas held on the private club grounds of the club. Even when my little Austin was finished I was not old enough for a licence so a good friend of mine, Rocky, used to drive her in rallies. He was to become part of my flying career as well and was to spend many hours in the air with me. The time we spent together forged a mechanical love in his bones and had an effect on his career as well. Ironically my first drive on a public road was during a promotion for "Those Magnificent Men and their Flying Machines".

The club had been approached to provide some Veteran cars for a promotional parade at the film premiere. I was a passenger with Mum in the 1911 Fiat, with Dad in another car. We joined all the other cars at the designated place and put the banners on our cars as instructed. We duly set off on the parade in twilight conditions. I remember that Dad was on gas and paraffin lights in the Ford Model 'T' and I had got the electric lights working on the Fiat in preparation for the event. In the city, among all the pedestrians, traffic lights and the general traffic, Mum was battling with the clutch and the heavier the traffic became the more flustered she got. I tried to help and encourage her but things got steadily worse. In the end I offered to drive and she accepted it with joy, as wrong as it was. I slipped in to the driver's seat and was soon cruising past traffic officers directing us towards the cinema.

After the parade, we parked in the places reserved for us, got out of our cars, assembled our group and went in to the cinema. We thoroughly enjoyed the film and needless to say I continued the drive home. That was my one and only 'illegal' drive even though borne of necessity and I still have the banner that was on the car as a memento!!! The film, however, merely added fuel to the aviation fire that was already burning.

I used to look through a few of Dad's old books, with pictures and articles about aeroplanes in them, and wondered what it was like to fly. I in fact even sent off for a brochure on a home built aircraft that seemed to be within my capability to build. The Headwind was a high wing, parasol aircraft, using a

Volkswagen motor mounted on a strange triangular fuselage, and the reply came back saying that it was unwise at the 5000 odd feet altitude where we live.

A number of family friends had either flown during the war, or were currently involved in it, and often the talk got around to flying. Dad was running the family shipping business and because of the national importance of shipping, he could not join the forces but was part of the Home Guard. He had always had an interest in flying and, even though unable to pursue it, he got to know many friends who had flown during the War. I often listened in awe to flying stories but even though I had never even seen a light aircraft up close, the bug was biting hard and soon the effects were evident. In my penultimate year at school an advert for an air display at Rand Airport caught my eye. Rushing to Dad, with the advert clutched to my soul, I used all my persuasion to get him to take us to the show as a family. As was always the case with him it was easy, the hard part was waiting for the day. I guess that schoolwork probably suffered a bit in the interim!

The day arrived and once we had parked and began walking towards the display line, the vibrant atmosphere grabbed me. The most amazing array of aircraft met my eye.

I cannot specifically remember too many types as I did not have the knowledge to recognise them, but I could not get enough of the Tiger Moths. I will never forget the sight of the silver birds, in a line, waddling out to the runway to take off. As soon as they had picked up some speed they were transformed into the most beautiful thing that I had ever seen. Their grace and beauty, as they drew perfect lines in the sky in a strange type of slow motion, put them aside from all the other machines that lacked their finesse and style.

There was a flypast of De Havilland (DH) aircraft, mainly biplanes. The other two DH types that interested me were the Fox Moth and the Hornet Moth. As they flew past I was amazed that I could see through the middle of the fuselage of the Fox Moth and it was only when I saw it on the ground that I realised why. A single pilot sat exposed above his four passengers, looking at them through a window between his legs, an unusual setup indeed. Even stranger, the four passengers sit facing each other with their knees interlaced. The overall effect is a creature that looks like a Tiger Moth with a rather distended pregnant belly with windows on the sides. The Hornet by comparison, is a rather more conventional, pretty, side-by-side, two-seater cabin biplane.

Once they had landed, we moved towards their parking area and watched them shutting down. I was amazed to look at the seemingly fragile craft, covered with fabric, reminding me so much of the balsa wood and tissue paper models that we all made in the years already gone by. Even the aileron hinges appeared to be strips of fabric. It was a source of wonder as the mechanical side of me shouted at the mere thought of only a cloth hinge. It was later that the real truth revealed that the fabric was only a seal preventing airflow through the gap between the aileron and wing, and hidden from view were good sturdy metal hinges.

An enormous desire to fly one of these delicate creations was born with only one cure, to learn to fly and try to get hold of one. I watched the array of craft from the small, agile aerobatic types to the large transport and passenger machines with a rising desire. But as much as I enjoyed the rest of the other aircraft, the Tiger was IT!!

Chapter 2

The next phase of my flying career came about as a result of an association with an American Field Scholar exchange student that was at school with me. He had been having problems with his surrogate family and the position was not very happy. Unless another family stepped in to assist and foster him, he would have to return home halfway through his year

Being in my class I felt terribly sorry for him, and so I asked my parents if we could adopt him for the remaining part of the year. This they agreed to do and so my younger brother Tony and I had a 'new' brother. While he was with us, we had many discussions about Soweto (South West Township) and they were talking about seeing some of it. I was telling him and his girlfriend about the schools, stadiums and parks that were there, when I had a brilliant idea. All the information was gathered second hand, as I had not had any first hand experience of the area. Because I was also interested, I suggested that rather than seeing a small part from the ground we could see it all from the air! The idea was an immediate hit and Dad set about contacting a long-standing family friend, Nick Turvey an instructor, and it was arranged.

On the appointed day we all arrived at Baragwanath Airfield. Bearing in mind that I had not seen a small airfield other than Rand at the air show, it was another new experience and I felt in my element as we walked up to the training school with the aircraft parked out on the apron. The atmosphere driving up to the flight school and inside the school was captivating. The aircraft that Dad had organized was a four-seater, and so there was a seat for me, as well as the two Americans. Other than one airline flight to Durban as a child, I had never been in an aircraft and the prospect was awesome. We walked out to a low-wing aircraft that we were told was a Piper Cherokee. I did not even know how to get into an aircraft. Nick showed us how to climb onto the wing and open the door. Thomas, the exchange student, and his girlfriend climbed into the back seat and Nick got into the left seat. He told me to get in next to him and close the door. I stepped down into the craft and settled into the seat and pulled the door shut. He leaned over me and showed me how the double latch at the top of the door worked. I looked with amazement at the array of instruments, and was particularly surprised at the duplicate set of controls in front of me.

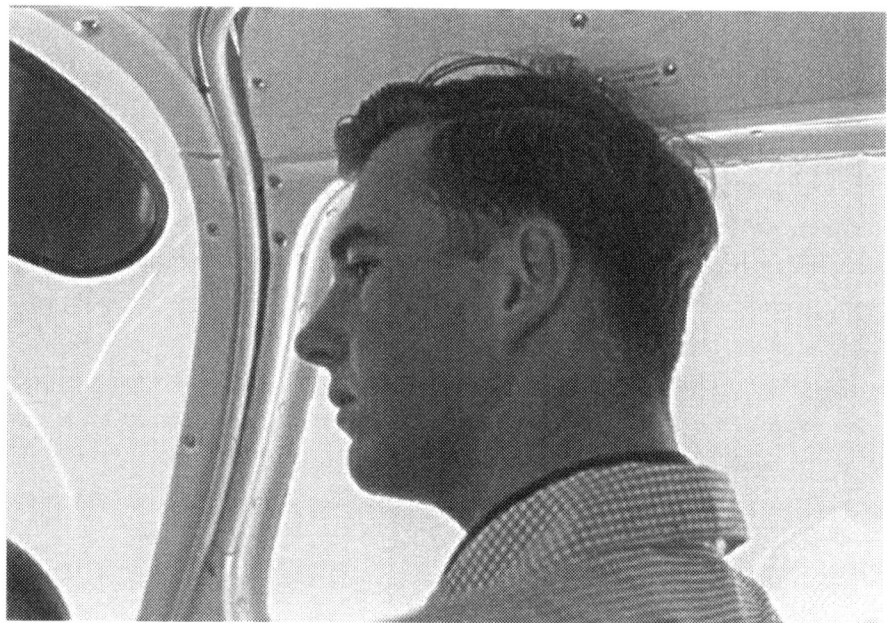
My first flight with Nick

We all strapped in as instructed, and Nick started the engine. He explained the basic controls to me and told me to put my hands lightly on them to feel how he taxied. I did so and was soon taxiing on my own. He explained how I must break the urge to try to 'steer' with my hands, and to steer only with my feet on the rudder pedals.

It brought me back to the time I read about aircraft controls in Dad's old book 'Dykes Aircraft Engine Instructor' that had a section on the theory of flight. I used to climb into the big tree in our backyard, get myself comfortable and sit reading technical books for hours. The information that had been carefully filed away in my brain now came alive.

As we taxied down to the end of the runway, Nick explained how to take off into wind, how the circuit was arranged and a few other basics. He carried out his checks, tested the engine and we taxied onto the runway. To my complete amazement he told me to continue holding the controls and he would talk me through the take-off and only assume control if it became necessary. He opened up the throttle and we accelerated down the runway. At the correct moment he told me to pull back the control column and I heaved back for all I was worth. My youthful glee at the prospect of leaping into the air did just that and with lightening reaction Nick pushed the stick forwards to save the day. Calmly, and with a degree of understatement, he explained that such drastic movements would leave us all in a pile of bits on the runway. I had no idea how gentle a pilot's movements must be. In fact it was a valuable lesson in how an aircraft must always be handled with care and respect.

Nick told me to carry on and we climbed out, with me again holding the controls, and I began to understand, for the first time, what an aircraft felt like. The freedom, flying like a bird, was the most amazing feeling. We just lifted into the air and the earth slowly fell away from us. My whole being was so absorbed that at that moment I did not remember that we were there to show the visitors behind me what the great Soweto looked like. Fortunately Nick had his head screwed on and he guided me over two huge cooling towers at a power station and on to the enormous area covered by the small houses all nestled together. I was amazed at the vast expanse of the township, and as we flew we picked out some schools, parks, sports fields and a huge stadium. As we circled over the stadium it seemed like we had only just begun when Nick said that it was time to head back to Baragwanath Airfield. I was enjoying the magic of flight so much that time had taken on a different dimension.

My attention was rapidly brought back to reality when Nick asked me to point out the direction of the airfield. I was suddenly aware that I had no idea where it was. I looked around us. In the distance was the great concrete jungle of Johannesburg. From this vantage point the huge buildings came alive, no longer merging into each other as they seemed to do viewed from street level. Each building stood proudly, reaching up to the very sky that, at that moment, was supporting us. To our left was an array of mine dumps contrasting sharply against the hills in the distance. The golden irregularity of the man-made dumps stood out against the rolling picturesque green hills.

Between the city and us, trying to conceal itself, nestled the airfield. I discovered for the first time how different they look from aloft. The features that seem so dominant from below are lost from above where they take on a different character. Nick continued his earlier explanation of what the circuit looked like and where to go to join correctly. I continued flying until we saw the runway stretching out before us. Much to my surprise he told me to continue flying as he talked me down. As he instructed, I eased back on the stick and we settled onto the tarmac, only then realising that I had been holding the controls during my very first landing in an aircraft.

We taxied up to the apron and switched off. I alighted from the aircraft with the most enormous sense of pride and joy. I felt as if my chest was puffed up like some giant bird in all its glory. My passengers at this stage were far from the front of my mind, but I was rewarded by comments of appreciation as they got out. We headed back to the flight school, two of us having enjoyed the aerial unfolding of the township experience for them, and the other one having had a new world open up for him. I was still floating on air, and I'm sure the instructor knew the effect he had had on all of us. Walking along the row of parked aircraft there was a feeling of being in another world, the new world of aerial recreation and air transport.

The trip home was lost as I was still in this new heaven that I had been introduced to. The gratitude that I owed Dad was enormous and I'm sure that it was plain for all to see. That day lived on with me for a long time, and was the architect of my future destiny. I was even more determined to pursue my career in mechanical engineering with some sort of flying flavour added in.

Chapter 3

By this stage the flying bug had really taken a firm hold on me. I used to look for any flying articles amongst the interesting bits and pieces in Dad's library. Invariably many references were to old aircraft, and that really inspired me.

My family's circle of friends included a few people who were either actively involved in flying, or who had flown during the Second World War. My interest in the cars seemed to close the age gap between them and myself, and while there was still the respect that age demanded, the common interest created a new friendship with them. Flying was always a keen topic with these friends, and in fact with anyone who would lend an ear.

One particularly influential person in this regard was Tom Zeederberg. Dad had known him for many years and it transpired that both families spent July vacations in the same coastal town, Scottburgh. Each day the two families would meet on the beach. Tom was always keen to tell stories of his flying past, and so he and I used to spend many days together walking on the beach and chatting about flying. Dad was not keen on swimming or getting his feet wet, and so Tom and I used to go and investigate the many rock pools while we chatted flying. He talked about his years in the Air Force and his later years in civilian flying. The one that I will always remember is of him landing on top of another aircraft and getting a huge gash on his forehead as a result of being flung into the propeller. His stories always stayed with me, and so when I saw an application for the Pupil Pilot Training Scheme, I felt that it was made for me and I spoke to him about it.

I took his advice and hurriedly applied. My application was accepted and in due course I was asked to present myself before the selection board, which I duly did. The interview went off really well and they said that I would be required to undergo a further medical with the military. By this stage I was as eager as could be, but my joy was soon to be shattered. I was horrified to see in the press that the whole scheme had been indefinitely shelved. I had got so far down the line creating visions and dreams, and to have them instantly shattered was drastic. So near and yet so far!

It must have been around the same time that I got involved with Nick again. He had moved from Baragwanath to Rand Airport and was busy setting up a flying school there. He had not yet established an infrastructure and all he had was a brand new Piper Colt that was going to be the basic training aircraft to start the school.

Dad, as always, was the most perfect father that anyone could ever wish for. He had obviously realised my huge disappointment at the scrapping of the Pupil Pilot Scheme and had organised for me to start training with Nick on Saturday mornings. He, like most people in those days, used to work on Saturday mornings, and his plan was that someone from the office would drop me off and he would collect me after work. It was quite convenient as Sipho, his driver, used to go out to Jan Smuts Airport and would drop me on the way.

As mentioned earlier, Nick had not yet established any infrastructure, so I used to meet him at Pop's Café in the terminal building after his Harvard flying each Saturday. It was rather a sore point as the Harvard Squadron at Rand was the last remnants of the Pupil Pilots Scheme that I so closely missed. I was his only student when he started and so we used do the pre-flight briefing over a coke or coffee in the restaurant.

My training in the Colt, ZS-DUM, cost a mere R4-50 per hour including the instructor, which by today's standards sounds a joke. One must however, remember the relative buying power of the Rand. Those were the days when a gallon (4.5 litres) of fuel cost a mere 32 cents. To put it into context, a few years later my first job as an engineer earned me R400-00 per month! Sometime later, once the school was going strong, a second aircraft, a Piper Cherokee was proudly added to double the fleet. The school had grown and there was a proper, staffed office. They could not believe it when I turned the Cherokee down, and they tried to persuade me to use it at an extra Rand per hour. I was not interested in the extra features as after all, what I was after was to fly a Tiger Moth, and the Colt with its limited panel was closer to my type of flying.

The Colt to me was a dear machine. She had the simplest of cockpit layouts, without any turn and bank indicator, radio or navigation aids. Only basic engine instruments, R. P. M. indicator, airspeed indicator and compass were fitted. It was a great way to get a 'Seat of the pants' basis for my flying, not having any slip indication.

Near the terminal Building was a huge motorised 'T' to indicate the direction of landing and take-off. The 'T' was even illuminated for night flying and the controller would turn it as the wind changes required new runway directions. The idea was to land in the direction along the long leg towards the head, rather like it represented the fuselage and wings of an aircraft. When returning to the field an aircraft was required to be 500 feet above circuit height to view the indicated runway direction before losing height to join the circuit at a height of 1000 feet. On windy days one had to keep a watchful eye on the 'T' as the runway changes were not announced, as radio was not compulsory as it is today. Instead the controller used a series of flashing lights to communicate with the aircraft in the circuit.

After I had been through the basic lessons with Nick, a special day arrived, although it was only later on that I realised its real significance. By that stage Mike van Ginkel had joined Nick, and he took over while Nick was away at the World Aerobatic Championships. I went out as usual and did a few circuits with Mike. After only 30 minutes he told me to do a full stop landing and return to the school.

I was mortified. All I could think of was what I had done wrong. What could be so bad as to cut the session short? Sheepishly I landed and taxied back. I parked the aircraft and started to go through the shutdown routine. Mike stopped me and explained that Nick wanted him to send me solo and how did I feel about the prospect. Did I feel ready for it? Not being part of a flying family I was not even aware of all the solo side of the training. It was a complete surprise. I said that I had no yardstick to judge by, but if Nick felt I was ready that was good enough for me. He hopped out saying that I should do just one circuit and meet him back at the office.

I taxied out with his earlier comments going through my mind. The winds on that day had been rather unpleasant and he had been pointing out how much faster we were on the downwind leg due to the wind. As a result it was very important not to leave the turn off downwind too late otherwise the aircraft would drift further away and it would take an unusually long time to get back to the runway. Also after take-off it seemed as if I was climbing at an alarming rate with apparently low airspeed due to the headwind and the decrease in weight being solo. As I turned out after take-off the aircraft got a sudden sideways drift all of its own. I completed my circuit under these somewhat challenging conditions, without room in my mind for much other than the flying at hand. After the 'craft was parked back on the flight line, I walked over to the café to get a coke. On the way back to the office I met Jeanette, Mike's wife. "Where is the huge smile?" She enquired, "Haven't you just gone solo?" "Yes I guess I have." I replied, accepting her congratulations.

It seemed strange that she expected a dynamic reaction, but then only did the penny drop. I had not been exposed to the solo ritual and so just accepted each lesson as it came along. I was not aware that in fact at least 15 of the compulsory

40 hours were to be solo, the thought was a bit horrifying. As I strolled back, the impact of what I had just accomplished began to sink in. Back home, my family was quite amazed at their child flying around the skies without even being old enough for a learner's driving licence. Interestingly enough, I went solo on the 20th February 1965, 19 days after my 17th birthday, and my Student Pilots Licence was dated 3 March 1965, which was my brother Tony's 12 th birthday.

By the time that the next Saturday's lesson arrived I had fully appreciated the significance of the solo flight. For some other reason I had to be more formally attired and, unusually for me, I walked in proudly sporting a tie that I had recently been given. With great aplomb, Jeannette pounced on me with a lethal looking pair of scissors and proceeded to cut off my best tie. I was mortified, and no amount of objection would stop her. She explained that that was part of the solo tradition, and I lost my tie. Had I realised, I would have worn an old tie rather than having to look at my severed one pinned to the wall each time I came in to their office.

Chapter 4

The next few flying hours were spent on consolidation. That is the term used for practising the circuit procedures. Most of the hours were spent solo, but each session started with a single circuit with the instructor to check me out for solo work. Thereafter I was to resume some upper air work, both dual and solo. The upper air work is carried out at a safe height above ground in the designated area for training, the General Flying Area, and it presents the opportunity to really feel how the aircraft behaves under a range of conditions and how to react to each of them. It is as important as all the other lessons that make up the course as the ability to cope with flying in emergencies is strengthened by it.

Nick knew how intense my interest in flying was, and that was probably why we got a good relationship going. I always felt that he was putting in that little bit extra for me, and that really made a difference. Out in the fields to the south of Rand we used to practice forced landings, precautionary circuits, stalls and spins. To this day I am not very partial to spins and the following event may be a contributing reason.

We had done all our pre-spin checks, and I had done a few spins myself. Nick took over to demonstrate something and we started another spin. As the nose dropped, we started to rotate and I saw something flash out of the corner of my eye. I stopped the spin and Nick asked what I was doing. Before I could explain that I had caught a glimpse of something, blow me down, there was a Dakota heading straight towards us! As we flew away from the area I looked in horror as it came blundering through the space of air that we were occupying just minutes before! We were in the correct place in the General Flying Area, at the correct height, and he had just simply not seen us!

It gave me quite a start. Firstly having the thought of all the solo flying to comprehend, and now this. The feeling of solitude and serenity was shattered. I could accept other aircraft in and around me in the circuit, but out in the open we should have been safely on our own. It was a good lesson to me and I suddenly realised how easily a mid-air conflict could arise if all pilots did not exercise caution all the time.

Once I was proficient in handling the aircraft in the air and on the ground, my next training step was to learn to navigate, by going on a series of cross-country flights. I had to do a minimum of four, two of which had to be solo.

Each route chosen was firstly to be flown dual and then repeated solo in the opposite direction. I had to learn to recognise ground features, as they were represented graphically, and thereby follow the route drawn on the map. An added complication was the effect of wind on the aircraft, which had to be taken into account in planning and flying the route.

Our first dual session took us to Rustenburg, a relatively small town north west of Johannesburg, a distance of around 60 miles. When we had taken off and were climbing away from the ground, I learned how to set the course and recognise the features. After less than an hour the town appeared as expected. Just as we turned over the Rustenburg Airfield onto our new course, there was a huge bang and a large object was flapping in front of us. I was totally unaware of what had happened and what to do. It was clear however that the place to be was on the ground. The noise was making every effort to offset the workings of my mind, and I was trying to resist its efforts. What had happened was that the engine cowl had opened and was flapping up and down, banging into the propeller. Experience was immediately evident as Nick took control and before any further damage took place, he established that, by sideslipping to the one side, the tortured cowling would stop its death defying gyrations. With the crisis now under control we could slowly return to Rustenburg and land. On the ground the damage was obvious. The one side of the cowling stood out horizontally, tortured and twisted into a strange shape. Both catches from that side had been ripped out, leaving the situation a bit interesting, to say the least.

I suggested to Nick that I could panelbeat the cowling into some sort of shape and wire it closed for the trip home. He agreed that we had nothing to lose as it was scrap in any event, and so I got to work. Being used to sorting out funny problems it was just a natural reaction for me. I walked towards the boundary fence, where I was sure to find some wire, keeping a lookout for a pair of suitable panel-beating 'tools' I found a pair of suitable rocks and some wire and returned to the 'craft. Nick had already started to do a thorough check of the engine compartment and propeller.

As soon as he was finished, using the two rocks as a panel-beating hammer and dolly, I managed to get the cowling into a reasonable shape, where both sides would at least close in an acceptable fashion. I then used the wire to firmly hold the cowling closed, making sure that there were no edges that might be lifted by the airflow. Nick was happy with the final product and so we got aboard and prepared to do a run-up and test circuit.

We took off and to our joy, the aircraft behaved entirely normally, so much so that he was happy to continue our cross country. The rest went without any further mishap, despite my thoughts about the result of my temporary repairs coming adrift. They had to be put aside while I continued with my map reading. From Rustenburg on, there was precious little to navigate by with the exception of the contour of the land. I was amazed that such a seemingly deserted area existed less than 100 miles from the city centre. My fears were unfounded as the dear little aircraft flew on without a falter and in fact flew for the rest of the weekend with my repairs. That was my first cross-country, and I went home hoping that better luck was to follow.

My next cross-country was the same route, but this time on my own in the opposite direction, and it was to produce a little surprise of a different nature! I arrived at the field and looked up at really dismal weather. As we moved the Colt to the flight line, I raised concerns about the weather and was reassured "Just remember to look down below you because the murkiness restricts your view directly ahead". Clutching this piece of information, I prepared to leave on my first solo cross-country flight. My first leg was to Fochville, a minute village 35 miles to the southwest, and it went well. I was within sight of a road most of the time and I was gaining a bit of confidence. Even though I was looking almost below me I was getting the hang of it, or so I thought. The second leg of 55 miles was then to Rustenburg, and I was about to learn why this was a favourite route. Unlike going in the opposite direction, there were very few landmarks and together with the poor visibility, I soon resorted to using the shape of a number of old mining excavations to identify my route, as I had been shown on the previous cross country. The salient difference was that when previously heading to Fochville, the town was visible beyond the larger town of Carltonville, whereas in the other direction there was nothing else to be seen, particularly under the poor visibility conditions.

Looking straight ahead, all I could see was a grey void, but armed with the knowledge from the previous lesson, I was looking below me to identify my position. It was after some time that the shapes of the old diamond diggings looked different from those on the map. I was a little concerned but with no other alternative, I soldiered on. I concentrated on trying to steer an accurate compass course, waiting for a sight of Rustenburg. Alas no joy. Although I was flying near the ridge of hills as intended, I saw no indication of the town and my estimated time of arrival (ETA) had now come and gone.

I was then in a bit of a stew, the books had not catered for this type of event (or perhaps non-event) and the only logical conclusion that I was lost did not help the situation. I knew that the longer I flew the more lost I would get. I decided to turn onto my planned heading for Rand as I would have the best chance of recognising the large city and a long time to possibly recognise a landmark on the way. As I was now tracking back to Rand on my planned course, settling down to a concentrated map reading session, I came across a little town that I could not identify. I circled the town and saw a large field that was suddenly very attractive.

My mind churned over the possibility and advantage of landing there. On the one hand there was the ever-present danger element, but on the other hand I could ascertain exactly where I was and prevent getting any more lost. Having made the best logical decision that I could, I carried out a precautionary circuit to check the surface, and to look out for any obstacles. It all seemed reasonable. There were a few cows grazing lazily on the one side and the rest of the field seemed suitable, with a hard surface, clear of anthills or any other obstruction, covered with short grass.

All my training was at my fingertips as I planned my circuit and came in for a textbook, near-perfect landing. Once I had parked the aircraft and shut down, I got out in the hopes of finding someone to tell me where I was. I looked about, and with consternation, saw that I was in a field surrounded by a huge wire security fence without any buildings inside the fenced area. I walked up to a few locals, who were staring at me through the fence, and they promptly fled in terror from the flying man. I realised that they had probably never seen anything other than a bird fly! I looked all around and called out, but to my horror I was all alone with the cows, without any form of communication. Oh for the modern day cell phone!

With little alternative I got back into DUM and looked at my map and flight plan. The one thing I had achieved was gaining time to think without pressure and without getting any more lost and using up valuable fuel. My only alternative was to continue on my way back to Rand while keeping my eyes peeled. At least I had gained time to double-check my route. I checked the surface of the field and got back into the aircraft to head back to the Reef. I lined up and took off in the utter amazement that I had landed at a place that I would never be able to identify! Having made my decision I stood by it and kept a keen watch for any landmarks that I could identify. I guess this typifies the expression that you are not really lost but just unsure of your exact position. Inadvertently I was thinking like that. I knew the area where I was and so my idea of following my planned course to Rand, until I identified something, was sound thinking.

I plodded along in this anxious state until I was due to see signs of the Reef. The first reference that I could identify was a lake. Fortunately the weather had eased up and as I got closer I saw that there was an airfield alongside it. Once I edged closer I could identify Robinson Lake and with a double check at the surroundings I got quite chuffed at being back on the map and revised my course for Rand. I was amazed at how far to the west of my track I had drifted, and realised that all the time I had assumed that I was east of track. If I had started a search at Rustenburg I would have assumed I was east and just aggravated the situation by flying a lost position search. Quite where I picked up such a huge error I will not know. All I could assume was that with all the bad visibility over the diamond diggings I had mis-identified something and an ever-increasing error had crept in.

I landed back at Rand a very relieved student and was met by a concerned instructor. I guess he was equally relieved to see his student and aircraft back in one piece. Whether his concern was due to the poor weather or due to my story, I will never know, suffice to say that his relief was most apparent. The one valuable lesson that I learned was getting lost and how difficult the way out was. The only way is to keep a meticulous position watch at all times. It was indeed a case of one good fright being worth ten hours dual!My other cross-countries went without any other problems, the only comments being around the new German instructor who took me for a few lessons. Just after take-off he would sit gazing out of the window with a look of apparent disinterest chiselled on his face. When he seemed to master it, and got bored with this simple routine, he would reach for his lunch box and flask. Then he would pour a cup of tea/coffee as full as he could, and place it on top of the dashboard in front of him.

"Don't spill my coffee," he would utter as he settled back to enjoy a handful of sandwiches.
My concentration was intense as I rode the mid-day thermals while navigating, all the while trying my level best (excuse the pun) not to spill his coffee. The good news was that my final cross-country went without a hitch and the hard-learned lesson was now behind me, never to be forgotten. Even today with the aid of the GPS (Global Positioning System) I am particular about keeping a map reference at all times.

Chapter 5

During my yearlong training, I was introduced to Grand Central Airport by a super chap, Arthur Mechin. Arthur's early years were spent working at the English De Havilland company that made the Moth aircraft series. I remember him recalling how, as an apprentice, his first task was to make flying wire acorns. They were designed to separate the wing bracing wires (flying wires) to steady them and minimise the noise that they would otherwise create. They are manufactured from wood with a series of complicated angles and must have been the most awkward and fiddly items to make. During his time at DH he progressed to being workshop foreman on the original racing Comet, a twin engined wooden wonder that won the race from England to Australia. Despite his background, he was unable to get his military licence, as he had to wear corrective lenses that were unacceptable to them.

Undeterred he went to one of the North African countries to get his licence. Subsequently, licence in hand, he moved to Rhodesia (now Zimbabwe), where he logged up thousands of hours in a range of aircraft including an amazing amount on Dragon Rapides. He told me that he had owned no less than 48 tail wheel aircraft over the years. On one particular occasion he was tasked to fly a rescue mission into the tropical forest to bring out a boy at night. The only aircraft available was a Fairchild, even old then, without any lights or navigation equipment. The medical rescue went wrong when he was flying along with a torch in one hand, map and navigation equipment in the other – darn, who was flying the beast? As could be foreseen, the fuel ran out before he reached the site. He had no option but to deliberately crash into the forest, tearing off both wings to stop the aircraft without minimal damage to himself. He woke up some time later and realised that his head was bleeding badly. He bandaged himself up and looked at the dense forest around him and realised that rescue was unlikely. As the aircraft went through the dense canopy of trees, it just closed up after him, and he realised that he would be invisible from the air.

To survive the evening cold, he stripped large pieces of covering from the aircraft, which he made into sheets by peeling off the dope (paint covering). With no hope of being found by an air search, he fabricated a homemade crutch and set out with what little supplies he could carry. He hobbled for five days until he came across an African village where he was compassionately received and given some welcome sustenance. They managed to get him back to civilisation, which took another few days. When he arrived home after his ordeal, he was greeted by his own obituary in the local papers. I read this only after his mother's passing when he gave me her scrapbook to read, including the obituary.

Even though he was somewhat retiring he came out with the most interesting snippets once I got to know him. He was the most well-balanced, sympathetic, supportive and likeable person, as well as being the most brilliant pilot. Although I would never have guessed it, I was to have a long friendship with Uncle A, as he became known, until his untimely death.

Once I had gone solo and had a few hours of solo flying to my credit, one of my childhood fears started coming to the fore, vertigo. Having had an association with many pilots over the years, I now realise that it is not an uncommon companion to a number of pilots as they conquer the elements.

As a child I had that terrible feeling of falling every time I looked over the side of a tall building or structure. The feeling of losing your balance and falling over the edge is something that is difficult to become accustomed to, either you have been there or you have not. As is often reported, if there is no contact with the ground, like looking down the face of a building or down a sheer rock drop, then the vertigo feeling is not there, so therefore it should not be a problem in flying.

During my initial training and various flights that I had had, vertigo never presented itself, presumably because of my application to the mere task of flying. It then came to haunt me in a big way. I will never know whether it arose as a result of insecurity or as a fear or some other reason. Suffice to say that it had arrived in an upsetting manner.

I was taken by the feeling of falling at strange times. During normal flight it was not a problem but as soon as I flew over a familiar area I was taken by the desperate need to be down there. During my training it would arise when arriving back at the airfield, and in later years it would manifest itself when I flew over the area where we lived, as it was so familiar from below. Joining the circuit was the most inconvenient time as that is when I needed my wits about me most and it seemed to manifest itself as a total lack of flying ability. This was probably spurred on by the fact that I was doing something completely new and away from my norm. Remember that at this stage I was not even old enough to get a driving licence and yet I was flying about the sky on my own. The reality of what

I was doing and the responsibility got the better of me and I suffered a complete breakdown of confidence.

Uncle A came to the rescue. Without any prompting, he had organised a Cessna 172 to take me up. He explained that this was not an unusual reaction and that he would show me that I should have no concerns. He was quite sure of my ability, certainly a far cry from my feelings. With a bit of persuasion from Uncle A, Mum got in the rear seat. We clambered into the front seats with me on the left (pilot's side) and I proceeded to start up and taxi. With all the checks complete I lined up on the runway, and took off.

As we were gently climbing out, Arthur turned around and started a conversation with Mum. As they chatted, I started my after-takeoff turn. The conversation immediately stopped and she blurted out. "Who is flying this darned thing?" Arthur casually pointed to me at the controls and immediately met a verbal broadside. "Take the controls back," she cried out, whereupon Arthur simply replied in his quiet simple manner. He explained that I was indeed a pilot, albeit in training, and that to assess me was in fact why we were in the air together. Mother was, at that stage, minutes away from jumping out the window and needless to say was never again one of my passengers!

We continued to climb and go into the General Flying Area to do a bit of upper air work (general flying exercises). By that stage Mum had started to relax a bit and she realised that I could in fact fly, even though she had been fully aware of my training schedule. Before we returned to the field to do a few circuits and practice landings, Arthur had pronounced me a fit and safe pilot and said that he was confident that the vertigo would cure itself in time.

Over the years it got progressively much better but I still had queasiness about flying over home or other familiar areas. Pilots are always extremely aware of the nature of what they are doing and the potential repercussions of things going wrong. That is probably the major part of the training, after all, when something goes wrong there is usually only one chance to rectify the situation. That, together with the fear of heights, is certainly what has kept me cautious enough to survive my colourful career.

A second flight that Arthur organised was my first ride in a Tiger. He was well aware of my interest in old aircraft and he had borrowed a Tiger from Leo Margo. This particular machine was a familiar sight at Grand Central and, little did I realise, was to become a closeby hangar occupant in the years to come. The Tiger, Stripes, was very dramatically painted in a gold and black colour scheme, a totally unimaginable presentation in the mid sixties. She had been painted for some filming work like that and kept the scheme for some years, being a stalwart of Grand Central skies with her equally dramatic owner.

I got kitted up in the flying suit handed to me, and took the leather helmet offered. Once I was told how to tell the back from the front of by looking at the elastic at the back, my next instruction followed. We walked up to the Tiger and I was shown a few basics including how to get in without putting a foot through the wing.

"Step only on the black walkway, and don't grab on anything but the struts as you get in. Speak to me through this speaking tube." I was to utter those very words countless times myself in the years ahead.

I sat in the passenger cockpit with a wonderful feeling of being part of the machine. Unlike other aircraft, you really fitted into it as opposed to those where you seem to sit 'on' and not 'in' the machine. Leo swung the propeller and after a few priming turns the engine fired, settling down to an even beat as it idled. We taxied away from the hangars and continued in an unfamiliar series of zigzags. As we taxied in this strange manner, I thought how like a waddling duck we must look. Looking around I became aware of the flying wires vibrating to the characteristic beat of the engine. Looking up at the centre section of the wing above me, with the flying wires on both sides going outwards to the wings, was a novel, new view.

As we lined up and took off she transformed from the waddling duck, to a bird of perfect flight. The transformation of any Tiger Moth at lift-off will always be a marvel to me. The effortless and gentle transition is unlike any other machine. There was no stick in the front cockpit so the option of holding the controls was not even there. The heightening of all my senses was an experience that I shall not forget. It was already late and there was only time for a quick circuit and so, too soon we were aiming for the runway on final approach, with the unique 'pop-pop' of an idling Gipsy engine.

I thought that my enthusiasm for Tigers was at its peak before the flight, but it brought a sense of urgency to the fore. The timing of the flight was a perfect sales ploy, the early evening stillness and the sunset with it's long shadows, as we pushed her into the hangar, made a perfect end to the beginning of a lifelong relationship with the perfect lady. I was sold.

Chapter 6

After the 172 flight, I was often at Grand central with Uncle A and got to know some of the flying crowd out there. As we arrived, driving up the road alongside the old racetrack entrance, I would often recall my childhood days spent at Grand Central Racetrack with Dad. I remember clearly looking out from the pits, across the track and seeing aircraft taking-off and landing. I have no recollection other than the memories of biplanes and a particular monoplane type where I could see right through the bubble canopy to the sky on the other side. I presume they were Chipmunks and for some reason I found it extremely strange. I never got to the airfield as a child, but my feelings were often with the aircraft.

The life at Grand Central was wonderful. The group of people were all interested in flying as a hobby and not as a tool, even though in retrospect a few were probably in commercial aviation, but their interest belied that. The weekends were a time to get together, talk flying and fly. As once was said, most flying is done in the hangars! The accent was on owning and cherishing your aircraft and honing your flying skills. That is not to say that we were particularly good but rather that we enjoyed the challenge.

We used to sit at the small clubhouse watching our friends in an array of Austers, Cessnas, Tiger Moths and Luscombe Silvaires, but easily the most impressive of all was Arthur's Dragonfly. Made by de Havilland, it was a five-seater biplane that used two Tiger Moth engines. Not too graceful on the ground, it transformed itself in the air to a very attractive machine. My association with Arthur was unfortunately at the end of his ownership of this machine, but at least I am one of the few who have been in one.

On one particular occasion I arrived at the field to see the Dragonfly in the air and we sat on the lawn in front of the clubhouse and watched. We saw the huge gracious beast come in to land and waited for the wheels to touch. No sooner had they contacted, than the bird took a 90-degree turn towards us. The aircraft continued to move along the runway albeit hopping sideways on only a single main wheel. We watched in horror as she hopped sideways with only the single wheel periodically contacting the ground. In some sort of miraculous manner the whole nightmare simply subsided as the aircraft came to rest as did the other main wheel and the tail wheel. It was amazing that the whole episode happened without any damage to people or machinery. I have not seen many ground loops but this was surely the most dramatic.

The door popped open and Arthur and his friend, Chick hopped out, laughing their heads off. I could not believe that they were not reduced to shaking wrecks. I almost was and I was not even inside!

They climbed underneath to assess the problem before taxiing further and immediately realised what had happened. A brake cable had jumped off its pulley and got caught between the pulley and structure. After a short time she was pronounced fit for flight and we were invited aboard. I climbed into the most amazingly spacious cabin. Two pilot seats were in the front with a large bench seat at the rear. In between them was a single seat, offset to the side to avoid a diagonal cross member. I climbed over the single centre seat to the right pilot seat next to Arthur. As I settled in I was aware of a very new sensation, that of looking along a very short nose. Looking down from this unusual height at an engine alongside, mounted on a wing well below, was also a new feeling. As I watched, it burst into life and we were soon taxiing out.

We lifted off in such a gentle, dignified fashion, without the usual noise, and climbed out steadily and surely. The aircraft was such a stable platform that one felt as if you were sitting, suspended in an armchair. The only thing other than the quietness and stability, was the heaviness of the flaps. Arthur warned us about the heavy reaction to the flaps shortly before he pulled the nose up to counteract them. He then reached down between the seats and heaved the flap lever with both hands and the nose dropped in sympathy.

The flight was fantastic. The quietness and serenity was totally new to me. The engines were far enough away that the vibrations and noise were quite insulated from the cabin occupants. At the time I was not aware of how fortunate I was to be one of the few ever to fly in a Dragonfly.

Soon after this episode, Arthur was to purchase a Beechcraft D17 commonly known as a Staggerwing. This was a magnificent beast with an enormous 450 hp radial engine on the front of a relatively short fuselage. The steeply sloping fuselage ended up in a very round rudder and tail feathers. The nickname 'Staggerwing' came from the very distinctive wing layout. Unlike conventional biplanes that have the top wing ahead of the lower, the Staggerwing has the top wing attached to the top of the fuselage, set substantially behind the lower wing, a layout known as reverse stagger. As a result when looking out to the side from the pilot's seat, your eye looks forward of the leading edge of the top wing. By contrast looking down, the lower wing blanks the view directly below.

I often flew with Uncle A in the Stagger and got to know her well. One of my first trips was to Baragwanath, the home of the Johannesburg Light Plane Club. As we got out of the aircraft his glasses slipped from his pocket and smashed on the apron. He bent down and picked up the pieces, I thought to throw them away, but he kept the frame and a few pieces of glass. After seeing the JLPC chaps and swapping stories over a cup of tea the time came to leave. We got in and fired up the radial with all the smoke and noise that they are notorious for, taxied out and took off. As we approached Grand Central he took a couple of pieces of broken glass and held them to his eye. Having chosen a suitable one he fitted it to his eye, monocle style, and peered down at the windsock to assess the landing direction. As if it was an everyday occurrence, he simply continued to join the circuit and land. I suppose that in his tens of thousands of hour's experience, he was used to working his way around such little problems.

On another occasion he had been asked to ferry an Auster from Brakpan-Benoni to Baragwanath. A friend of his had bought it on a military surplus auction and, without a Certificate of Airworthiness, he needed a commercial pilot to fly it with special permission. Leo Margo, Arthur, Tony, and I left for Brakpan-Benoni. I had also never been there and was looking forward to seeing the airfield. Leo would fly the Stagger from Brakpan-Benoni to Bara to fetch Arthur.

We landed and taxied up to the apron area. The airfield was less sophisticated than I was used to. I seem to recall that both runways were grass. Parked outside the largest hanger was the Auster. We all went up for a good look, Arthur, because his safety depended on it, and the rest of us just out of interest. It was finished in a camouflage colour scheme and looked quite sound. I had not yet seen a true camouflage scheme in the flesh, as there were none flying in the civilian sector.

After completing a thorough inspection he got in and the prop was swung for him. The machine burst into a healthy burble, and we looked with dismay at a stream of fluid coming from inside the cowling. He shut down, got out and opened the cowling. He soon detected the problem as being a leaking petrol pump diaphragm on the second pump.

His solution was just to put in a few extra gallons to make up for the loss through the drain. From a safety point of view, having double pumps, the likelihood of the second pump quitting was slim. His parting words were "I will start my take-off run and if I continue you will know all is well and I will see you at Bara" and with that he left us to follow him. Leo and I taxied out behind the Auster and watched him take-off.

Once airborne we soon passed him and carried on ahead. We flew over Johannesburg and without warning, as we got overhead the railway station, he pushed the nose down. I was totally taken unaware and did not know what was happening until he said, "This is what it was like in the war when we were strafing the stations." With that we plummeted towards the ground in a howling dive. As the Stagger came screaming towards the platform I remember at least one porter, pushing a baggage cart, abandoning his charge and running for cover. As Leo pulled out of the totally reckless dive and regained his lost height, my heart was racing but I felt a bit better than being in the porter's shoes.

As I composed myself I thought that, although a touch impulsive, he had been a top pilot in the Second World War. I recalled the days as a child when Leo lived near us and used to ride around on a horse, wearing a cowboy outfit and shooting a six-shooter into the air. In those days we had no closed gates and high security walls as we do today. I would be alerted by the sounds of gunfire and would look down towards the driveway entrance. Almost invariably I would see the horseman galloping past with his gun blazing! I now realise that they were most likely blanks, but at the time I was petrified and it left a permanent memory behind.

I gradually accepted that he was known to my folks, and so could be dismissed as an eccentric neighbour. Some years later on he used to greet us on weekends with a low pass over our house in a twin-engined Beech 18. It would invariably be early in the morning when we would hear the rumble of radial engines. We had just enough time to leave our breakfast and go outside to see the huge aircraft flash past at chimney height. But my thoughts are wandering; we will go back to Leo and the story.

Much to my relief we landed back at Bara. We wandered up to the Auster and met the proud new owner who was delighted with his purchase. He was so happy that he offered to fill the Stagger up with fuel. He quickly swallowed his comments when Uncle A said that the tanks could take over a hundred gallons! A compromise was soon reached and we got back into the Stagger and headed for home.

Chapter 7

By this stage Arthur, despite our age difference, had not only become a real friend to me, but he also began to realise that my dream of one day having a Tiger was realistic. He was probably testing me out when he took me up in Stripes, although I never thought so at the time. The hours that we spent together at the airfield, as well as the rebuilding of cars that I was doing at home, must have reassured him that I was capable.

One Saturday morning he pitched up at the house, in his Triumph Spitfire, and told me to get in as we were going on an expedition. Despite every attempt at an explanation, I could not get out of him what was afoot. As we drove south I could not help wondering what he had up his sleeve and where we were headed. As we trundled down the road I began to suspect that we were going to Baragwanath. I was itching to know what was in store for us. As I expected we arrived at Bara, but instead of going to the flight office or clubhouse, we turned into the entrance near the hangars. I expected him to turn right towards the hangars, fuel bay and clubhouse, but amazingly he turned left towards the maintenance hangar. We stopped outside the large, open, hangar doors and got out of the small sports car. Looking inside I saw a number of elderly aircraft. Austers, Tiger Moths, and Piper Cubs seemed to be the regular occupants.

I followed Uncle A inside and he introduced me to Harry Sharman, who operated the outfit. I soon realised that he had the most amazing vocabulary, and that the rules of his speech obviously required him to use the more colourful side at least as often as punctuation. The resulting adjectives emanating could easily strip off a good coat of paint! He was the official maintainer of the JLPC (Johannesburg Light plane Club) fleet. The two Tigers that the club had were ZS – DLK and 'BSF. Harry proceeded to explain to us that 'BSF had some years earlier suffered a broken crankcase and as such was in pieces.

What transpired was that the pilot had a propeller break on him and he was not quick enough to react to the situation and throttle back. The result was a cracked crankcase. I put myself in the pilot's shoes and could not imagine how I would cope in a similar situation. The vibration must have been horrific, I wondered if he still had some teeth in his head.

As we looked at the sorry sight of 'BSF lying in pieces all over the hangar, Harry kept on explaining the situation. The club's demand for Tiger flying had dropped off and as a result they had cannibalised 'BSF to keep 'DLK flying. They were looking at selling off what remained of her.

"What," I thought, "is going on here, how do I fit in?"

They started talking price and soon a figure of R500 was thrown about. As an illustration of current value, I can barely fill the Tiger's tank for that amount today.

Uncle A took me outside and said. "You have always said that you want a Tiger, now we will see how serious you are. What I propose is that we get her together. I have two engines that have been taken out of the Dragonfly and we could use one of them. If you are prepared to undertake the rebuild, I will put in the engine as my part to offset your work."

I could not believe what I was hearing. As he continued to explain that he was a licensed maintenance engineer and had cut his teeth on Tigers at De Havilland, my ears and eyes nearly burst from their sockets in exuberation. I could not wait to get home and see my folk's reaction.

We left the airfield and my mind was soaring. We arrived home and I burst in on Dad, blurting the whole thing out. Once all the garble had been straightened into a sort of logic, my father came forth like was his form. Being the most wonderful father he came up with the support that all dreamers dream of. Not only did he readily come forth with the required R250 for my share, but he was fully supportive of all my efforts in all the years to come.

As I write these words some 35 years later on, it is quite ironic that my Tiggy has just undergone her second rebuild in my ownership and both my sons are itching to get their conversions on her.

We then made a second trip back to Bara, this time accompanied by a truck that Arthur had arranged. At Bara we started the loading process. All the major components were easy to identify and we were aware that many instruments and undercarriage components were missing, but some smaller ones that were not readily apparent slipped through our net. Later we were to meet the Strecker family in our quest for spares and establish a relationship that was to test the passage of time.

Even though overjoyed at the acquisition, it would be many years before I realised that I was only 17 years old and embarking on such an ambitious project was quite unusual. I was in first year engineering at university and with all my rebuilding interest, it just seemed natural to me. This was just going to be another rebuild project, although this time without four wheels.

When we got home I proudly walked in with a most tremendous grin to announce our arrival. Everybody came out to see this amazing 'aircraft'. Although Dad was right behind me, I am sure that the general feeling was not a reflection of my own optimism. We offloaded and made a huge pile of bits in the back yard. All I can recall is a mixed feeling of intense happiness and confusion, with little idea of where to start. I was blindly confidant that, with Uncle A's help and Dad's support, anything was possible and that I would succeed.

The next point of discussion was where would I work and keep all the bits. Dad agreed to let me use one car space in the garage and that was all I needed, I was on my way. I was itching to get started. The other problems would just have to be solved in time. Without a driving licence I was not very mobile and was quite happy to work on projects at home. The long Christmas university holidays were on the horizon and my thoughts wandered to completing the overhaul during that period. With Arthur's expert guidance it seemed an achievable goal.

I started work and soon realised that space was a major consideration. Two of the neighbourly children, who had been a couple of years below me at school, began to take a huge interest and became my 'official' helpers. Seeing my space problem they spoke to their father and came up with a wonderful solution. They had a three-car garage with one space empty. I was offered their spare space in the garage and soon all the bits were under cover.

When the rebuild was in full swing, I often had to move large components between the two garages. As a result it became a common sight to see me and my friend or the gardener carrying a wing up or down the road past our five neighbours. We would then stop at the stop street, turn left and carry on past the next four properties before turning into their garage. In time the fuselage was on wheels and I used to repeat the process, this time just with me holding the tail wheel, rolling her on the main wheels. In retrospect I wonder what they must have thought, while to me it was completely logical and normal. One wonders what a policeman would have thought and done!

Arthur then came in with his enormous wealth of experience gained at the De Havilland factory in the years that they were building 'Moths. We isolated missing components, and the tasks that I had to do. I got stuck in and soon was working all day up until at least midnight. I remember taking a weekend off to socialise when a friend's sisters came up from Durban. (More about them later). Other than that break I worked as if my life depended on it.

When the time came to spraying, I was very grateful to Dad. Earlier when I was rebuilding my Austin '7', he had volunteered me as an apprentice to a panel beating and spray-painting business so that I could become the local fundi. Dad was the most amazing father, always supportive when I came up with my strange ideas. Many years later he is still with me in spirit and I realise how valuable he was to me. He would always help with the bits of junk I brought home as lovingly I made them into useful objects. I can't remember getting useable gifts like other kids. My pride was in the junk that I could work on, and it was always a source of gift ideas for me.

The painting using the dope technique was quite a revelation to me. The steel tube fuselage and wooden wings are covered in a fabric to which layers of dope are applied (initially by brush and later in the sequence with a spray gun) to provide the finished taught weatherproof surface. The whole process is lengthy as there are many coats of dope, all to be rubbed down and prepared. Only when I did it myself did I realise how big the job actually was.

Stored in a friend's garage

Chapter 8

During the period that I had been with them, Avex Air had grown significantly. Gone were the days when I used to meet Nick at the café as the office. They had put up their own mobile office on the grassed area next to Pop's Café, and Jeanette was working for them full time. I was approaching the basic requirement of 40 hours for my Private Pilot's Licence and, unlike being caught out when I went solo, was anticipating the flight test and would soon be ready for it. Fortunately, I was talking to Jeanette and she told me that Nick was going overseas for an aerobatic contest and would be away for a few weeks. It came as a blow as it would mean that he would probably not be back by the time that I would be ready to take my flight test.

When he walked in, I asked what I should do as I really wanted him to do my test. "Are you ready for your test now?' was his reply, as he casually picked up some forms, "I just happen to have some test sheets right here. We can do the test now and you can complete your hours while I am away." With little to lose I was soon in the seat with Nick next to me, this time as the examiner. Under a new type of pressure with this 'new' person next to me, I taxied out, took off and flew to the best of my ability. The test required that the examiner sits next to the pupil with a clipboard on his lap, calling the shots. It all seemed to go smoothly, although the feeling I had with him next to me ticking a series of blocks to indicate my ability or lack thereof, was a bit intimidating. When we landed, not knowing what to expect, I was very gratified to be told that I had passed. I returned to the office, a surprised but very happy student, now with a successful flight-test behind me.

I spent the next few sessions doing a bit of general flying practice on my own making up the required hours. It was really the first time that I was alone in the aircraft without a set practice exercise and able to just enjoy the pure thrills of flying. It was wonderful being master of the machine, looking down on the world below. I had a new sense of freedom as I flew south of the airfield and along the ridge of hills. Below me, as I flew along the valley, were a few farms with their patchwork fields. A feeling of serenity came into my flying being able to appreciate the beauty below. Little was I to know how often that I was to see this ridge over the years, from a variety of different aircraft.

The fear of heights that I suffered from never worried me in the General Flying Area but as soon as I flew over the field to look at the huge motorised 'T' to get the landing direction, it seemed to bother me a bit. On one occasion a Harvard was standing on its nose below me, surrounded by a team of ground crew, and I was given a red light from the tower to indicate that I must wait to land. I had to circle overhead until the team managed to pull it onto its wheels and away from the active area. I then got the green light and landed. It appears that the one Harvard pilot was too close to the lead aircraft as they taxied out and was doing up his belts. He looked up just as the lead aircraft stopped at the threshold and got such a fright that he pushed too hard on the brakes and ending up in a rather embarrassing situation on his nose.

I spent hours either watching the military Harvards and other traffic, or around the hangars speaking to people as they worked, cleaned or prepared their aircraft for flight. I felt complete and I had a feeling of really being part of the airfield and all the happenings. Because of the age of the airfield there were always old aircraft around and there was never a shortage of things to keep me occupied.

In due course Nick returned from an enjoyable contest with some amazing stories. He had been using a Stampe that he had borrowed in England. The one in particular that I remember is of him ferrying it out of England and all the way to behind the Iron Curtain. He, together with a group of other Western aircraft, had to follow a huge Antonov in a loose formation. He described how they were not allowed to cross the border and so special permission had been obtained for them to follow the huge biplane to their destination. The sight of the formation must been rather impressive and I always feel that it must have seemed like Mother Goose with all her goslings.

Once the hours that I required were complete, we sat in the office and filled in all the necessary paperwork. I sat and looked around, spotting my severed tie forming part of the growing collection on the wall as the school grew. I had to admit that it was, in fact, worth the loss. I was aware of a type of homely feeling that existed there, almost like a big family of the sky. The registration of the Colt was ZS-DUM and that prompted a particular greeting. Dad used to announce his arrival to collect me with "Are DUM and Dumb back yet?" Jeannette used to take offence at the reference and pulled Dad up, but she never succeeded in stopping the standard greeting. I had a strange feeling because as of that moment I was no longer part of the familiar training scene.

With the paperwork all completed, we left the airfield. The next day a very proud father took a very happy son to Pretoria to the Division of Civil Aviation to get his licence issued.

Chapter 9

Another new friend who was to become a very close companion was Rocky. He lived across the road a few houses up. I cannot remember exactly how we first met, but I imagine he was probably intrigued by the goings on at our home and it finally got the better of him. As we got to know each other, the friendship became closer and his involvement and interest in our crazy hobbies increased.

Being a bit older than me, he was out and working, managing a plating plant while I was even too young for a driver's licence. I had completed the rebuild on my Austin '7' and he was the first person to use it on the road. He even used to drive her in rallies and other events and it was his first exposure to old vehicles.

He was a wonderful help when it came around to plating and polishing, particularly on my type 35c Bugatti that I was busy restoring. Those who have seen photographs of them will realise how much aluminium polishing goes into any Bugatti, particularly when building it up out of a pile of corroded scrap like I was trying to do.

His eyes lit up when he saw the Tiger bits and he kept a close watch on the progress and was often to be seen working with me. During the three months that I was concentrating on the Tiger, his sisters came up from Durban for a week and I was persuaded to take a weekend break from the project to be with them. I don't remember all the details of what we did over that weekend except going out to Rand Airport and taking each of them flying.

I had just got my licence and had not really thought about taking up a passenger until we got chatting. Without any persuasion they had volunteered to be my first passengers. The aircraft was booked and the team was soon out at Rand and ready to go. I had taken up my first passenger and it was all going well until I got airborne with my next passenger. We had taken off in the Colt uneventfully and as I steadily climbed away from the field, I started my turnout. As DUM banked my passenger shouted words to the effect that she felt as if she was falling out of the aircraft. Having been subjected to similar feelings of fear I related to her concern and continued to fly on straight ahead away from the airfield, without knowing how to handle the situation.

As we flew on my mind was working overtime until I came up with the solution. I carefully explained to her that if I could not turn we would just carry on straight until we ran out of petrol. Once she accepted it I continued to explain how an aircraft banked in a turn and how she would not be falling out of her seat. This she accepted (at least logically, if not physically) and I demonstrated the controls and started rolling as I would into a turn.

After some persuasion I seemed to win the point and with much trepidation I started a gentle turn, explaining my every move. I slowly let the aircraft drift towards the General Flying area. There I carried out a series of left and right turns to show her that we were safe and neither of us would fall out, nor would the aircraft fall out of the sky. Once I had gained her confidence we returned to Rand Airport and I put down a very welcome landing.

As she was only my second passenger the reaction was a bit disturbing but it made me realise that as a pilot one is always in a learning process. The situation highlighted the need for a briefing before each flight, particularly in the case of someone unused to flying.

Even though Mother was a bit apprehensive, my family joined me in my moment of pride in getting my licence, particularly as I was not old enough to hold any other licences. For me the freedom of floating around the sky was wonderful, rather a different approach to my peers. I had written my Matric (final school year) younger than most and had not been conscripted to the Army as I was too young. In time, when I turned 18, I was to join the Commandos and do my military service with them. As a result I was years younger than my colleagues and was the only one at university without a driving licence.

I recall a girl who used to catch the same bus as me going to university. I used to watch her each day with a longing to get to know her. The day came when I plucked up enough courage to sit next to her and start talking. Over the next few days things went well, and I imagined a friendship developing, until the conversation got around to hobbies. When she enquired about my hobbies I told her about my aircraft and the cars and offered her a ride in the Tiger.

She looked at me sceptically and upon hearing that I did not even have a driving licence, she immediately cut me off her 'social' list and I was never able to talk to her again, even though I continued to see her every day on the bus. It was a huge blow to my confidence and I could not understand how such a simple discussion had turned her away from me. In the years to come I was to have more lessons highlighting how different I was from the so-called norm.

Chapter 10

Dad had managed to get me a manual from a friend who worked with Hawker Siddley. They had taken over all the De Havilland affairs including the technical manual section and they had provided Dad with a brand new Operating Manual for the Tiger Moth from their stock. Rather sadly this was to be lost in later years with a loan to a 'so called' friend.

The Tiger had got to a stage where the fuselage and wings were now almost complete. The fuselage was standing proudly on its wheels with the engine installed. I was finishing off inspecting the undercarriage and was browsing through the manual looking for any related sections. I came upon a reference to checking the tightness of the axle. To facilitate maintenance/repairs, the axles are separate items bolted in place and easily removable, contrary to the normal practice. They referred to removing the bolts to check for wear.

This sounded like a good idea, so I started to follow the procedure in the manual. Jack up the aircraft and remove the two bolts. "What could be simpler?" I thought. So I jacked up the one axle. Not being used to regular aircraft maintenance procedure, I did not realise that they meant jacking up the whole aircraft on the fuselage jacking points.

With her jacked up under the one undercarriage leg I carried on with the task. When I was pulling out the second bolt I remember thinking how tight it was. No sooner had I got it out when there was a huge bang and the next thing was that, dazed from a bang on my head, I was on the floor looking into the front cockpit.

What had happened was that the bolts were not only holding in the axle, but they were also holding the collar where the suspension leg attaches to the undercarriage leg. As soon as I had removed the bolts the whole of the one side of the suspension collapsed and the aircraft fell on me! I had been struck on the side of the head by the exhaust as it went past but at least was not pinned underneath as the exhaust had pushed me aside.

This was a blow (literally) as the V-strut was bent, as was the axle I was trying to check. Another axle and V-strut solved the problem, but not the feelings! They were procured and with some application the fuselage was again on its wheels. The lesson about the undercarriage collar attachment is indelibly imprinted on my brain.

Soon the time would come to plan the trip to the airfield. I was a bit daunted by the thought, but Uncle A assured me that he had towed aircraft on the road on numerous occasions and would have it all well under control. He recalled an incident in Salisbury (now Harare) when he was towing a rather large Dragon Rapide through the town and got stuck at a traffic circle. The arm of the law soon joined him and after some intense discussion, they then escorted him on his way.

He was the one with the experience, and so I left him to it. On the appointed day he arrived with a bakkie (open light delivery vehicle). With the fuselage riding on its wheels, we lifted the tailwheel onto a wooden beam across the rear of the vehicle. As the tail surfaces were already fitted it was quite wide and it restricted the turning of the bakkie. We then lifted the tail onto the protective frame behind the cab. In this way the tail was free to turn on the corners using the movement of the tailwheel, the overall length was less, and the wide tailplane was unlikely to come into contact with any obstructions.

With the tailwheel secured to the frame, and with me in the back looking after the whole contraption, we set off. I had to bang on the roof to alert Uncle A if anything went awry. Dad came along in his car with the old 8mm cine camera to record the occasion and keep an extra eye on the transporting. Looking at the developed film later it was an amazing sight seeing this apparition moving backwards down the road. It was just as well that I was in the back as the tailwheel jumped off the frame going over the hump into Grand Central. Dad captured me on cine as I quickly jumped up and put it back on the frame.

Once off the LDV the fuselage was pushed safely into our allotted hangar. We locked up and set off to collect the wings. After an uneventful trip the whole aircraft was in the hangar. It was a new feeling being part of our very own hangar even with an aircraft (albeit a bit dismantled) inside.

The next job was to rig the wings, a fancy name for fitting the wings and lining them all up. This was a far greater job than I had anticipated. The problem was that the top wing must be attached and held it in place while fitting the bottom wing and attaching the flying wires. The whole assembly is not rigid until the bracing wires are screwed in. In the interim the wings have to be supported by many hands. At last we got all four wings with all the bracing wires installed and put her to bed until the next weekend.

The following weekend Arthur arrived with a sort of spirit level with an angle measuring ability. We set up the whole assembly with the fuselage level according to the levelling pegs fitted on it's one side for that purpose. We then used the spirit level to measure and adjust the wings to the angles required in the manual. Once all the measurements were within the prescribed limits, we locked up all the adjustments with the lock-nuts on the flying wires and turned our attention to the engine

The engine that Arthur had provided had been removed from his Dragonfly when he had replaced them with slightly more powerful engines. He had purchased a pair of Gipsy Major series 10 engines that made the two out of the Dragonfly redundant. At least we knew that the engine chosen had a known history. Arthur checked out all my work on the all the hoses, piping and wiring and had a second complete inspection of the engine and installation. We poured some fuel in and pushed her out.

My excitement was all but getting the better of me. I was past the butterfly stage, I had great eagles soaring inside me! When Uncle A told me to get in while he started her, I almost lost grip of reality. I leapt into the cockpit, now so familiar from the hours spent working on it, and looked out. Even though I had not yet finished the cowlings, the vista was wonderful. As with many of the older aircraft, one has to swing the propeller by hand to prime and start the engine. This is a rather tricky manoeuvre, as the proximity required makes it easy to lose a limb in the turning propeller if adequate care is not exercised.

After a few priming turns the time for the real test came. I was asked to switch on. "Contact" I proudly called for the first time in my life and with that he gave a healthy swing and she burst into song. What a superb sound it was. As she gently idled I looked down at the instrument panel as the oil pressure rose, and let her warm up. Arthur came around and stood next to me, looking into the cockpit. My feeling of pride was indescribable; my rib cage was about to burst. Even more so when he said that I should try a gentle taxi. As she moved on her own, for the first time in many years, the atmosphere was electric. I had never before taxied a tailwheel aircraft and so I was very gentle as I taxied around. I shut down and climbed out full of pride. Reluctantly she was put to bed and I went home to resume the repairs on the cowlings.

The next outing was to fit the cowlings and get her ready for flight. Once the cowlings were fitted and we peered inside the cockpit and inside the engine compartment, a crowd had assembled around us. My friends, family and the neighbours who had watched the almost daily excursions of bits and pieces up the road, could not be kept away. This was surely a day to be remembered. Soon the time came when there was nothing else to be checked and she was ready for flight.

Uncle A ceremoniously emptied his pockets in a rather sombre fashion and gave the contents to Sheila his wife. I felt as if he had suddenly realised that he was about to fly an aircraft built by a youngster who had not even got his driving licence. His face was definitely telling a tale that we were not privy to. He got in and I hand swung the propeller as I had been shown. The engine fired up immediately and he did an engine check. Once I had removed the chocks he taxied along and we all followed him to the clubhouse rather like the Pied Piper. After a short wait we saw him enter the runway. Trusty Dad was there with the cine-camera capturing the moment.

We heard the engine note increase as the throttle was opened fully and in an amazingly small distance we watched the gentle lady lift gracefully into the sky. Even though the engine note was perfect, as she flew passed in front of us, I began to have my first ever doubts. Was everything done to the required standards? Was it all safe? Arthur soon landed and taxied up to me. He climbed out and said that that she was perfect. Once he had made a check for any leaks or obvious problems he told me to jump into the front seat and strap in.

We had no form of communication, as I had not yet made up the speaking tubes (Gosport tubes). As we lined up for take-off I looked alongside to see Chick in his Cessna 120 with Dad in the passenger seat and we carried on to take off in formation. The day was full of surprises. Uncle A opened the throttle and the engine note smoothly rose in obedience and as he eased the stick forward the tail rose.

As we rolled along the runway she gained speed and I looked across to see Dad, his face half hidden by the camera. I could not believe that this machine that I had assembled was taking us aloft. We completed a circuit and lined up for the final approach. Arthur throttled back and the characteristic 'pop pop' made me feel as if I had now arrived. I watched his technique of brakeless steering with interest as we taxied past the rows of parked aircraft down to the 'T' hangar.

When we got out Arthur complemented me on my work and said that she flew perfectly and that no adjustment to the rigging was necessary. Those were welcome words, particularly in view of the ceremonious pocket emptying before the flight.

This was surely to be the greatest day of my life, but I was to discover that it was just the first of a series of firsts. It was the 20th February 1966 and it was exactly one year since I had done my first solo in the Colt at Rand. Each flying first in itself has the great euphoria that dreams are made of. Flying was to become a new talent taking me to a new series of heights of emotion and feeling.

Chapter 11

The time now arrived for my conversion to the Tiger. She was finished even down to the Gosport Tubes used for communication between the cockpits. I had mixed feelings of pride and anxiety as the time drew closer for my first tail-dragger conversion. In fact it was also my first conversion ever! One was always aware of the stories of the difficulty of tailwheel aircraft, particularly in the more demanding situations.

At this point it may be wise to point out the different handling characteristics to those readers who are not familiar with tailwheel (or so called 'conventional') aircraft. This type of aircraft rests on the small tailwheel at the rear of the fuselage, indicating that that the Centre of Gravity is located just behind the main wheels. When the aircraft is in motion it causes instability in both the horizontal and vertical planes because the momentum of the aircraft acts through the Centre of Gravity and the drag of the wheels is in front of it causing an unstable set of forces. The momentum is continually trying to 'pass' the resisting drag, so to speak.

This means that if the aircraft swings on the runway, the tendency will be to aggravate the swing, the main cause of the so-called 'ground loop'. Similarly looking at the aircraft from the side, if the aircraft is landed slightly hard, with the tail in the air, the momentum will drop the tail severely. This will in turn increase the angle of attack and she will start flying again, only to run out of airspeed shortly thereafter unless the pilot's reactions are sharp. With all this tumbling about in my head, I set out on my conversion.

My instructor was a most delightful old chap called Cecil Starke. We met at Grand Central and went to the hangar to get Tiggy out. After a thorough inspection and a few tips on handling, he got in to the front seat and I prepared to start her. Starting a Tiger is a bit of a ritual due to the procedure required and potential hazards.

Placing chocks in front of the wheels was the first necessary requirement because there are no brakes fitted. The next step was to switch the fuel on, and check that the magneto switches are off and throttle is wide open. Then, around to the front to open the RH cowling where there is a handle to be given a turn to clean the oil filter. Also inside the cowling on top of the carburettor is a button to depress the float to allow extra fuel into the engine for starting. Check that a little fuel dribbles out of the drain at the bottom of the engine. Close the cowlings and go around to the prop.

This is the point at which you must have confidence in your magneto switches. It is reassuring to know that you were the last person to shut down and that you did do your mag. check before shutting down. This is the part of the procedure that breeds stories about aircraft careering around airfields out of control, or standing on their noses. The prop swinger then pulls the propeller through 6 blades to get the fuel into the cylinders ready for firing, with someone in the cockpit for safety. It is then back to the person in the cockpit to set the throttle to idle and to switch the magnetos on. With the engine now 'live' a couple of brisk swings usually starts her and she settles down to a gentle idle.

With the chocks removed, I settled into the rear cockpit and strapped myself in. The next challenge was getting used to the old Gosport tubes, the only form of communication between the cockpits. Gosport was the name of the training base where the 'new' form of communication was first used. Quite simply each person speaks down a tube that ends up in the earpieces in the other person's helmet. This was a major breakthrough in its time as it was the first time that communication in the open cockpits was possible, illustrating the point that the simplest solution is often the most effective and practical. Nonetheless one can imagine that it is not the easiest and clearest form of communication. So often an instructor was left somewhat hoarse after a tough day's instruction.

For the first time I was now subject to instruction this way, and to say that it was a new experience was putting it mildly. In time however, like so many things, I got used to it. As instructed I taxied very cautiously using the soft areas of grass to slow me down. As an added complication, it is all but impossible to see directly ahead due to the tailwheel configuration. This demands a unique method of weaving from side to side to view the area ahead of you. It rather reminded me of a field mouse darting from one clump of grass to the next to avoid detection. The big secret is at all times to avoid going too fast because the soft areas will then not be able to slow the aircraft down enough. In this odd manner we got to the holding point.

Having no radio, we waited for a lull in the traffic, looking towards the tower. With a green light from the controller, we lined up for take-off. I was staggered at how little of the runway ahead I could see. Feeling the controls with Cecil, and with the stick back, I gently opened the throttle fully. With full throttle I felt the stick go forward to raise the tail. At 60m.p.h. he eased back the stick and we were airborne. With a slight forward check we settled to a climb at 65 m.p.h.

Again I nearly split my sides with pride. I was in my own aircraft that I had rebuilt, and was now learning to fly my dream machine. We continued the circuit and I was totally absorbed with the whole process. My total exhilaration of the next few lessons blanks out what we actually did with the exception of the simulated engine failure, my oil problem and my subsequent first solo in the Tiger.

As per normal instruction routine, after a few circuits he pulled back the throttle after take-off to simulate an engine out. As I eased the stick forward and, as Arthur had suggested in anticipation, I reminded Cecil that with the very coarse propeller there was quite a delay before the engine power took hold. He was obviously caught out because we had precious little height in hand by the time we had recovered and started to climb away.

Not long after that, during a regular session of circuits, without warning I heard over the tubes 'If you haven't landed her on your own now is the time because my feet are in oil and it is seeping further into the cockpit. I have my feet up on the seat so you better get down fast."

With that, I glanced at the oil pressure gauge and was relieved to see it showing a steady pressure. I was on the downwind leg of my circuit and so I just continued my circuit, keeping an eye on the pressure. As I looked out on the right lower wing I saw great waves of oil spreading along the top surface. As the pressure was still good I proceeded to complete a regular circuit. I landed very cautiously, and, no sooner was I firmly on the ground, than the pressure gauge dropped to zero. I switched off and had enough speed to coast clear of the runway. We pushed her back to the apron and opened the cowling. The problem was evident. A small seal had for some reason ruptured on the pressure line. We were both relieved to find that it was such a minor problem and that she had not suffered any damage. The lesson however was substantial.

With a new seal in place Cecil said. "You were on your own last time, go and do it again." And with those words I set off on my solo circuits.

Another memory that stands out during my early solo circuits happened at a flying competition at Grand Central. My family was out and we had all been watching the spot landings and flour bombing, and I decided to do a few circuits. All went well until I got into a real galloping goose. This happens when you put the 'craft down a little too hard and too fast. As explained earlier, due to the tailwheel configuration, the tail comes down and you are immediately in the air again. You try to rectify it as she comes down and the same happens. This carries on, getting progressively worse until you decide to go around and start again. The whole affair looks much worse than it is, and as always there is a crowd to witness your worst mistakes. On that day, not only did I have a good audience, but also Dad had it all recorded on the cine camera. Nonetheless I was in seventh heaven. I had the aircraft that I had dreamt of owning, and had a machine I was proud to park alongside any other aircraft (especially other Tigers). Little did I know what was around the proverbial corner.

Shortly after getting her all together I was to have a rather serious mishap that was to have rather long-lasting effects. A very good lifelong friend of mine, Paddy, had been my driving tutor, and in fact even took me to the testing grounds to have my test in his mother's car. With the rebuild and getting her flying, driving had not been a priority and we fitted it in, usually on the way to the airfield to work on the Tiger.

I had just got my driving licence and Paddy and I were coming home from Grand Central when it all happened. I was using my mother's car at the time, and Paddy was following me. Mum had had a flat tyre the previous day, which I had changed for her. The spare tyre that I put on had not been replaced with the last set of tyres and was an older cross-ply tyre, while the newer tyres on the car were all radial-ply tyres. Unlike today when the danger of mixing them is well known, they were the newest development, and the potentially dangerous condition resulting from mixing tyres, was not common knowledge. What in fact happens is that the single cross-ply causes a severe deterioration of road holding. I had put the cross-ply on the right rear and on the way home entered a long turn to the left.

The car started sliding, and I turned into the slide. The last that I can recall is trying to keep control and prevent it spinning, but the car kept drifting towards a line of trees on the edge of the road. Suddenly there was no more road left and the car rolled. The rest of the tale is recalled by others as I have no recollection. Paddy was following me and saw it all happen. As the car rolled, the driver's door opened and caught the road causing the car to lift up sharply and I was thrown out and over the car, landing on my head in the middle of the road. He stopped his car and as he came to pull me off the road he was amazed to see me sitting up and collecting bits of my broken watch. As I appeared only to be a bit shocked and the car ended up well off the tar, he took me home.

As I went in, my mother was resting. I walked into her room and told her what had happened. I apparently told her that I was not hurt, but that the car was a bit broken and left on the side of the road, and with that I started to leave the room. She looked at me as I turned and saw that my whole back was caked in blood. She leapt off the bed, staggered that I had said that I was not hurt, and followed me to my room. By the time she got there I was lying on my bed, collapsed and seemingly dead to the world. She immediately got hold of the doctor, an ex-World War 2 veteran, who pronounced me quite ill, so much so that I would in all probability not survive an ambulance journey to hospital.

Because my mother was an ex-nursing sister, he advised that she could nurse me at home. This she did and I will be eternally grateful to her, in fact the book would stop here if not for her nursing me. I believe that the next few days were crucial as my pulse was unstable, going from high to low over a ridiculously short period. My bed was continually monitored day and night and soon I showed signs of recovering. The radio played continually and the song of the moment was ' Those boots are made for walking'. It will always bring me back to those days whenever I hear the song. The only other thing I remember is a recurring gloomy vision of a hooded man wrapped in a dark shawl in a long boat. He would appear out of a dim and misty haze towards me at the water's edge. The only sound was the gentle lapping of the small waves on the shore. As he punted with a long pole he would say that he would break the gentle lapping with his deep rumbly voice saying that he was coming to get me. Each time this happened I would reply that I was not ready to go. He would then slowly turn and depart, saying that he would soon be back.

Only in later years would I realise that he must have been the mythological Hooded Reaper on the River Styx, who was sent to transport us all across the river of death into the next life. Quite eerie in fact. Eventually I recovered and my family started to talk to me about flying. Apparently I was quite reasonable until they started talking about my flying training and I would insist that I was still in the process of training at Rand. When the suggestion of me having a licence, being at Grand Central, having rebuilt a Tiger and being a Tiger Pilot was raised, I simply dismissed it. I would insist that it was only a wild dream and that I was currently still training with Nick.

No amount of persuasion would convince me otherwise. When I was well enough they took me out to Grand Central and opened the hangar door. Even then I took some convincing that the magnificent aircraft inside was mine, never mind the fact that I had rebuilt her! It appeared that I had lost virtually a full year's memory. Some time later Arthur took me flying and I remember circling over the Veteran and Vintage Club in Tiggy. Even then it felt that I was in a dream world.

From there I made an almost full recovery with only a few skeletal and mental scars remaining. The memories of the year that included the rebuild were slowly recovered thanks to what friends and family have told me, and they don't seem as real as my first hand memory. My flying then got back to full swing, I had used my long university vacation to the full, and I was on a roll again.

Chapter 12

I had got back into the flying and the life at Grand Central. The Star Newspaper had advertised an Air Race and a number of us had entered. Each night as a run-up to the race there was a small insert introducing each entrant in the paper. I even got one, and a mention that I was the youngest pilot and a current engineering student at the University of the Witwatersrand. As the time drew closer my preparations for the air race were not quite as feverish as one might have expected, probably because I had only a vague idea of what was to be done for the race. I tried to imagine what was required from me, from the aircraft, and all I could think of doing was a thorough flight plan. The route was known, so I set about looking at the maps. We were required to take-off at Grand Central and fly the first leg across the suburbs of town to Baragwanath. Thereafter we would continue to Vereeniging, Krugersdorp and back to Grand Central. The total distance was over 200 miles, which was close to the Tiger's maximum cruising range.

When I asked Arthur for a few tips, he simply said that to get maximum performance, I must fly as low as possible to remain in ground effect. In other words to be so low that the air is compressed between the lower wing and the ground. This sounded quite dramatic to me, and I could not imagine map reading at zero feet while flying at the same time. A bright idea struck me; I would ask Rocky if he would accompany me in the guise of a navigator. With glee he agreed and we arranged a training session around the dining room table.

We sat down and I started off with my lesson on navigation. The idea was that Rocky would do all the navigation, as I would be too busy flying at zero feet. I did not even want a map in the back with me. I opened up an aeronautical map and showed him the legend on the back explaining the symbols to him. I went over the route that I had drawn on the map and explained what to expect. As we were going for speed I did not bother to go through many calculations with him, rather just concentrating on recognition and map reading.

We would fly the route together a few days prior to the race as his final training exercise. That should show us what would be in store for us and from that I would be able to generate my final flight plan for the race. In retrospect it seems a bit of 'the blind leading the blind'. However the enthusiasm of youth always seems to conquer all! The most frightening thing, although not to us at the time, was that I had less than 50 hours total, and a mere 6 on the Tiger and yet we were boldly setting out on this crazy venture.

With the two of us on board we must surely have been the most inexperienced crew ever to enter an air race. Nonetheless nothing was going to stop us and we were totally fuelled by our adrenalin, inexperience and enthusiasm. We did the practice run during the week at normal heights and Rocky's navigation went well. I remember him getting out with copious notes and little sketches of landmarks along the route. How he kept them all together I will never know. Before the race we had to produce the aircraft for scrutineering. This entails each aircraft, in its race configuration, being flown by an experienced pilot and individually timed over a set distance. This would enable them to calculate a handicap speed. Even though I knew that we were using the coarse Dragonfly propeller, I was staggered at the handicap speed of 97 miles per hour that was allotted to me. After that all the machines would be impounded until after the race.

The night before the race there was a gathering for all the competitors to get to know each other. Among all of us locals were a few from around the country. One well-known person who was to become a household aviation name was Pikkie Rautenbach, the owner of a crop-spraying outfit based in Durban. Everyone was in good form and the obvious discussion topic was the forthcoming race. Rather gingerly I asked the assembled crowd what sort of heights they would fly at over the city and their unanimous call of 2000 feet was not quite what I expected. Arthur's words of 'as low as possible' echoed out in contrast. I could not envisage this lot taking all the time to climb up to that height and thought that 500 feet was a safe, attractive figure. In addition having such a restricted range, any time spent climbing was not going to help much.

The day of the air show and race dawned and my whole family came out, suitably equipped with a whole picnic. In those days the clubhouse was very small and there was a small lawn in front of it. Rocky and I left the family to settle on the lawn and we went to check up on Tiggy, who had been out all night after the scrutineering. She was all safe and sound with all the other competing aircraft, although we were not allowed access to her till later. By this time the whole field was buzzing with activity, the organizers were putting the final touches to the barricades and the stall operators were laying out their wares. There was a constant stream of visiting aircraft coming in to land, adding to the atmosphere.

When we could get to her, we proudly put the race number on the tail, did our pre-flight checks and, at the required time, moved her to the flight line. In due course Rocky pulled over the prop and our world sprung into a life of vibration and wind. We taxied out in our allotted turn and waited for our flag-off time. We sat there idling with scarcely enough flying time left to get a good flight of butterflies going in our stomachs. I remember being flagged off and opening the throttle with gusto. We had not been restricted at the briefing on our first turning point. We were taking off on the old runway (35 I think it was) and so barely halfway down we had the tiny red and white striped control tower on our left.

I approached the tower, knowing that we would be well off the ground by the time we reached it. I saw it coming and as soon as I drew level, I cranked the stick to the left and heaved back. I remember thinking that I would go through the floorboards, and my vision went a bit funny. I realised at that point that I had overdone it a bit, but to my surprise, she did not bat an eyelid. We executed the sharpest, smartest 90-degree turn that I would have imagined possible.

With my heart in my stomach, the adrenaline pumping through my veins and the wind whistling past my ears, I straightened up and set course for Baragwanath. As we passed over the suburbs rather sedately but somewhat lower than normal, my thoughts wandered. I suddenly realised how close I had been to creating an ugly spectacle as I turned after my take-off. I wondered if Rocky knew how close to disaster we had been. I am sure that it was a classic case of ignorance being bliss and that he was none the wiser!

Getting closer to Bara the housing density decreased, and so did my height, but I was aware of the minimum height on the turns being at 300 feet above ground. I flew towards the windsock (the turning point) and as soon as I got overhead pulled into another knife-edge turn. This was what Arthur had said would minimise time loss in the turn. I knew that I was 300 feet up so I felt much better than at the start. As we set course on the next leg to Vereeniging I got bold enough to try the low stuff. At the new height the whole vista changed from the normal cross-country view. The horizon got so close that it was like looking out of an upstairs window, and the trees became huge monsters looming over us. The only thing was that we were now hurtling along the ground at little short of 100 miles per hour. There was no way that I could do anything except keep my wits about me and keep the aircraft in the air. Rocky seemed confidant that he knew where we were and so I had to leave it at that. With the coarse prop, I was flying at full throttle and she was not exceeding the rev. limit, so I kept up the monstrous pace.

I watched the trees and fences come hurtling towards me, and eased the stick back just to slide gently over them and resume our low-flying crouch on the other side. My mind was so busy with the task at hand, just keeping us safely in the air, that I had no thoughts of navigation. Rocky kept a calm, continuous report of where we were, so much so that I was not sure whether to be amazed at his talent or just consider us lost.

Soon enough his credibility was reinforced as he called the approach to the next turn. I eased the stick back to regain our 300 feet minimum and executed another bone-jarring turn onto the next heading. With a gentle descent we were on the next leg.

A handicap air race is based on the aircraft being set-off at different times to attempt a simultaneous arrival at the finish. To achieve this, the speed obtained on the test flight is used to calculate the expected flight time. This time is taken from the finish time to give each entrant's start time. Thus the first aircraft over the finish line has beaten their handicap time by the greatest margin and so is the theoretical winner. As a result you don't see anyone until close to the end when everyone tends to bunch up.

Our last turning point was Krugersdorp, and as I approached, I saw my first fellow competitor ahead of me. I had a bit of height as there were a number of industrial buildings below and I looked at the high wing aircraft ahead of me to try my aircraft recognition skills. As we both approached the turning point I realised that potentially we would be there together. My problem, however, was that the Air Navigation Regulations say that I must overtake on his right. If I did that I would then risk cutting inside the corner, unsafe, and risking disqualification. I guessed that perhaps this was different and so planned to pass him on his left. As we approached I saw that it was a J3 Piper Cub and as we turned simultaneously I passed him on his left. I could not believe that anything was so slow, and I seemed to scream past him, waving as I did. The little yellow bird seemed so effortless and gentle with the 65 hp motor protruding from the sides of the nose. I could only presume that he also was doing all he could, but the ease with which we passed him was amazing.

As we crossed the mountain ridge, I looked at my compass to make sure that I was on track, and as I looked up I saw the valley beyond the ridge. It was a beautiful sight, the squares of farmland in the lush valley were all different shades of green and it all unfolded before us like a patchwork quilt.

The final leg to Grand Central was relatively short and I looked back to see how the J-3 was doing. He had already dropped back quite substantially and I saw more aircraft in hot pursuit. Too far away to recognize, some of the black dots were obviously coming up at a great rate of knots. I checked the throttle to see if there was any more travel, but alas it was fully open. I adjusted the mixture to get a few more R.P.M. to strengthen my position but no, all I could do was to fly as smoothly as possible and helplessly watch them pass me. I maintained the ridge height and looked ahead, wondering about the merit of going lower to benefit from the compression effects of the air under my wings. I was weighing up the situation in my mind, my main concern being that of fuel. We knew that it was critical, and I was reminded of that as the indicator attached to the float bobbed up and down, only just visible. When the indicator disappeared completely we would have 20 minutes of flying time left.

As we crossed the last ridge I realised that it would be wiser to keep the height that I had, as an engine stoppage at zero feet would be a bit embarrassing, to say the least. As I looked ahead I saw a glint on the horizon, I checked my compass, and yes, I was on track. As I strained to identify it, I saw a few specks also concentrating on their progress. Looking back I saw the specks of the pursuing aircraft getting bigger. Would they pass me before I got to the finish? Who were they? They were too small to recognize. Could I pass any of those ahead of me?

Heading straight towards the glint, it seemed likely that it was in fact the reflection of the afternoon sun on the hangars. As we got closer, this was clearly the case as the airport became identifiable. The sky was filled with aviators stretching their machines to their limits. There were eight ahead of me, and a whole gaggle behind. This got the adrenaline going in my blood again and I eased the stick forward to best utilize all the energy I had. The aircraft ahead were at a variety of heights with a number visibly below the specified 300 feet.

My final attempt at pipping the others to the post resulted in me zooming over the finish line at hanger height to finish 9th. I was ecstatic. I seem to remember that I was also the first Tiger home. In the briefing, the Tigers, due to low fuel at the finish, had requested landing priority and with that in mind I immediately turned onto an early downwind. I gently converted my speed into height, without zooming, climbed up to a gentlemanly height and carried out the pre-landing checks. After a final, gentle turn onto final approach, and a landing, my body was on a high as I taxied back to the aircraft park.

We got out of the aircraft and it felt as if we were still flying. We were walking so tall that it was not true. This was my first-ever flying competition and I had come in ninth. My family was overjoyed to see us back in one piece, and so proud of our achievement. They had enjoyed watching the air show in the two and a half hours that we had been away. Later on, when we viewed the developed cine that dad had taken, I was quite embarrassed at how low we actually were at the finish. We seemed to come almost 'through' the large hangar.

The rest of the day was overtaken by my elation and all I can remember was seeing the aircraft lining up to leave at the end of the show and all I wanted to do was fly again and try some aerobatics.

I found Nick and a few other aviators drifting across the lawn towards the clubhouse. I gave chase and caught up with him. "Nick, how about giving me a lesson on some aerobatics while the weather is so good." I challenged him.

"What? Now? You must be crazy. The only thing I am going to do is relax in the pub!" was his immediate retort.

As determined, as I was to persuade him, he was equally set to prop up the pub. At last he relented and said that I should go and try some loops myself.

"Just get up high, clear the area as you do in the General Flying Area, and push the nose down to get some speed. When you get to 120 miles per hour pull the stick back and watch the horizon disappear beneath your feet, look above you and when you see it again, slightly centralize the stick and when you cut the horizon you will have done your first loop."

It all sounded so easy. I went back to the family and invited Rocky to join me. Most of the visiting aircraft had left to get home before sunset. We seized the opportunity and leapt into Tiggy and prepared to go. Once airborne, I climbed up to 2000 feet above the ground, headed out to the West and surveyed the area.

Having done all my flying that day at zero feet, this now felt as if I was up with the Gods. I carried out my 360-degree lookout turn and checked out for loose items, tight straps etc. I called to Rocky. "Are you ready." His affirmative reply was all I needed. Easing the nose forward I watched the speed build up and pulled the stick back at 120mph. Not ever having been in a loop before I did not know what to expect as I felt the G-force build up on my body, pushing me into my seat. I saw the horizon disappear below me and continued holding the stick back. As we went over the vertical we were faced all around by blue sky, and it was then that I was aware of things going silent as the speed fell off at a most alarming rate. Not knowing what to do I wisely figured I should not try anything else but just kept the stick back.

We went over the top with both of us hanging in our straps. I will never forget the helpless feeling I had as we sat inverted with almost no airspeed. I sat there with the stick in my stomach hoping that the airspeed would recover. Gradually the speed increased and, to my relief, the aircraft was flying again. With airspeed back the feeling returned to the controls and I pulled out of the resulting dive.

With glee we talked over the Gosport tube and decided to give another one a go. I reasoned that my error was not applying enough back stick. The second loop still resulted in a soggy patch over the top but was a slight improvement. Looking at the long shadows a wise decision returned us to the field. With a mixture of butterflies, joy and pride we pushed Tiggy back into her hangar for another week.

Later in the pub, as we recounted the events, we were greeted with much mirth and laughter. I think that Nick probably did not expect me to take him so literally! All the happiness in the pub that night marked the closing of another chapter in my flying, probably one of the most influential airshows in my career.

Chapter 13

Chick and Arthur were my closest friends among the flying group at Grand Central. The club, though rather small, had a vibrant life. Sunday was the traditional flying day for us and was usually spent formation flying, bog roll cutting (nowadays more politely termed streamer cutting), or just flipping a few friends.

The formation flying was more often than not with Chick in his Cessna 120, 'Penny". I was not yet good enough to give it a try myself, but by contrast Arthur and Chick would often be seen flying around with the Tiger and Cessna tied together with a long piece of white ribbon. To take-off, fly a circuit, and land again without breaking the strings at the ends of the ribbon was no mean feat, something I was to aspire to in the years to come, but without the proficiency that they had achieved.

Bog roll cutting, by contrast, was something we all had a bash at. We would climb to 2 000 feet and throw out a roll of loo paper. The next step was a trifle dangerous. A series of steep turns would be executed in an attempt to cut the now unfurled roll as many times as possible before it touched the ground. I used to thoroughly enjoy this particular activity. The secret was in the way it was thrown out. In the Tiger I used to throttle back, hold the stick back to reduce speed and gently throw it up above my head.

I would then get my speed back as smartly as I could and pull into a steep turn, looking for the roll. If you were lucky it would have unrolled into a long streamer. Invariably a first timer would expect to see it far below them, but it is amazing how slowly they fall. A series of turns and straight runs clipping the top off the streamer each time would do the trick. Anywhere around 5 – 6 cuts would be a score to be proud of. If inadvertently the streamer was cut too far down, the effect of the aircraft flying through the streamer would cause it to bunch up into a scruffy ball making other cuts more difficult. I can still see myself doing my last cut ever at Grand Central.

My last pass found me approaching from across the field towards the fuel bay. As I cut through the tip for the last time, the other end was just gently settling onto the apron in front of the fuel bay. As I flew over the fuel bay this marked my last ribbon cut at Grand Central as thereafter it grew far to big and commercial and such activities were dissuaded.

I recall the day when an American aviatrix was watching us on one of these occasions and she came up and introduced herself. She was out on holiday with her husband and had been watching our crazy antics. Soon she was in the front of Tiggy with me and as we tumbled and turned cutting the roll, she was madly taking a cine film. As usual, when we got down I checked the aircraft for bits of roll caught on the airframe. As I walked around Tiggy, she followed me and collected a hand full of oily tattered bits to take back home and show her fellow pilots what went on in the remote continent of Africa.

One day I had been checking the valve clearances and filling the rocker boxes with oil when Arthur appeared out of the blue. He asked how soon we would be ready to fly and said that he and Chick wanted to try a bit of wing walking as soon as Tiggy was ready. As soon as I had finished, the two started a pre-flight inspection and clambered aboard. The only difference was that Chick was sitting ON the wing, with the leading edge behind his knees. I was amazed as all the airshow routines I had seen started with both occupants inside the machine. He was going to take-off with Chick on the wing! As they taxied out I casually thought that half of the uninsured Tiger was mine. After all, they had so much experience that hopefully nothing could go wrong! They lined up on the runway and I heard my half of the Gipsy engine doing its best to help his half get the strange sight into the air.

As expected, I watched the ground fall away from the aircraft, but not quite as fast as I would have liked. To my horror, as they got out of ground effect, the climb stopped and as much as my two cylinders battled to help his two cylinders keep the spectacle airborne, it did not happen, and I watched helplessly as the 'craft lost height and disappeared from view steadily losing height. I leapt into a nearby car and one of the members drove me to the main road that was roughly parallel to the runway direction. After a short space of time that felt like forever, we were amazed to see the aircraft climbing steadily back towards the airfield.

By the time we returned they had already landed and I leapt out of the car. My emotions of seeing Tiggy climbing steadily curdled in my stomach as I wondered what had really happened. As always the two got out, laughing and joking, despite my total horror at what may have happened. What had happened was that Chick thought that Arthur was just trying to give him a bit of a start. In the meantime as soon as they had taken off Arthur realised that they were not climbing and, with no communication, he was trying his level best to attract

Chick's attention. The more he tried, the more casual Chick was, thinking it was just a bit of their continual bantering and jibing.

Now that they were back safely, it conjured up quite a picture. Arthur shouting at Chick to get back in the cockpit while Chick was casually sitting on the wing, waving at the people below them, and me in a frenzy wondering what was going on and what I could do to help the situation. The harder Arthur tried, the more Chick waved, even as they passed over one particular woman hanging out her washing, and periodically turning to grin back at Arthur, who was desperately trying to save the day.

With Arthur's usual cool head, unflustered by the situation, he turned along the Olifantsfontein Road and landed safely. He asked the first motorist on the scene to turn the aircraft around so that he could take-off. The stunned motorist complied, Chick was told in a few curt words to get into the front cockpit, and they took off and headed back to Grand Central. In Arthur's inimitable style everything worked out well, and my blood pressure slowly resumed its normal beat.

Another one of Uncle A's amazing ideas came about in our own home when Nick and Arthur were at a dinner party that Mum and Dad had arranged and of course after dinner the conversation swung around to flying. Arthur was explaining his concept of a small, all aluminium, aerobatic aircraft to Nick. His graphic descriptions were supported by a series of highly technical illustrations on the back, inside and all over his cigarette box.

The biggest advantages, he went on to describe, were cantilever biplane wings with negative stagger, and a nose wheel to avoid those tricky situations. He felt that his concept would reduce drag and weight significantly, and would give a good performance on 130hp. The evening made all his thoughts gel and inspired him to put them into action the next day.

A group of us enthusiasts got together at Arthur's factory, and with a donated case of wine to seal the occasion, the 'Spirit of ----stein' was born. We all had a part to play, meeting in the evenings at the factory, and soon the bits of metal started to take the shape of a rather unique aircraft.

The remaining Gipsy major engine from the Dragonfly graced the front, and behind that was a cantilever top wing with the leading edge at the pilot's eye level. Forward of the top wing, at the level of the aircraft floor, and without any struts or bracing, was the lower wing. The stubby little side-by-side machine was like nothing that anyone was used to, it had a strange look all of its own.

After weeks, or rather, months of working the day for it to be transported to the airfield dawned with Chick and I in the air in Penny. We were patrolling above Louis Botha Avenue waiting for it all to happen. Arthur had arranged a low-loader to transport the 'Spirit of ----stein' with the wings on, while we watched from aloft. I remember Chick's advice. "When you do things like this, always cover yourself." And with that he talked into the microphone and reported ZS-BBZ for low flying between Louis Botha Avenue and Jan Smuts Airport. As we all knew that BBZ, the Staggerwing was in for maintenance and was having all her wings recovered. The theory was that if anyone reported another aircraft (us) for low flying it would be assumed to be the aircraft that had already been reported.

In this manner, we 'supervised' the relocation to Grand Central for its final finishing off. Things went well until Uncle A was doing the taxi tests, and rather tragically they were to lead to its final demise. Severe nosewheel shimmy was experienced, even at very low speeds. It was so severe that he did not even get anywhere near lifting the nose.

Hours of discussion followed and everybody had their input. I disagreed, based on the fact that the post was leaning forward thus not allowing the wheel to centre. Despite trying to get my thoughts accepted and a chance to be tested, the impasse remained. The stalemate was so severe that everything came to a halt and the aircraft remained in the hangar.

One day I was at 'Central, and I decided to check up on the 'Spirit of ------ stein', and I found the hangar empty. I immediately phoned Uncle A who thought I was dreaming. Of course I was dreaming, I must have just had the wrong hangar. Sure enough, a few days later he checked up himself to find it gone.

Some years later I tracked down the engine that had been used in the aircraft, and therewith the amazing story. The engine had been purchased in a scrapyard. I went to see them and they admitted that they had bought an aircraft that had been sold off in pieces. It transpired that one of Arthur's disgruntled employees had taken it and sold it for scrap – what a disaster. Cut down in the prime of youth one might say!

Strangely, one of the home-designed and -built aircraft that is seen regularly at events bears a strong resemblance in its fuselage, and I often wonder if the constructor bought it from the scrapyard. I did confront him once to be assured that it was entirely his own design.

One happy thing that did come out of it was that I now had the two original engines and logbooks from the Dragonfly in my possession, complete with their consecutive numbers. Who knows, in the years to come, the new owner of the dragonfly might even be willing to buy them and fit them back where they belong.

Chapter 14

The following year The Star decided to hold a second air race. This year the event was to take place south of Johannesburg. I can't help thinking that the change may well have had something to do with the number of aircraft screaming over the city the year before at slightly below the prescribed height. The airfield chosen was Baragwanath Airfield, the home of the Johannesburg Light Plane Club, which is the oldest flying club in the southern hemisphere and is still active today. It was started in 1936 and has operated successfully on a piece of ex mining ground, until the airfield was rather tragically closed down when a road was constructed through it. Another piece of ground was secured from the Johannesburg Council and a new field was constructed. I am part of the club and we still operate J L.P.C. at the 'new' Baragwanath, slightly further south of Johannesburg than the original location.

The air race, as in the previous year was part of their air show. The proposed route would avoid flying over built-up areas, to the east, towards Bethal and Delmas. Most of my flying had been to the west of Johannesburg and so the whole area would be new to me. This, together with the memories of the previous event, inspired me and so I was an early entrant. I remember the number allotted to me as being 51, which I proudly applied to the rudder. We spent the previous weekend polishing the aircraft to get every little bit of performance out of her.

The day of the air show dawned with a collection of us flying over from Grand Central Airport to Baragwanath for the event. Some were taking part in the air race while some were just spectators. As is most often the case, the airfield is closed to anything, other than the current display, at an early hour so there is invariably a mad dash to get in before the field closes.

As I approached, it was amazing to see the dust rising up from all the motor vehicles jostling to get in to the field and all the stall-keepers setting up their positions for the day. Being the first time that I had flown into an air show, I was amazed at all the activity that one normally takes for granted. From above you could get a real feel of how much effort is put into a large show.

The ground below was a picture. It looked like part of the scenery of a huge train set. There were stalls that had been erected; cars parked in orderly rows, and lines of neatly arranged aircraft either on static display, as visitors, or participants. All the air shows that I had been to by road lacked this special approach view. With it came that wonderful feeling that you were really part of the show. Even today, many years and many shows later, I still get that special feeling when you look down at the ground so wonderfully decorated, a feeling of pride, belonging, and of being a bird.

I flew away to the downwind leg and, by the time I was established in the landing circuit, there were a number of aircraft ahead. With the differences in speed each was juggling the size of their circuit to maintain the separation so that they could land safely in turn.

We spent the morning relaxing (as much as one could with the race ahead of us) and enjoyed the early part of the air show. The airshow opened with a most impressive fly-past of the new Boeing 707. Little did I realise that in the years to come I would actually be flying one of those birds. SAA had just received them and they were the new pride of their passenger fleet. We watched in amazement as the huge bird swooped down onto us, its silver wings, looking as if they were able to shield even the crowds on either side of the runway. This was the first jet airliner any of us had seen and to see it so low and in such a dramatic presentation was a first. They were to supplement and eventually replace the DC 7's and Constellations that were currently in service.

As the race start time got closer, the adrenaline began to manifest itself and by the time it came for us to go, we were on quite a high, although still on the ground.

We taxied out at the time allocated to us at the briefing and waited our turn. When the flag dropped I opened up and started the take-off roll. We were airborne and at the end of the runway I rolled in to a steep turn and set course. We had been warned at the briefing that any crew turning out up before the end of the runway would be disqualified.

The flight itself followed the same lines as the previous race, except that we now had a better idea of what to do. As we sped along the green fields, we were each absorbed in our own thoughts. One vivid memory was that of us speeding along and approaching a road at a slight angle. As I looked to my left I saw a Mini speeding down the road that we were due to cross. As I did a mental projection it seemed apparent that we would both reach the point where our tracks were due to cross simultaneously. I could see the driver clearly and I was pretty sure that he had not seen us - yet.

We continued as we had planned and at the moment of crossing I pulled back the stick to leap over the Mini by a safe margin. Just before I pulled back, my last glance saw the driver's eyes widen as he observed us as leap over the top of the car. I am sure he probably got a bit of a start, but I looked back and saw nothing unusual and the Mini was continuing down the road without a problem. Now, years later and being much more mature, I realise that I owe him quite an apology. But, kids will be kids, and youth does not always display the most responsible side of life.

As we turned onto the last leg the position became rather crucial in fuel terms. The Tiger was fitted out with Arthur's Dragonfly propeller and so I was able to cruise at full throttle without over revving. We had checked the fuel gauge and had set it to read zero with a reserve of 20 minutes.

For safety I climbed up to a modest height on the last stage of this leg and waited for the gauge indicator to disappear. I was almost within sight of Bara when it vanished. So I knew that I just had a safe margin on fuel. As on the previous year, as soon as I crossed the finish line we gently executed a climbing turn onto the downwind leg and came in to land.

As before, the Tigers had priority to land due to their expected fuel shortage. As I continued in the circuit I looked at the aircraft in the air around me. I counted a total of six aircraft, some in the circuit and others giving way for me. That meant that I had in fact come in 7th. As I came in to land, the relief at touching the ground with a minimum of fuel was complete.

I taxied up to my parking place and a saw Mum, Dad and my brother Tony, come up to greet me. We settled down to watch the rest of the show. After a few hours watching a series of aerobatic presentations and commercial advertising flights, the time came to pack up and get my parents off home by car. As at every air show it was a real bun fight to get out and on the ground all the cars were rushing to try and beat the traffic jam. As they drove off I could already see the traffic building up ahead of them.

I stood with Chick and Tony as the show came to an end, slowly getting our minds into the mood to get into our aircraft and fly out.

I put on all my flying kit and climbed into the Tiger as Tony started her for me. He took his seat and we taxied out to join the queue of departing aircraft. When our turn came I lined up and opened the throttle. As I raised the tail I was again aware of the dust clouds made by the cars as they crept along at a snail's pace towards the exit. The exit track took them across the end of the runway and I could see the long snake of cars crossing the end of the runway.

As I continued my take-off roll, and gained airspeed, the wheels gently broke free from the grip of the land and I began to climb. Looking at the cars crossing the runway I gave way to that naughty temptation that all of us children have from time to time, as young or old as we may be.

I pushed the nose down and flew parallel with the runway, and zoomed over the cars with a wonderful feeling of exhilaration. I saw the eyes of the people in the cars follow our path as we crossed them, barely feet above their heads. I wondered what they thought as they were locked in to the queue crossing over just before the end of the runway. I was amazed that the organizers had agreed to them using it as an exit.

I soon forgot about them and a wonderful warm feeling flowed through my whole body as I thought about the day's flying while we made our way back to Grand Central. On arrival we slotted in to the array of aircraft in the circuit and landed in turn. With the Tiger safely back in the hangar we drove up to the clubhouse for a chat and sundowner before setting off home.

The pub was full of stories as each participant relayed his or her perspective of the day's flying. When my turn came, I was standing next to Chick, and I started to relate my take-off. As soon as I mentioned seeing the cars crossing the runway, Chick looked at me and said:

"Did you do that too?" and we had quite a laugh when we realised that a number of us had zoomed over the poor spectators. It just goes to show that the child in each of us never really dies.

Another air show that got my heart going was down at Klerksdorp, another small town where Arthur had offered to fly a radio-controlled Tiger act. Arthur was staying over for the night and so I was to fly Tiggy down and return as a passenger in the RSA 200 with Arthur's friend Peter. During the Tiger Moth's wartime years, an attempt was made to produce a radio-controlled aircraft to be used for target practice. The Tiger Moth was equipped with a massive radio set with huge servos driving the controls. This resulted in a full-size aircraft to be used as a drogue, known as a **Queen Bee**. Around 600 of these were built and I don't think any were ever shot down.

This is probably where the idea originated, and in due course the public announcer was heard to say that this radio controlled aircraft had recently been resurrected. At the time, Arthur was busy fitting a huge black box to the back cockpit, and he squeezed himself into the cockpit underneath it. On each side was a gap at the front that hopefully he would be able to look through and fly his sequence. I was horrified. Here was my pride and joy and uncle A was going to attempt to fly, peering through his little holes barely the size of a large toothpaste tube. The slots were covered in a black fine mesh and the whole black box was adorned with a series of knobs and strange-looking aerials.

Never having seen anything like this before, I had to climb into the front of the aircraft and taxi out of the hangar and on to the flight line. Just to make things worse they were using the taxiway in place of the main runway for the display. I lined the aircraft up on the taxiway and climbed out of the cockpit, leaned in and secured the straps in the empty front cockpit. I moved to the back cockpit and made pretence of setting up knobs and making the radio ready for flight, and told Uncle A to be careful. I was so worried about Tiggy.

The engine note picked up and the aircraft started to move. To my absolute horror, the Tiger started doing the most amazing gyrations all over the runway and headed towards a Dakota. Without any play-acting, I started chasing the wild aircraft with all the power in my limbs. The crowds must have loved it. My heart was racing and the comical scene of me chasing the aeroplane randomly around the airfield was probably more than money could buy. This was definitely not part of the act. I was rushing around, the aircraft would then turn on me, and I would jump out of its way, and then continue my desperate chase. I eventually managed to grab hold of the edge of the cockpit, and climbed in.

I taxied back to the start of the taxiway and lined the aircraft up again. As I got out for the second time, I brushed past the back cockpit and in no uncertain terms told Arthur to stop messing around. With that I slipped off the wing and walked away, hoping for the best. I turned around as Tiggy opened up again and began her take-off roll, this time without too much messing around. The sight of the seemingly pilotless aircraft, with its tail up and taking off, was quite amazing.

He took off and proceeded to give a wonderful display of crazy flying. The supposed 'pilot', who stood alongside the taxiway, in front of the large black box, apparently wrestling with the radio controls, kept the crowds on their feet. Prompted by the commentary over the public address, the antics of the aircraft and those of the 'pilot' would get wilder. "He seems to have lost partial control," the commentator would say and almost on cue the aerial antics would get wilder and the 'pilot' would struggle even more, until the announcement that it was all under control calmed things down.

The 'pilotless' machine turned onto an erratic final approach and the crowd was silent. The aircraft rounded out and we saw a number of bounces, from one wheel to the other. The crowd's anxiety was fuelled by the announcer's comments and everybody heaved a sigh of relief when the crazy aircraft finished its dramatic, wild landing and came to rest. All the antics ceased as the propeller came to a halt, and I ran up to the aircraft. What a sense of relief at seeing my Tiggy in one piece. I must say that at times I was having serious doubts.

I climbed in and got a swing to get her going. With the 'radio equipment' still in the back I taxied to the hangar from the front seat. Once the dummy radio apparatus was removed and Arthur could climb out, we all had a chuckle. Only an outstanding pilot could pull of a display like he had just done, and I was proud to have him as a partner. I felt a bit spare in retrospect at having doubted his ability, but it had made for a good show.

Soon it was time to consider my journey home with the chaps in the locally made RSA 200. Even though Arthur was the driving force behind the manufacturing project and although I had seen them on many occasions, I had never been in one and was quite looking forward to the flight. The RSA 200 was a Partenavia design, built (or assembled) under licence in South Africa by Atlas Aircraft. Arthur had flown out this particular one out from Italy as the prototype to start the operation. I sat in the front next to Peter, somewhat different from my usual open cockpit sensations and really enjoyed the flight back. We chatted about the aircraft being somewhat like a very powerful Cessna 172 with a variable pitch propeller, but not quite in the 182 league. I always feel that the project was dealt an unfair blow by circumstance early on in its career, before it could reach its full potential.

Chapter 15

Up to this stage my flying career was restricted to the Colt and Tiggy. Always having an aircraft at hand and not seeing myself in a commercial role, I was not in the queue for getting conversions on as many types as possible. At that stage I had been flying for five years and whenever there was something on the go, I invariably used my own aircraft while those that did not have that privilege were amassing a multitude of different types listed on their licences. During one trip to Natal, my number of types doubled from two to four. I was on holiday on the Natal north coast with my family and during one of the day visits to Durban I stopped off at Virginia Airport.

Virginia, one of the older airports in South Africa, just north of Durban, was often the host to a number of interesting machines. As was custom for aviation visitors to an unfamiliar field, they wander around peeping through cracks in the hangar sheeting, talking to anyone remotely close to aeroplanes and generally getting to know as much as possible about the field.

That was how I came across Pikkie Rautenbach's establishment. He ran a very successful crop spraying organisation operating out of Virginia, and having met him previously at the air race at Grand Central, I had no compunction in going into his office for a visit. He gave me a hearty welcome and we chatted away. Never having flown at the coast before I asked him if he knew of any aircraft available for hire.

He took me and showed me a Turbulent that he had and said that I could rent it from him. A Turbulent is a rather attractive wooden, single seater aircraft with a Volkswagen engine. Being a low-wing tailwheel aircraft it sits quite low on the ground and looks like a big radio controlled model. I was as keen as mustard and said that I would come back to him. The problem was firstly that the Turbulent was a single-seater and secondly that I had no experience at the coast. Although Pikkie was confident that I could handle it very easily, I had my doubts. I said that I would soon be back, and went away with a few thoughts in my head. I walked past the flying school and one solution became very apparent. They had a Cessna 150 that I could hire with an instructor. That way I could get a conversion and get a bit of coastal flying at the same time so that I would be a bit better prepared for the 'Turbi'.

I was used to flying up at 5500 ft where the density altitude on a hot day went up to 8000 ft. This in simple terms means that, when taking the daily temperature into account, makes it the same as flying at 8000 ft under normal conditions. Effectively it is like taking off or landing at an airfield at 8000 ft above sea level. The air in those conditions is so thin that it reduces the performance of aircraft rather drastically.

The next day I was off to the training school. After producing my licence and filling in the required paperwork, we strolled off to the Cessna 150 parked on the tarmac.

To most people this is a simple run of the mill aircraft, but to me it was my first all metal aircraft. As we walked around doing the pre-flight check, I was amazed at the difference between it and the fabric aircraft that I was used to. The Colt was bulky and purposeful with short, stubby, fabric covered wings while the Cessna was rather sleeker and with a bigger wingspan. The overall effect was much more dainty and spindly. Once inside, the feeling of finesse carried on. There were even proper door panels, unlike the Colt where the sides were covered in fabric. The effect of creating shapes inside the cockpit was much more like a motor vehicle. The seats carried a little bit of artistic design, and when one looked at the instrument panel the comparison was amazing.

The array of instruments was something I had never flown with before. I was used to a very basic panel without even a turn and slip, but here I even had an artificial horizon, radio, and radio navigation aids.

Undaunted, but amazed by the display, the instructor and I boarded, and prepared to set sail. It was dramatic as the aircraft screamed into the sky and it felt very awkward keeping the controls back far enough after take-off. The aircraft felt like a World War 2 fighter to me as it climbed into the sky at an incredible speed. It felt so unnatural having to pull the yoke back so far to get the climb speed to stabilize in the super dense air. When everything had settled down, the horizon was below the nose of the aircraft, a very unusual situation for me in a climbing attitude, quite a revelation for a Reef pilot.

When we came into land, I was equally taken aback at the feel of the aircraft in the thick air. It seemed to float forever and have an amazing force keeping the wings aloft. After a few circuits I got used to this new way of flying and was given my conversion on the 150.

As I walked over to Pikkie with the ink still wet on the conversion in my hands, I could not help wondering what happens in the opposite scenario when a coastal pilot comes up to the Reef. How could they possibly be prepared and how could they adapt themselves to fly in the thin air that we have up there? How could they cope with their first landing at high altitude? Even more so, how would they cope with an aborted landing in air so thin? How would they cope with having to keep the nose lower than at the coast, when they applied power?

Pikkie took one look at the conversion and questioned why we had done so much time. "Just get in and fly it" he said "with all your Tiger flying you will have no problem at all. Hop in and I will sign your conversion as soon as you come down."

I inquired about speeds and he reiterated his earlier comments about me being very capable. In any event he said the airspeed indicator doesn't work correctly it was about 30 to 40 mph out. "The rpm limits don't really matter because it is only VW engine, keep it going and it is OK."

With all the enthusiasm of youth I climbed into the tiny cockpit. I was amazed at how small it was. The engine felt as if it was bolted to my feet and looking on either side the wings seemed to be extensions of my arms. I taxied out in a state somewhere between amazement and terror, and got to the end of the runway. The runway at Virginia is parallel to the beach with only a series of large bushes growing on the sand dunes between it and the sea.

As I opened up for take-off all the drama I expected came to naught, and I climbed out effortlessly in the most delightful aircraft. Sitting in the open cockpit without even a helmet, with the damp, salt-laden air blowing on my face, I felt like a bird. I continued the circuit keeping a respectable distance on downwind and came in for my first landing. I concentrated on my approach; lined up well, and carried out a good landing. Amazed at how easy it was I did the obligatory three circuits and taxied up to Pikkie's hangar. To this day I can remember the feeling that, even though Tiggy had little to do in the cockpit, this had even less. Pikkie was waiting with a big grin on his face and my conversion in his hand. We agreed that I could come and fly her on occasions while I was down there and agreed on a figure of only a few Rand per hour.

I had a number of wonderful flights up the coast over the next week, and even got involved in a little bit of low flying. On one occasion a friend of ours, who was at the local hotel, was even heard to comment on the little aircraft that he had seen on a few occasions. Bert had in fact been a Spitfire pilot in the Second World War and when he saw Dad, he recalled how he had seen this funny little aircraft zooming along the surf towards the bathing area below his hotel. He had been watching from the balcony and swore blind that he was looking down at the aircraft. Enough said, or perhaps it was that the front garden of the hotel was built very high off the beach!

My final flight in the Turbulent was the most memorable, if not for the best reasons. It was also going to be my last as it was the day before we left for home. I was returning to Virginia after my usual flight up the coast, and was doing everything by the book, but I was in for a surprise.

Downwind at Virginia was always out at sea. Aware that all the pilots that flew the Turbulent ridiculed at how close they made their circuit, I was making a nice generous circuit. Armed with this and the other relevant information, I turned overhead and throttled back.

I had almost lost the 500 feet to join downwind at 800 feet, and was just about to open the throttle when things felt a bit funny and the engine note changed. I throttled back and, even though the difference was almost imperceptible, I realised that something was wrong. I tried in vain, by opening and pumping the throttle, to get the motor going again. My training sprang to the front of my mind - fly first and then problem solve later. I looked back at Virginia as I began to turn, and the airfield off my wingtip seemed to jump up to eye level.

Even at this early stage of my flying career, the absence of fear was evident. I did not have that screaming fear that humans normally have, but merely a deep concern. This is part of one's basic training where a pilot is trained not to be surprised when things go wrong. Well, my time was now. The cards were down, would I get back in one piece?

I was at barely 800 ft but at least I was heading back directly to the airfield, scarcely one kilometre away and things did not look so rosy. I figured out that I was going to swim, so I might as well get as close as I could and keep my swim as short as possible, and get poor Pikkie's aircraft as close to shore as I could.

Without a working airspeed indicator it was difficult to try different speeds to get the best glide, but I seemed to be winning. All I could do was be aware of the sounds and the wind in my face to judge my speed. As seconds went by they felt like hours, but things soon began to look better. I realised that I would at least make the breakers. Not a pleasant thought, but that is what it was. After another short space of time I realised that I would even make the beach and I began to plan an approach to try a landing there. I almost cried with joy when I realised that I had a chance of getting back to mother earth.

My thoughts were jolted as I was suddenly aware of the new landscape unfolding ahead. My whole world had condensed into the small space between the runway and me and I had a sudden feeling that I would be able to scrape over the bushes and get to the airfield. I was now very fortunate that I had not tried to make a circuit and had headed directly for the field. There was now no time or space to plan anything other than to creep over the bushes and turn on to the runway. As I turned over the bushes, almost on cue, the propeller stopped windmilling and I sank out of the 90-degree turn onto the welcome hard surface of the runway.

That tiny craft seemed to stop almost instantly and I got out rather sheepishly, but with the most enormous burden off my shoulders. I was safe! As I pushed the Turbulent off the runway some figures came running into view. Leading them was Pikkie, with the biggest grin I have ever seen, probably because I could not see my own.

Unbeknown to me, my antics were all being watched from the 'field and Pikkie was certain that he had seen the last of his little aeroplane. With much relief and thanking my ever-faithful Guardian Angel, we all pushed her back to the hangar.

A little investigation showed that I had a severe case of carburettor icing. This was a lesson never to be forgotten, as the little Turbulent had no carburettor heating.

With much thanking and farewells, I left Virginia and drove back to our cottage at Salt Rock. As we were leaving the next day I had no chance of ever flying that delightful little aeroplane again, and in fact I have never flown in or out of Virginia since that day. The memory of the Turbulent will never be forgotten. She was a real little lady, so responsive, and with such a wonderful feedback to the pilot and the time I spent zipping up the coast to Salt Rock was very special for me.

Chapter 16

Life at Grand Central had taken a turn and there were a few changes that painted a new picture. Arthur Mechin had tragically died while in the Mediterranean on his yacht, and was to be sorely missed by everybody. I took over his share in Tiggy and continued operating at Grand Central. I had got to know a few of the chaps at Baragwanath and in fact a number of the old crowd had moved across there.

Club life had changed dramatically as it had taken on a far more commercial approach. A new, large clubhouse had been built and there was a large swing away from the type of club activities that we had been used to. Grand Central Flying Club became little more than a name attached to a big commercial venture. In fact, in the preceding years, the future had looked so settled that Dad had given me a life membership of the club. Years later as I write this book, it no longer exists and I have outlived the club!

The fun-loving aircraft crowd no longer felt as welcome as we had been in the past, and as we were not buying vast quantities of fuel nor supporting the maintenance activities as much as their financial forecasts wanted us to do, we were literally being squeezed out. The lack of club activities meant that visiting old aircraft were far less frequent, and their visits were sorely missed.

I considered the feasibility of moving to Baragwanath and getting a hangar there and when one became available I took it with rather a lump in my throat. It was one thing talking about moving, but quite another actually uprooting and moving on. The day came and I got all my goods together and left my faithful hangar at Grand Central for the last time. I flew over to the now familiar airfield and, while I was putting her into the new hangar, I wondered what the future held, how long I would be there, and was I doing the right thing? Was this the best place to be? One big plus was the fact that I had got one of the new hangars facing the main runway and immediately there was a good vibe, being able to see all the activity.

Baragwanath itself was also going through some changes. The airfield was being cut down in size and the old hangars and T-hangars to the East were being replaced by a new series alongside the runway. The future looked good, the clubhouse would remain untouched and the only real loss was the cross runway. There were a number of members who did not even fly but used the club rather like a country club.

The club was accommodated in the most magnificent, thatched building that had a large lounge with a lovely fireplace at one end and an adjoining, well supported, dining room. On the weekends the dining room used to produce the most wonderful homemade meals, and in the evenings in winter we used to sit round the warm fire with our sundowners. The overall result was that one felt truly at home and like a family. Outside the main building were a series of 'igloos' for out-of-towners to rent. I always got the impression that there were more full-time residents in them than there were visitors.

It was a very active sport aviation club, the home of the Johannesburg Light Plane Club, and it supported two parallel runways. The larger runway was hard paved and was used for the power aircraft, while the other runway was used for the gliders. Consequently, the power circuit was always to the East and the glider circuit was always to the West. It was quite something getting used to flying on base leg, about to turn onto final, looking at a glider coming towards you on his base leg.

The general hum, particularly in the old aircraft scene, was far more active than it had been at Grand Central, and certainly more than in recent times. There were quite a few Tiger Moths resident on the field and it was more often the case that at least one other Tiger was active on that part of the weekend that I had chosen to come out to fly.

There was also an active aerobatic contingent and, all in all, I felt completely at home. There were even a couple of chaps constructing a pair of Pitts Specials on the airfield. There was an old building on the airfield, near the 'igloos' where they lived, that was used to house the two aircraft under construction. The maintenance organisation was also far more geared up to looking after the older aircraft, and much to my relief, I soon realised that my new home was a vast improvement to my type of flying interest. The maintenance hangers were always worth a look because there was invariably something old or interesting there. The bits and pieces all around were so much older that there was always something of note lying around.

The first air show and air race, after my move to Bara, was already on the cards and so naturally I wanted to get involved. Due to the large interest that the previous air races had drawn, the race distance was increased, which put all the Tigers out of the running. However, as a compromise, they had organised a separate air race just for the Tigers. This seemed even better as we would all be competing on an even footing. It was due to be a race over one hundred and fifty miles, which would be within our scope.

The day dawned, and as we drove out to Bara we were dismayed at the weather. The cloud base was low, but the visibility was not too bad. When we got there we were greeted by a group of long faced organisers. All the aerobatic slots were in jeopardy due to the low cloud base.

It was not long before we were officially notified that both the races had been cancelled. Disappointed, we had no option but to sit on the grass under our aeroplanes, bemoaning the weather and watching a handful of commercial fly-pasts keeping the crowd amused. I wandered over to the large hangar and saw Hansie Haraf, the Aero Club chairman. I had met him previously with Dad, and so greeted him and commiserated with him over the unfortunate situation caused by the weather. He vocalised how distraught the organisers were at the way it was turning out. I had a suggestion. With the enthusiasm that is only brought about by the naivety of youth, I suggested that, as the Tiger Moth race was cancelled, we should replace it with a pylon race. He emphatically rejected my idea, pointed out that pylon racing had been banned since before the war and wondered if I was crazy.

"Was I talking on behalf of the entire group of Tiger pilots?" He inquired.

I said that I certainly could not talk on behalf of every pilot, but those that I had spoken to were very keen to participate. As I looked north I saw Brixton tower.

"We can do our first turn around there," I said pointing and looking to the West I continued," and then we could fly around Orlando Power Station and back here. A few laps of that I am sure will keep the crowd cheering and us pilots happy."

We parted company, with me having firmly planted a seed that I was sure would grow over the next hour or so, and him shaking his head at us pilots. All I had to do now was to get the word around to all the Tiger pilots. I was confident of success.

While we were idly chatting and watching the remnants of the air show, I repeated what I had suggested to Hansie, and explained my thoughts to the group. A few enthusiastic pilots soon got the mood going and it was not long before all the Tiger pilots were right behind me. All we had to do was wait. I was confident that before long we would be called.

Some time later Nick Turvey caught up with me. As I had expected, out of desperation, the organisers had reluctantly agreed with my pylon race concept. Nick had been sent to find me and arrange a briefing outside the large hangar.

I rushed off and soon gathered all the Tiger pilots together to attend the briefing. I will long remember Nick's face as he gave the briefing. Concern was written all over it as he talked to us. His reservation about the race was clear as he told us not to go anywhere near Brixton Tower, but to turn around the end of the mine dump on the extended centre line of the runway. There was already a marshal on his way to the end of the dump to erect some sort of marker. From there, as per my original suggestion, we would turn around the towers at the power station. Thereafter we would return and turn around the old control tower on top of the hangar. Five laps of that would keep us happy and should keep the crowds cheering.

His final words were: " Remember chaps, be careful, don't crash, its ugly."

To this day those words will ring in my ears every time the situation warrants it. He then produced a hat and we were invited to draw a number to get our starting positions. He then got more marshals together and left us to our own thoughts and preparations.

Like a group of naughty school kids, we chatted as we wandered back to our aircraft to get ready. A marshal was due to flag us off in the order that we had picked out of the hat. We lined up all the Tigers in that order and waited with butterflies doing aerobatics in our stomachs. We all donned our flying kit and were soon ready to go. We each looked enviously towards the lucky guy at the front who drew number one, and waited. The marshal, with a white flag, got into position and we all strapped ourselves in and waited for our respective starters to swing our props. As the aircraft engines started one by one the number one guy was flagged off.

I cannot remember my position among the 15 Tigers, but I just remember being near the end. Tigers surrounded me, with their engines running, and my brother was swinging my propeller for me. For the first time ever my Tiger would not start promptly, with all the noise he must have been unable to hear the fuel while he was priming, and flooded her. Murphy was against me. I watched in horror as a string of aircraft took to the skies ahead of me. At last she fired. I was last in line. I taxied immediately to the runway and lined up on my take-off roll. As I turned I remember seeing three aircraft all with their wheels on the runway simultaneously.

The last aircraft was still on the runway as I slotted in, with my throttle fully open, and began to raise my tail as the speed built up. I was on my way. As she picked up flying speed I kept her low to allow the speed to build up and also to cope with the slipstreams of the other aircraft. I headed straight for the mine dump with all the speed I could squeeze out of her.

As previously, I was using the Dragonfly propeller giving me a good turn of speed (in Tiger terms of course!) at the expense of my climb. Heading straight for the minedump I saw the turning marker ahead, and as soon as I got there I pulled into a steep turn, and set sail off on the next leg for the cooling towers.

Another max rate turn over the towers and I was on my way back to the 'field, heading straight for the little object on the top of the hangar. At this point I must explain that the old control tower was a small hut perched on top of the hangar roof on the centre of the crown. Up the side of the hangar, and running along the one side of the roof to the hut, was a long staircase with a handrail along the outside.

A number of newspaper reporters had congregated inside the hut, in their efforts to get the 'perfect' shot, and as I pulled into a steep turn just above the hut, I had a wonderful view of a bevy of bodies tumbling down the staircase. They were obviously setting themselves up and had been totally petrified by the sight of the crazy airmen (and one woman) in the biplanes approaching at eye-level as fast as each entrant could go. I watched a human cascade pouring down the stairs and across the hangar roof all fighting to exit as fast as possible. I must say that even though the moment of rounding the corner was tense, it brought quite a grin to my face and perhaps had a little to do with how low I was.

We then proceeded to repeat the course for another four laps. I recall trying so hard to pull up a few places. One turn over the control tower with two other machines was quite dramatic. On one lap as I approached the hangar it became evident that three of us would arrive simultaneously. As we got closer we all maintained our positions and started an unplanned, max rate, formation turn. I remember Myrtle was above me as we turned and I looked down at the other Tiger below me. All three of us were in perfect formation, in a near vertical turn and I remember thinking what would happen if one of us slipped or skidded in the turn.

Between the mine dump and the cooling towers, we flew over a long slimes dam (a long narrow dam of slurry deposit that gradually hardens), and I was trying all I could to get a few extra m.p.h. out of her and to save a few seconds on each turn. As I roared along the slimes dam on each lap I got lower and lower, trying to increase the benefit of ground effect. At the edge of the dam I saw a ridge of bushes presumably growing on a mound of soil. On each lap I pulled up slightly to clear it, each time getting a little bolder (or more stupid depending on how you see it!). On the penultimate lap I was as pleased as punch, I had passed a few machines and was somewhere near the middle of the field. I was just clearing (or so I thought) the bush when there was a sharp bang and I felt the whole aircraft shudder. I had collected the bank!

I had no option but to press on, still trying my utmost until I crossed the finish line. Then my thoughts would concentrate on the landing task ahead.

On the ground things were happening as well. The table where the DCA (Division of Civil Aviation) officials were sitting had been placed directly in line with our route between the hangar and the mine dump. As we came out of our turn over the hangar we had the full height of the hanger to convert into speed as we zoomed down low over the airfield to again get max benefit from the ground effect. Our minds were far away from DCA and their table. In fact, as we passed over them, they were getting spattered with drops of oil, and their tempers were being tested. Nick told us afterwards that they were jumping up and down, calling to stop the race. He just maintained, with a smile on his face, that he had no communication with us and in any event anybody with a radio would have it off or not listen to it anyway. So the race continued unabated.

As I came over for the last time, my family saw long tentacles hanging from my undercarriage and they were a bit perplexed. They were not privy to DCA's tantrums (probably so much the better) and so were only concerned about the bits hanging from the underside, wondering what it was, and what it meant.

Back in Tiggy, as I completed the last lap, I continued straight on to join the circuit. The undercarriage is not visible from the cockpit of a Tiger and so I had no idea what the state of it was, and even if it was all still there. All I could do was continue and make the gentlest landing ever and hope for the best.

I will never forget the hollow feeling as I rounded out and held the stick back for my landing. With glee and relief I felt both wheels contact the runway. I taxied off the runway and, as soon as I could before getting back to the crowds, I stopped and got out to assess the position. The axles were covered in mine dump sand but fortunately there was no sign of damage. I brushed off all the sand and removed the few bits of remaining foliage and taxied sheepishly up to the apron.

Once we were all parked, we got out and gradually the reaction of what we had just done began to filter through the insulated pilot skin to our inner emotions. A feeling of excitement, fear, pride, and relief at still being in one piece all boiled in the pot together to give that special, inexplicable feeling. The mixture that was boiling up was soon spiced with the chatting and swapping of our individual stories.

As the weather improved, the organisers were able to resume the programme, but our minds were active as we half watched the aerobatic displays. The rest of the day may have been good, but it was quite mild by comparison to our experiences. We all lived that race over and over again.

The air race had been a winner with the crowds and had saved the day. So much so that it was to be repeated on another two occasions before being banned forever by DCA. We had succeeded in getting the better of the weather and created a new highlight to the flying scene.

Another less formal series of shows arose from our motoring interest. Dad was invited to house some of his collection in a museum set up on the edge of Hartebeespoort Dam, some 30km from home. A local developer was selling off a number of stands and had set up the museum as a focal point in the area. Once we had moved the cars across my attention focussed on the adjoining land. I paced out the length between the base of the power pylons next to the museum, and the road at the opposite end. It came to five hundred of my paces, and even though it was a bit uphill I reckoned that I could make a strip there.

I approached the developer on the basis that if he sold those few stands last, I could clear out a strip. He agreed which then left me with a mind full of ideas. One day I was looking at the road workers and a spark jumped into my brain. I got hold of one of the drivers of the large road rollers, and after a bit of persuasion, I was soon driving it up and down my runway. I based my thoughts on the concept that I would have pushed any big rocks into the ground and end up with a reasonable surface.

It worked out a treat, and soon I had affixed a wind sock to one of the telephone poles on the side of the runway. The next weekend I brought Tiggy in and the strip was born. It was always a little tricky as I had to sideslip over the pylons and land short, but it worked well. I did not have many visitors but we often had a few of my friends flying in for the day. I would fly in each weekend and meet the rest of my family there.

The manager of the museum, Arnie, was all enthused and we had little *ad hoc* airshows most weekends to add to the festivity. Arnie even got a paraglider and he used to tow guests along the runway behind his beach buggy.

As with so many things, it all came to an end and today the ground is all built up and the museum is the local supermarket, but it was good fun while it lasted.

Chapter 17

The next 'pylon' race was to be held at the opening of the Westonarea airfield. It is a small town to the South-west of Johannesburg. The air shows away from the main cities and out in the country were always great fun, and this was no exception. The crowd that attended these country air shows were not as sophisticated as they are in the larger towns, and so they were happy just to see the flying take place. You didn't have to try to kill yourself to get their attention.

This was a real country show complete with the beer gardens and stalls set up all over the place just like a village fair. There was the usual array of ball throwing, shooting, running races and other activities. Food stalls sold hamburgers, vetkoek (a dough deep-fried in oil) and mince and anything else that you could think of. Over and above that there was a most enterprising guy who had bought a scrap car from the local scrap yard. He was charging a fee for the bystanders to take a swing at the car with large hammers that he provided. It was amazing to see his first few customers having a go at all the glass parts. They were vying to have the privilege of the first crack at the windows and headlights.

Tigers at Westonarea

As they struck, huge splinters of glass were showering all over the place. Thereafter his customers had to be content with heavy blows to various parts of the bodywork with not quite the same therapeutic effect. By the end of the day the car had been reduced to a heap of randomly shaped metal.

The fair-like ambience was super to enjoy while we thought about the race to come. We had lost a few contenders who had obviously had a few memory jogs telling them that it was perhaps not the best thing to do.

To the rest of us, sanity did not prevail over the sheer exuberance, and so we were back for the next adrenaline fix. Our numbers had dwindled down to nine, and to their joy the organizers managed to work out that three times three equals nine. As a result we were set up at the end of the runway neatly in three rows of three aircraft each. As explained to us in the briefing, at the drop of the flag the nine aeroplanes would start to roll simultaneously, quite a sobering thought.

Although a touch apprehensive, we were all determined to make it work. Tony, my brother, was again given the task of starting the engine, and then filming us with the cine camera. As the flag dropped, each and every mind was focused on the output of our engines. If one of them so much as faltered we would have ended up in one darn big mess.

Afterwards, I recall looking at the newly developed film, and asking Tony why he did not film our take-off. "I did" he insisted " it is on the film," and with that we laboriously rewound the film, re-threaded it and tried again. After a few attempts the penny dropped. What we saw each time was not a perfect nine-ship formation that came later in the afternoon, but in fact the mass take-off. It looked so much like a deliberate formation that we were completely fooled, and thought that it was a formation that we put up later on in the day.

The pylon race itself was not quite as exciting as the first one. As is most often the case, the newness, the anticipation and excitement of the first one always takes the wind out of the other's sails.

This time I had not had as bad a start as previously, in fact I was plum centre. I was in the centre of the centre row, totally enclosed by aircraft. Once we were all started and ready, our assistants moved away, and the starter dropped the flag. Having the coarse prop did not affect my acceleration up to lift-off to any great extent, and so I was soon airborne amongst the 'formation'. Soon the coarse prop began to take effect and I was able to pull away from most of the field, and catch up on those that had out-climbed me.

I was soon among the front-runners and I clearly remember battling it out with Brian. We were both determined to do our best and were challenging each other for first place. Turn after turn we would swap places and each time seeing the other aircraft ahead, we would get the extra bit of courage to pull a bit tighter on the turn to get in front. Sure enough on the next turn the roles would be reversed. I recall entering the turns just behind him. Obviously to avoid the turbulence I would be to the side or above him. As we approached the turn, if I remained alongside as we turned, I would then have a greater distance to cover so I adopted a technique of using a bit of speed and pulling well above him before the turn. I could then turn steeply, looking down at him slightly ahead of me. I was then able to convert my height into speed and pass him on the next leg. At the next turn I would do a steep low-level turn and he would pass me. And so it went on, until he got the better of me on the last turn. Happy, I settled for second place. The real prize however was the fun and the adrenaline rush that it gave us all.

And so we sat down to watch the rest of the show. One of the aircraft there was a Stampe. This was virtually the French equivalent of the Tiger Moth. It was also a biplane of more or less the same dimensions, but not quite as high. A readily visible difference, particularly in the air, are the rounded wingtips, contrasting to the Tiger's squared off tips. Originally fitted with a Renault engine, most Stampes now have Gipsy motors fitted. This was the only one in the country and so we all took a keen interest, particularly noticing the ailerons fitted to top and bottom wings, and waited to see its rolling performance.

The Stampe then put up a fine aerobatic display in the hands of Scully who was a friend mine from University. With a huge wealth of flying experience, he was to become one of our senior SAA pilots in the years to come. We all marvelled at the way she rolled much faster and smoother than a Tiger. She was also fitted with a fuel system that allowed the engine to continue running upside down. This meant that the engine did not cough and splutter when inverted in the roll, making quite a difference.

The programme included a wing walking display and so we waited eagerly. We then watched a Tiger Moth take off with a passenger aboard. The passenger was none other than the same budding SAA pilot, but he was not to be a passenger for long. As we watched the series of flypasts, he climbed out of the cockpit and onto the wing. At each pass Scully was on a different part of the aircraft. On one instance he came past sitting on the rear fuselage with the tail plane behind his legs, flapping his arms like some huge bird. How he manoeuvred his way to that position was beyond my comprehension.

I approached him later on and asked him how he managed the feat. He explained how he had worked his way along the fuselage, holding on to the edge of the cockpit. It had not been so bad going down to the tail, but on the way back to the cockpit, he missed his handhold and nearly went for a solo flight, sans aeroplane. Needless to say I don't recall any other occasion when he ventured out onto an aircraft in flight.

As the air show drew to a close, we all prepared to depart to get home before sunset. We all flew back with that wonderful glow, keeping us warm in the chilly open cockpit breeze. We were to have only one other pylon race before DCA stopped it totally. It took place at Bara with a very small field of entrants, not turning out to be a very memorable occasion at all. We had been given ridiculous minimum height restrictions, and we were started off with huge separations that made the whole race a parade. We were held back and only flagged off when the previous aircraft's wheels left the ground. Rather a sad end to these events that were so much fun.

A very different weekend's entertainment found me at the old Vereeniging airfield with a group of parachutists. One of my friends at university was a parachutist, and she had invited me to come and spend a day with them as some of the more experienced parachutists had wanted to jump out of a Tiger Moth, but had never had the opportunity. Believe me there was no way that they could reverse the situation and get me to jump out of an aircraft, but a day with them sounded like fun.

She was a super girl and during the time I knew her had a tragic accident when her chute failed to open. Despite all her efforts she plummeted into the ground without managing to open her reserve 'chute. Some time later she told me how she felt when she was falling helplessly. She knew that she would be hurt, but she remained conscious, even after hitting the hard airfield surface, until help arrived. As soon as she saw them arrive she drifted off. Amazingly some weeks later she was back at 'varsity, full of life, and I even danced with her only months after the incident. Sadly I lost contact with her and wonder what she is up to today.

The old airport was on the edge of the town, right next to the major access road from the North. The airfield had a rather homely atmosphere with lots of activity. One such activity concerned people voluntarily jumping out of perfectly serviceable aircraft. This to me was amazing. A parachute in my eyes was a safety accessory only, and the situation would have to be quite disastrous for me to think of it as a serious option. However, each to their own, they always say.

I had been warned by some of the older chaps that some parachutists had a similar feeling about our aircraft. They thought that they were only there to take them aloft to jump out and some of these guys had what they thought was a great trick. They would switch off the front mag switches as they got out of a Tiger, just to say 'thanks'. The poor pilot was then faced with a dead stick landing for his troubles.

I personally did not feel the need for my forced landings to be tested thus, and so found a long piece of thin aluminium tubing that I kept down the fuselage next to me. As rehearsed on the ground, it was the correct length to reach the front switches from the back and flick them on again if required. Needless to say, I never had to test the effectiveness of my solution for real.

I made a point of giving a good briefing to the parachutists before they got in, based on the assumption that their getting onto the wing and then jumping off was a show of agreement that they were happy with the height, position and conditions. In no way was I going to be held liable for some broken body lying on the ground below. I also insisted that they get out onto the right hand wing to keep them away from the mag switches.

After a climb to a minimum of 8 000 feet (3 000 feet above ground), I would indicate that they were free to jump at their own discretion. I throttled back and they would raise themselves up in the front cockpit by holding onto the cabane struts (the struts going up to the fuel tank) on either side. As they grew in stature before me they would block out all forward view and I would have to exert a serious amount of forward stick to offset the pitching up that their bodies would cause. With parachutes and all their clothing blowing in the wind they looked like huge grizzly bears. Once on the wing, as requested they would close the front cockpit door and stand on the walkway and when ready they would wave farewell and jump off.

As their weight left the aircraft it seemed to leap up in the air, and they would disappear from view in the most amazingly short space of time. As I got bolder I would throttle back completely and try to match their descent rate. I soon found out that the only way to lose height fast enough was to spin. As there was no danger of hitting them I used to wait until they jumped, and then boot the rudder, causing a spin.

Only once was I able to beat my passenger down. He was one of the Springbok team, and so it was quite a challenge. I had also dropped him a few times so we both knew the ropes. Watching him go, I initiated the spin and continued until I reached a safe recovery height. Then I proceeded to get into a huge sideslip, like only a Tiger can do. I watched his canopy open and pull him above me as I continued slipping onto finals. I estimated where he would land and projected my run to end up in that direction.

I managed to land and to taxi up to where he was about to touch down. I sat idling next to him, while I watched him land and I waited for his reaction. He started gathering his canopy and then he looked at me. His face showed absolute horror as he realised who I was. "It is impossible," he said "I have just jumped out of that aircraft." "Yes" was all I said with a huge smile on my face.

We all had a huge laugh at my efforts, but the last laugh was on me. Trying to beat the chaps down had taken its toll. I was left with the most splitting headache as I flew home, and it was some years after this occasion that I dropped parachutists again. Probably due to the airspace restrictions, the parachuting stopped and soon the field was closed and a much larger airfield built further from town.

Chapter 18

One of the Baragwanath stalwarts was Bob Hay. He got his Tiger Moth a few years after I did and we had often attended events together. He and I had become close friends over the years. He bought his Tiger from Mozambique and rebuilt it himself and then moved it directly to Bara to get her flying. When I moved permanently to Bara, our time together increased and the friendship was sealed.

At Baragwanath, because we had a number of active Tiger enthusiasts, we often had formation flying sessions, and usually both of us were part of the goings-on. One of the members of the group had a video camera, quite a modern innovation at that time. We used to practice while he would video us. After the flight we would congregate in a hangar where he had set up a television screen. We would then be able to have a constructive de-brief, something quite new in the times of the 8mm movie camera! We also frequented various air shows with the group, or even occasional *ad hoc* excursions as the mood would take us.

I always loved formation flying, and to this day it is a wonderful exercise. It demands a fair concentration in the air and a thorough briefing before taking off. Flying formation on another aircraft demands looking at them the whole time, to the extent that one has to rely implicitly on the leader's judgement. The leader on the other hand has to fly as if the formation is one huge aircraft, taking all obstacles and limitations into account. It becomes apparent that each pilot must have great confidence and trust in the leader. With it all together, flying along, the feeling of being the components of a huge flying machine takes some beating.

One of the memorable exercises was arranged to publicise the film 'The Great Waldo Pepper'. We were tasked to put together a formation to follow the Agcat (a Grumman crop spraying aircraft) that would be towing a huge banner advertising the film. A group of some twelve Tigers agreed to take part and we all waited patiently for the day.

On the first flight we all took off as soon as the Agcat flew over Bara and we tucked in behind him as he guided us over the outskirts of Johannesburg city. After a successful flight in a tightish formation over the suburbs we landed back at Bara all fired with enthusiasm for the next flight scheduled to cover the Pretoria area the next weekend.

The day arrived to find us again waiting for the Agcat. Formation flying as mentioned earlier requires that each pilot concentrates on their individual position so that the whole formation operates as a single large aircraft and so the individual relies on the leader to position the formation. We all took off and slotted into position as we were led over Pretoria. I distinctly remember seeing the huge steelworks passing below at one stage and presumed that permission to pass through the restricted area had been obtained by the leader. We had also passed over one of the military airfields, also a big no no, a bit earlier, but I was confident that it was all in order. After a good flight we all broke formation and headed back to Bara. On the ground we had tales to swap and our usual debrief session in the restaurant and headed home to resume the working week to pay for our hobby.

Monday morning heralded a surprise when I got a telephone call from the Division of Civil Aviation asking me to explain our flight over the forbidden areas. I was rather stunned and explained that we were all following the Agcat as per pre-arrangement. It transpired that a senior inspector had been playing golf next to the steelworks when we all flew over. In a quiet manner he took out his diary and wrote down all our registrations. In the end he said that we were fortunate that all our stories agreed and that I was the last pilot that he contacted and so he would let us all off with a warning. Apparently the Agcat pilot was not Nick that we had expected, as per the previous flight, but a substitute who denied all knowledge of the Tigers behind him, and was not even in radio contact to get clearance!

The Tiger club was invited to fly in to Jan Smuts International Airport on a particular occasion. I cannot remember the reason and what it represented but only what happened that day. I had been chosen to lead the formation of four aircraft on the day. By that stage radios were compulsory and we had all had them fitted. The briefing was that I would call for the whole formation, and that we would all keep formation until we landed. By so doing and with the huge runway we would all be able to land without executing a circuit. We met out at Baragwanath, got our aircraft out of the hangars and ourselves ready. One of the pilots was a real character. Alan was a diamond cutter by profession and a pilot/artist for recreation. He always wore a hairpiece to disguise his baldness and we observed his caution while taxiing with certain amusement. He would taxi without a helmet with his grey hair gently waving in the wind. As the aircraft slowed down he would retract his head like a tortoise and give a blast of power on the throttle. Immediately his head would pop up and look out either side of the cockpit.

We all taxied out with Alan and the tortoise act and prepared to get airborne. Once the formation was aloft and positioned I led them Eastwards. The formation of four Tigers and one Stampe steadily passed over the northern part of Johannesburg towards the large airport full of commercial jetliners, wondering what was in store for us. I had called up the airport and been given clearance to enter the pattern on a left base for runway 03. All had been going as per plan, when suddenly my earphones went silent. A quick scan of the radio showed that it was properly set up, and so I assumed that I had a power supply problem. Reassured with the confidence that I could rely on one of the other pilots taking over the radio work I signalled to the Tigers on either side of me. By clapping my open hands on both ears and holding open palms upwards they surely would get the message I figured. I cupped my hand over my mouth and pointed to them in turn to get them to take over transmitting, but in vain. As we flew on I resorted to reaching down to the battery box beside me. Hopefully the battery had just become dislodged. Leading the formation while fiddling with the battery was no mean feat. With none of the pilots understanding our plight there was little other option. I well understood the need to fly steadily and the disastrous consequences that erratic flight could have on the two aircraft on either side of me. Suddenly Alan peeled away from the formation seemingly without power. I watched him go down and carry out a forced landing on an open field near a road. Relieved it was obvious that he had executed a good landing seemingly without any damage. I had no option but to continue with the other three aircraft still in position around me, although my thoughts were very much with him. Fate was kind to me and soon the radio was working, and by that stage the airport was well within sight and we were on our base leg. They cleared us onto finals and soon we looked down the huge runway. It felt as though we could even land across the runway and onto the apron it was so huge. I kept the power on for almost the full length of our normal runway before throttling back and we all settled onto the tarmac. We followed the instructions and stopped next to a Boeing 727 airliner that completely dwarfed us all. All the biplanes were arranged around the Boeing while we were offered refreshments accompanied by the usual multitude of questions from the onlookers. The time came to leave and soon the formation was on its way back home to Baragwanath, still with thoughts about Alan. Once on the ground we got news that Alan was all well, had got a lift home, and was planning the next step to recover DNP.

I went out with him the next day to check the engine out. There was no compression in one cylinder and so I took off the one rocker box to expose the valve rockers. The problem was apparent. One of the studs had broken. I went to Brian's factory and borrowed one. Back in the field I replaced the broken one and soon she was running well again. Alan and I reccied the field and I was stunned at how the long grass had broken his run and how short the landing roll was as a result. There was no part of the field good enough for a take-off so we looked at the road. We manhandled the Tiger onto the road. After a good runup we monitored the ends of the road for traffic and soon the familiar Gipsy sound heralded the start of his take off. We watched him get off and climb overhead as arranged. Soon a wing waggle told us that all was well and that he was off back to Bara. Relieved we drove home to mark the end of a successful day.

On another occasion my brother was riding his 1928 Indian motorbike back from Durban on the 'DJ'. Short for Durban to Johannesburg, it is a run for pre 1936 motorbikes to commemorate the race that was held on this route up until 1936. I had taken part in the first two commemorative runs and it was now his turn. As always, the lunch stop was to be at Standerton and I thought that it would be a good idea to fly down, have lunch with all the bikers, and fly back.

When I mentioned it to Bob, he immediately jumped at the idea and it was all on. Mum and Dad were also driving down and so we would have transport from the airfield to the lunch stop. Jane, who was later to become my wife, came down in the front seat of Tiggy, despite coming from a non-flying family. I can't remember if it was her first flight, but it was certainly new to her. We flew down together in the two Tigers and landed at the airport where Mum and Dad were waiting to collect us.

After a super meal with all the bikers, we watched them set off one by one, and then were taken back to the airport. In due course we took off and followed the bikers on their trusty steeds all the way back to Johannesburg. Most of the way back we flew quite low, one on either side of the road, watching the bikes on the road below us. We flew in a loose formation so that we could see each other and the road at the same time. We were enjoying ourselves and I am sure that the bikers enjoyed it almost as much as we did.

Each time we got to a small town with its own airfield, we would peel away from the road, land and have a browse around the airfield. As all aviation enthusiasts know, we all have an instinct to prowl around, scratching behind hangars, and peeking through gaps in their doors.

As a result of all the stops we would keep passing Mum and Dad and all the chaps on the road. At one stage mother was driving the old 3.8 Jaguar, and she looked into the rear-view mirror to see the two Tigers approaching her from the rear. Despite the concern that it raised, we were having a wonderful time. As we flew along we felt almost as if we were part of the event below us, and the two Tigers flew along as one. Jane, who suffers from terrible airsickness, was on her usual medication, in the front of Tiggy. I remember her actually sleeping in the open cockpit while we were flying, certainly a first in a Tiger Moth. At one stage I even had to tap her on the shoulder to wake her up before we landed at one of the funny little strips.

It was on this flight that we even learnt that chickens could fly! We were approaching a clump of trees on either side of the road, and in our usual style pulled up simultaneously to clear them. When we descended on the other side, the air was full of chickens. Bob maintains that they were mostly on his side and the air was absolutely full of chickens around him, but in any event it was quite an eye-opener for both of us. Afterwards, chatting, we were amazed at how they just seem to appear all around us. They had probably been alerted by the approaching sound of the aircraft, and as soon as we appeared they took flight (and fright). The whole incident was over in a flash of white feathers, fortunately without incident, and we continued on our way. The rest of the flight was uneventful and we landed after a good day's fun and put the aircraft to bed.

On yet another occasion we had both intended to fly down to Lesotho for an air show, and the weather turned bad. We decided to share a car and drive down instead. After watching an enjoyable airshow we drove home and again, this time by car, popped in at all the little strips on the way. We ended up at Brakpan-Benoni airfield. Scratching around and peering into the hangars, we found a rather sad looking Aeronca 7ac. Fired by enthusiasm we made enquiries and soon had the full story.

The aircraft, commonly known as an Aeronca Champion, was a tandem (one behind the other) two seater with a 65 horsepower engine. Yes the aircraft was for sale at a price to be negotiated. The engine had seized, needless to say ending up in a forced landing, and a sad looking aeroplane. The wheels caught in a ditch, damaging the undercarriage, causing the aircraft to go over onto its back on a fence that was fortunately not yet strung. What had happened was that the aircraft had been used for some air-to-ground photography with the photographer in the front seat for better visibility. The pilot, who normally flies from the front seat, was flying from the back and so could not see the instrument panel. We were told that the pilot, unable to see past the passenger and huge camera, had flown too slowly, for too long, and the resulting lack of air-cooling had caused the seizure. It sounded a bit strange but nonetheless we persevered.

We negotiated a price and agreed to buy the aircraft as a project between us. We then made arrangements to collect her the following week and take her back to my family home. We spent the following weekend collecting bits and bringing them back in a truck. Jane, who by that stage was my fiancée, came along to keep us company and was amazed at the endless number of bits-and-pieces that we brought back. When we got home with the first load, we realised that we could not get through the gate with the truck loaded, and so we dumped all the bits onto the pavement and went back for a second load.

Sunday evening at home was a social occasion for all the young and old alike. On that day Jane's folks had been invited to spend the evening with my family and I will never forget the look on my future in-laws faces when we arrived home with the second load. They had arrived shortly before us, and we found them peering amazingly at all the stuff on the pavement. They had not yet gone up to the house and so I got out and started to explain what it was all about. We started carrying everything up to the garage and they scratched their heads in amazement. I can't help thinking that it was probably a good thing for them to see what my life was about and what their daughter was in for. Nonetheless, little more than a few words of surprise were uttered.

When all the bits were up at the house, they were totally amazed at the fuselage that looked like little more than a jungle gym frame with a tattered cloth covering. Not being used to aircraft, the delicate framework was beyond their comprehension. At least the minor amount of damage was able to reassure them, if only slightly, that these strange craft were in fact safer than their first impressions indicated.

Over the next few months the bits began to resemble more of an aircraft. With the fuselage stripped we were able to assess the repairs required. Bob called on a certified aircraft welder that he knew and had used previously, and the repairs began in earnest. All the damaged sections of the fuselage tubing were cut out and replaced with new pieces of 4130 (The specification of the steel) and welded. While the welder was busy, we tackled the damaged undercarriage and prepared it for welding. When she was proud to stand on her own wheels again, the fuselage outline emerged. Once we had painted the frame and started recovering, the skeleton began to disappear and was gradually replaced by the gentle curves of an emerging aircraft.

When we turned our attention to the engine, the reason for the engine failure was clear. The pilot was totally blameless because there was a pad of carbon on the ends of the piston rings preventing the ring gap from closing up. The mystery was what had allowed the carbon to build up so strangely. Looking in the logbook, the engine had recently had the cylinders removed and new rings fitted. What appears to have happened was that the ring grooves were not properly cleaned. When the new rings were fitted the carbon was pushed into the ring groove, preventing the ring from bedding in the bottom of the groove on expansion, allowing the carbon to build up on the ends of the rings. Operating for some time like that, tough carbon pads had built up on the ends of the rings, and the first time they got slightly hot there was nowhere for the expansion to go and the piston rings seized.

It was amazing and a good lesson for us that such a simple oversight had had such disastrous consequences. Once it was cleaned, the barrels machined, fitted with a new set of rings, and it was all assembled the motor was as good as new. We then fitted the engine onto the blunt end of the fuselage, and with the cowlings on, a real aircraft emerged.

The next step was to straighten the propeller. There was only one slight bend in the one blade, well within the acceptable limits for straightening. Bob proceeded to pick up the prop and to walk around the garden looking at the trees. I could not work out what he had in mind, but it soon became apparent when he found two large limbs correctly spaced. He proceeded to put the blade between them and apply a gentle force. After a few attempts and checking against a template made from the other straight blade, we had a propeller that when put on the engine, tracked perfectly true. (In other words the propeller tips followed the same line as it rotated).

Once the prop was wire locked, we prepared to start the engine. The other members of the family were tasked to keep the animals out of the way while we pushed the fuselage outside and got ready. Standing outside the kitchen, with the tail secured, we gave her a swing and the engine burst into a most welcome purr. Once she was warm, we opened up and checked for any vibrations through the rev. range. Not a sign. I, for one, was amazed at how Bob had managed to get the prop so straight.

The next focus of attention was the wings that fortunately had sustained very minor damage. The fence posts had amazingly passed through the fabric without causing any structural damage. One wingtip and the fabric covering had to be repaired and when that was finished, the wings were fit for flight.

At that stage, Bob had an Austin 1800 with a tow hitch. We got a trailer and took the fuselage out to Bara, followed by the wings on a second trip. We then started the assembly, first the empennage (flying tail surfaces), and then the wings. Carefully each wing was offered up to the fuselage and the wing struts fitted. She looked like, and in fact had become, an aeroplane!!

The next seemingly simple task had a rather humorous element. The aircraft had to be weighed before being certified fit for flight. The closest scales were at Rand Airport, and new rules said that it had to be weighed. I had an idea. As each main wheel only carried around 400 lbs, I could make a jig to span two bathroom scales for each wheel. We could jack up each wheel, place the pair of scales under it and each scale would only be weighing the mass of one overweight body. With another one put under the tail in the level flight position, Bob's your uncle (or so they say).

Well, I borrowed bathroom scales from all and sundry and made up the two jigs, and off we went. Well, I set up all the scales in front of the wheels and zeroed them with the jigs in place. We lifted each wheel up and positioned the scales. We took the readings under the watchful eye of the AME (Approved Maintenance Engineer) and all was well. I must add at this stage that the whole exercise had now gathered a few spectators, and the AME took quite a bit of persuasion to agree to my method. In the end he did and he left us with his signature.

The problem then came when we moved BBS off the scales and I stood on the first one to check if it was still working correctly. To my horror the number in the window bore no resemblance to my weight, and when I hopped off, the reading remained far from zero. Despite all my efforts at making a large pad to spread the weight over the top of each scale, the top plates had distorted and the mechanism was sticky. Dismayed, I checked the other scales in turn to find that they had all suffered in sympathy. Rather relieved that the AME had not seen the problem, I was faced with an embarrassing task to rectify the situation.

Shortly thereafter Bob took BBS on her first flight and came back to report that she was a delightful lady. I did a few flights with Bob over the next few weeks and agreed that she was indeed a lovely plane. She would easily perform as well as the Tiger on less than half the horsepower. The fuel gauge just did not seem to move and unlike the Tiger we never seemed to have to put fuel in. Unlike more modern, high power machines, she had a quiet serenity about her. She was not noisy and full of vibrations, there was no wind noise and she was very stable. I only flew her on my own on one occasion when I took Jane for a ride and sadly she did not remain in our ownership for long.

Jane and I had set the big date and were getting married on 15th December 1973, and it unfortunately led up to BBS being sold to help other expenses of a more permanent nature. As a result I only had enough of BBS to begin to appreciate the super little aerie and never got fully acquainted. BBS disappeared from action for a few years in the hands of the new owner. He kept her on his farm strip and she was not seen around for some time.

One day I was ambling down the apron at Grand Central when I heard the distinctive note of a low powered engine, and was surprised to see BBS taxi past. Intrigued, I followed her down to the hangar and was rather pleasantly surprised to see a blonde lady get out. I introduced myself to her, and explained that we had rebuilt the aircraft and told her some of BBS's past.

Sally had bought her while she was still on the farm strip. The owner seemed not to use her after he had bought her from us. Sally was to become a personal friend of our family as well as a regular member of the flying scene for a number of years. We were to spend time together at various functions, but the friendship really got going at one of the EAA conventions.

Chapter 19

The Experimental Aircraft Association (EAA) is a body of aircraft enthusiasts started in the USA, that has spread to many corners of the globe, including South Africa. The membership is spread to other areas through a system of chapters. Chapter 322 was started in South Africa by a small band of aviators, and has since gathered momentum in a big way. One of the major EAA events is the Annual Convention held in Oshkosh in the 'States. This event, over the years, led to us holding our own South African Convention.

The Association caters for both experimental aircraft and restored vintage aircraft. The term Experimental is a term that includes homebuilt and vintage aircraft, and it is not used in the true sense of the word. The principal aim is to help the person who purchases a set of plans or a kit and sets about building his own machine. In more recent years, due to the similar requirement where spares, manuals, and updated certified documentation are not readily available, some older aircraft have also been put into a similar category.

One of the early conventions held in South Africa was in the little town of Swinburne. The organisers had found a volunteer farmer who would prepare a field for us and would be our host for the weekend. The town itself lay between the larger towns of Harrismith and Ladysmith. The idea was also to bring the gathering closer to Natal to encourage some of the coastal pilots to participate. My supportive wife Jane decided to go down with a friend of hers by car so that her husband could fly down with me in Tiggy.

On the appointed day the two of us were out at Bara getting ready to go. With the marginal range of the Tiger dictating that it should be possible to get there, a map with a cross on it, and a good deal of optimism, we set off. Without the modern navigation aids, we had little idea of what was in store for us. Without the guaranteed assurance of being able to get there on a tank full of gas, as well as the fact that we were heading for an unregistered, temporary field, I was taking a very cautious approach. I figured that, as I knew I could get to Harrismith, it would be my safety haven. I would fly directly overhead so that if I had to divert I would know the exact route and the conditions there. From Harrismith, if anything was wrong with my cross on the map, I could literally follow the road directions given to Jane.

After nearly two hours we saw the distinctive flat top mountain at Harrismith appear, reminding us that the other benefit of not routing direct was not having to cross over the mountain. We would have to be above 8 500 feet to have adequate clearance and the cold that it would bring in an open cockpit, is not what you want nearing the end of the journey.

Overhead Harrismith I had a good look at the field and wind conditions and made a mental note of the dominant physical features. I then followed the main road towards my cross on the map. Without any fuss, I soon saw a large mown field on my left, exactly where my cross was. I joined the circuit and landed on the smooth grass. I must add that there is nothing like a grass runway. The ease it offers, particularly when putting down a three-point landing, is an extra bonus, and the feeling as you touch down is very special. I was recently reminded of that when my son was doing his conversion to Tiggy on a grass runway. He came home amazed at the cushioning effect that grass has on a landing.

As we taxied up and chose a parking spot, I was aware that there was already a good few aircraft that had already arrived and were proudly on display. Sally had brought BBS down, together with a large number of other regulars. As we disembarked, we watched more aircraft arrive, join the circuit and land. Some, like me, were just arriving while others had been out exploring the area and generally having fun. In particular, we watched the huge Beaver doing a series of fly-pasts.

The Beaver, made by De Havilland Canada, is a high wing, tailwheel aircraft with 450hp radial engine hanging on the front. The end result is a large, dramatic aircraft that always gets heads turning. This particular one was owned and operated by DCA (Division of Civil Aviation) and had been brought down to do airfield inspections in the area, as well as joining us (guess which had priority!). One of our friends had got in there, (how, we will never know), suffice to say that there he was, in the L/H seat (main pilot's seat) having a ball.

Most of the other aerobatic chaps were down as we were also holding a minor competition in conjunction with the convention. Even though I had been doing aerobatics for some time, I had never entered a formal competition. As a member of the club, I knew most of the chaps and had been brushing up on my aerobatic manual as to the requirements of competition.

In a competition, the accent is on presentation of your sequence to the judges as a picture drawn in the sky. In order to achieve it, all the individual manoeuvres are linked and, unlike normal aerobatics, all the horizontal, vertical and 45 degree lines in the sequence must be accentuated. This was an ideal opportunity for a first time entry as they had introduced a Primary Class, just including the four basic figures (loop, roll, stall turn, and spin) specifically for beginners. This was followed by the next step, the regular sportsman's class, which I also entered.

I took off on my first flight, and as I climbed up I was aware of how different the view was compared with the Reef. We were in between the flat-topped Harrismith Mountain and the huge Drakensberg range. There were no towns visible and the higher up I got, the more the mountain vista increased. I came back over the field and waggled my wings to indicate that I was starting my sequence. As required from a beginner, I started with the four basic manoeuvres unlinked, and then came in again to repeat them, but this time linked without a break in between the manoeuvres. I felt happy as I waggled my wings to indicate completion and came in to land. Later on I took off again to fly my sportsman sequences. Being my first competition, the relief afterwards was amazing, I had not realised how tense I had become.

As I sat watching the other competitors, I was aware of the continual running commentary from the ground. Each competitor seemed to be sub-consciously verbalising his observations. One comes to realise that it is a common feature at contests and practice sessions, seeing a whole group of observers all commenting to no one in particular as they watch a competitor flying. I wondered what was being said during my flights, wouldn't I love to know! Listening to the comments, I felt not too bad about my efforts and could not wait for the results to come out.

In due course I was amazed to be called out as being the winner of the Primary Class, and third place in the Sportsman's Class. This was certainly a feather in my cap, even though it was partly due to the small numbers in each class. Needless to say that was the last time I was ever to be 'on the podium' so to speak, suffice to say that I was the winner of my first trophy. An aircraft company sponsored the competition and I remember the official photograph of me, proudly holding the cup, surrounded by all the other competitors. As it will probably not happen again I will have to keep a mental picture of the occasion.

The convention had been a huge success, the informal airfield, with only our crowd around, was stimulating. The area that had been prepared for us as a runway was superb. There were no complaints and we all thoroughly enjoyed the absence of Mr Joe Public, although in hindsight, not as much as we should have. Had we anticipated what a huge part of EAA that the public was destined to become, perhaps we would have been back to similar, less formal spots more frequently. This particular convention forms a sharp contrast with a recent one held on a licensed large airport, where EAA was the subject of a claim. A pilot of a spam can (modern metal aircraft) inadvertently taxied into a hole and then tried hard to hold EAA liable for the damage to his aircraft even though EAA had no control over the airfield.

Sally was totally enthralled by the aerobatics in particular, and in fact got herself into the middle of the aerobatics picture, with me holding up the cup. Once we were back home she was determined to get into aerobatics. She lost no time, and soon managed to get the use of a Cessna 150 Aerobat. FXH, or Foxhole, as the 150 became known, was soon a familiar sight among our gatherings. As Sally progressed with her aerobatics, each of the aerobatic pilots were tasked to pass on a bit of their knowledge to her.

As much as I liked her, my aerobatics were just above par, punctuated by healthy doses of fear, and I was certainly not instructor material. This, together with the fact that I was self-taught, kept me well clear when she was around looking for aerobatic help.

The day came when I was fresh out of excuses, and I had nowhere to duck off to. I got into Foxhole, next to her, and was tasked to go through stall turns. As Sally already had a fair bit of coaching from the others, I felt a little better and after a bit of ground briefing to ensure that we were both on the same wavelength, we took off. After a climb to height she carried out all the safety checks and started her dive for stall turn speed.

All went well as she pulled up into the vertical, and I looked at the wing tip as normal. I saw that she was a little on her back (ie. she had pulled past the vertical), but not enough to comment on during the manoeuvre, or so I thought. As she kicked rudder, the little Aerobat went on its back into an inverted spin. I nearly jumped out of my skin. I grabbed the stick and pulled back to regain flying speed, and we began to recover. It was only once we had recovered fully and I looked at the wing tip that I realised what went wrong.

The 150 Aerobat was fitted with performance enhancing, droopy wing tips. The resulting effect was that, with the visual reference cutting the horizon at 90 degrees, the actual wing was over 90 degrees, resulting on her going over on her back. Fortunately my reactions were not too bad. The little 150 gave the feeling that it would easily settle into a stable inverted spin! Like they say a good fright is worth 10 hours dual.

Sally persevered and soon progressed from the 150 and bought a share in Bob's Pitts Special, ZS-FUN. She was doing well and certainly had more dedication to competitive aerobatics than I did. I really did it for fun rather than from a desire to get the Big Cup. Nevertheless I was drawn into the fun and ended up entering the Jet Stores Aerobatic Contest in both sportsman and intermediate class. Even though a couple of Tigers had entered in the past, intermediate was a bit beyond their capabilities. As a result we were permitted a free re-climb during the 11-manoeuvre sequence. We also had to do flick rolls, not really permitted in Tigers. Having said that, the general feeling was that as long as they were not done too fast, it was really only a high-speed spin. Done at a low speed they are in fact quite gentle. After the competition I counted up that I must have done around 48 flick rolls, either practising or in the contest itself.

During the lead up to the contest, Sally and I had spent quite a lot of time together as we were both in the beginners league. She soon showed her determination to be a top performer and left me behind to enjoy my amateur status. I enjoy aerobatics and the competitions, but I was (and still am) nowhere near as dedicated to getting to the top as she was. I did, however, have a little contribution to make.

It was at this time that she was finding out about the training limitations of single seat machines. For the contest she had to learn to do flick rolls. Neil Williams was at this stage our mentor as we all read his book from cover to cover, but Sally was reluctant to put his theory to the test on her own. This time, being able to use my own machine, I was quite ready to help. I offered to take her up in Tiggy and show her her first flick roll. I explained that the Tiger was very gentle, but at least it would show her the way forward. She jumped at the offer, and soon we were buckled up and ready to go.

At height I showed her a series of flick rolls and returned to the field. Even though they were very gentle and, I'm sure, not very precise by Pitts standards, they did the job and she was soon flicking all over the sky. I can probably say that this amateurish introduction paved the way to her success. She continued for many years and has been the one lady in our midst who has made an impact in aerobatic competition. She sadly no longer flies competition but remains to this day a flying enthusiast with her own aircraft, now a family four seater.

I continued to compete in my small role as a real amateur/enthusiast and enjoyed the competition. I was always keen just to participate and be happy just to give a reasonable account of myself. Looking from another side, the more competitive you are, the greater the load on the aircraft, as well as the need for finances to pay for it all. Having neither vast amounts of spare cash, or fancy aircraft, I was happy as a rank amateur. I always feel that I am giving the other competitors someone to beat, after all someone has to make up the bulk of the competition. Most of my aerobatics were self-taught; book in hand like the German chap in those Magnificent Men in their Flying Machines. There were no organisations teaching aerobatics, as they had no machines, and just a few instructors that were prepared to get involved.

One of the two occasions that I had some instruction was just before a competition at Bara. I felt that my cuban eights were not as tidy as they should be. A cuban eight is a figure where you go through seven eighths of a loop, and you are then inverted on a 45 degree line. While maintaining the line, a half roll is executed to bring you to the upright position. Then a second loop is entered, again stopping on the 45 degree line, followed by another half roll and a 45-degree round out to horizontal. In effect you draw a vertical figure 8, lying on its side.

Peter, who offered to help me out, and in fact was to have an influence in years to come, had been a friend for many years. We had all grown up in Tigers and he was one of those that carried on immediately to pursue a career in flying. Unknown to me at the time he was to be a major contributer in my flying career, some 25 years later. As he was an instructor I had had a few renewals with him and here he was offering to help with my cubans. Having flown many hours in Tigers, he would seem to be an ideal tutor. It is important to understand that, in a Tiger Moth, each person sits in their individual cockpit with a Gosport tube as communication. A funnel type mouthpiece sits in front of each person with the ends connected to the other occupant's earpieces to transfer the sounds. With a good imagination and interpretation skills they work quite well, however you can imagine the odd misinterpretation.

It is thus vital that a good ground briefing and a series of stick shakes shows who is in control as the control passes from one pilot to the other. A firm shake and the words "I've got her" is the usual routine. That is the theory but I was to learn a new meaning to 'feeling me through'. This is the term used when one pilot is flying and the other lightly holds the controls to follow the other pilot's movements. The other thing was to remember what was said in the briefing.

Peter gave me a good briefing, explaining that, once at height, after the lookout, he would start with a cuban on his own. Then he would do a second one with me lightly feeling the controls. I would then do one on my own and we would come down for a debrief.

We took off, climbed up and got ready. Peter took control and executed a superb cuban. It was the only time I had been in one with someone else flying and it gave me a good feeling of what was required. I then lightly held the controls and waited for his next one. It was a large figure in the sky, rather lazy and slow but not too bad. I then proceeded to do my bit. It was tighter and more positive and I was pleased with my efforts.

We landed and taxied to the hangar for a de-brief. "Your last one was quite good" he said "but the previous one was too big and sloppy." I was struck dumb. "I was not flying the second cuban, you were," I retorted. It turned out that neither of us was flying, but with both of us 'feeling' each other through, we had performed a complete, almost passable manoeuvre. This was a valuable lesson to us both. I had taken him at his word and he had changed his mind and expected me to do the second figure.

Although now rather humorous, it was a valuable lesson in briefing before a flight.

Chapter 20

The aerobatic scene at Bara was quite active. We had four Pitts Specials and a few other machines, all flown by a rather spirited bunch. One of them who shall not be forgotten was Warren. He was not only the friendliest soul one could wish to meet but also a good pilot and a wonderful friend. He had a Piper Pacer as well as a share in one of the Pitts specials. His particular signature at the airfield was to come screaming from behind the hangar inverted and shoot over our heads at minimal height. The sound reverberated between the hangars making it very difficult to detect where he was actually going to arrive from until he was directly overhead. Warren was an active participant in the EAA functions, aerobatics and any other flying that was around. In fact, he was the chap that managed to wiggle his way into the Beaver belonging to D.C.A. at the Swinburne convention. Very tragically Warren was to leave us some years later as a result of leukaemia. He will always be remembered for his fun and participation in many events.

One occasion that springs to mind was a Tiger gathering at a farm near Hartebeesport Dam. While all the Tiger owners were sitting having lunch under the trees, Warren decided that it was time to liven things up with a bit of flying. He grabbed me and led me to the Pacer. As I got in the right hand seat he reached into the back and handed me a flour bomb. I must hasten to add that being a passenger was a very unusual occurrence for me as, having my own aeroplane, I seldom found myself in that role.

We took off and proceeded to turn and head back to the trees where everyone was having lunch. As we screamed towards them, at what seemed to be their eye-level, I opened up the right hand window and put my arm out holding the flour bomb. Calmly sitting there with my hand out the window, my eyes got bigger as the trees approached, and I let go of the bomb. Whether by design or sheer fright I don't know but I just let it go and he pulled up to clear the trees by a few leaves. Well, his judgment must have been better than mine because I could have sworn that we were destined to plough into those trees. I was very grateful to feel the wheels touch the ground when we landed and we taxied up to the crowd who, by then, had certainly finished their lunch.

As humorous as this little event was, tragedy was soon to strike. I had organised the whole day's event and the afternoon was to be filled with some gentle competitions. The first was a toilet roll cutting competition, as mentioned earlier, nowadays more politely called streamer cutting.

I had highlighted the cautions and difficulties in my briefing, and stressed the need for a good 2000 feet at the start of the cutting. I explained how to throw it up so that it unrolls completely and I stressed that if it was not fully unrolled it was a hard object and to avoid contact with it. I tried to think of every detail. Bunty was the first to have a bash, and after his cut he would then come in for a flour bomb and end up with a spot landing. Well, little did I know what was in store for us all. Bunty was a very experienced aerobatic pilot, someone I regarded as far more capable than me, and even though he had not been so much part of the EAA scene, I was happy that he was leading the way.

We all watched him climbing up until he gained the height he wanted, and he threw the roll out. I was a bit concerned as I felt that he did not have the 2 000 feet that I had requested, but I still had confidence in him. I watched in horror as he lost too much height and presumably could not see the ribbon. He caught sight of it and pulled back on the stick to zoom up to try and get it, the mistake I had warned them all about in the briefing. In horror we watched the Tiger lose speed and stall in a very nose high attitude and it started spinning. I immediately thought of all the spins he had done in competition. "Stop the spin" were the words going through all our minds, but he could not hear our pleas.

Despite his experience, we watched one, two and three turns before a slight hesitation. It was not enough to get the wings flying again and the Tiger started spinning the other way. As on command, but with the silence only broken by the sound of the Gipsy as it tried to pull him out of the spin, we knew, and all started running. We felt a huge thud under our running feet as he hit, barely 400 metres from us. We felt sick. I gave a spurt and was the first of our crowd there. He had hit the flat earth alongside a local's hut, and the villager was pulling him out as I got there. A very sorry sight met me. He had broken one leg, his face had come into hard contact with the compass, and he was indeed very poorly. Warren's wife, Annie, was soon on the scene and, as she was a nurse, I turned my attention to the wreckage while she attended to him. Once I was sure that there was no chance of fire, and a few people were stopping spectators smoking, I turned back to Bunty. Anne was magic, she had makeshift splints and he was soon lifted into a car and taken to Krugersdorp hospital.

We then looked at the machine and realised how lucky he had been to suffer as little injury as he had. The front cockpit was totally destroyed, the cross members had broken and the fuselage had opened up on impact with the two sides spread apart. The smouldering engine occupied the front seat. Ironically, one of the girls had been trying desperately hard to go up with Bunty. For some reason, luckily for them, fate made sure that Bunty insisted on going alone!

The craft had hit so hard, and so close to the vertical, that an imprint of the four wings and fuselage was left on the ground. The wreck had bounced back from the point of impact a matter of feet, so that it lay with the front view impacted on the ground ahead of it. The fuel tank, supported in between the top wings, had struck the still-turning propeller from the rear as the wings hit the earth. The aluminium prop, that he was using, cut open the tank and the whole area was covered in fuel. The wings were totally destroyed and the rear fuselage was little better. The following day Tony helped them dismantle the aircraft. The fork ends of the flying wires were even opened up so that they had sheared off the split pins. The wreck was recovered and some years later, with lots of new spruce and steel tubing, she again took proudly to the air to join her friends and is with us to this day.

Annie was forced to come to the rescue on another occasion as well. A whole crowd were due to go down for the EAA Convention/air show at Welkom. Three of us in Tigers met to fly down together. When we looked at the weather, the one chap who had little Tiger experience immediately opted out, much to our relief. Bob and I stood at Bara looking first at the weather, then at each other.

Bob asked me what my thoughts were. "If you look at the gap between the hill and the cloud it looks fairly stable."

I said, "I am sure that we will find out that from there the clear space opens up as the ground gets lower. We all know the area well and we know that the ground falls away to the South, and there are no large hills for some way. I think that we should fly to the crest of the hill and if it looks good we carry on, if not we will keep a lookout behind us keeping the field clearly in view." As we watched, a Grumman aircraft took off for a circuit and was soon reducing height to keep out of the cloud base. We now knew how high (low!) the clouds were. Bob agreed with my thoughts and so we prepared to go, keeping a good eye on the weather.

With Jane in the front, we took off and climbed towards the hills. Low and behold I was right. As we got to the hills we saw that the cloud ceiling stretched ahead, and the clear space between ground and sky opened up on our route as far as we could see. Later on Jane told me she was so petrified that she just closed her eyes and prayed all the way. Under the thick cloud cover we were quite safe but it was bitterly cold and clammy. We had planned all our options on the facts and had come up with a safe workable plan, without being stupid. As predicted, the flight had an increasing ground clearance, but the further along we flew the colder we got. Eventually the cold was overbearing. We approached Parys, just over midway on our journey, and Bob clearly indicated that he was landing.

We landed behind him and taxied up to the clubhouse area. He got out and announced that he did not need fuel, as the attendant assumed, but was frozen to the core and needed a hot cup of coffee. We felt the same way, and as it was easily rectified, we each sat down to a cup of warmth.

After a short time our bones became a touch less brittle, so we climbed in and got ready to go. I normally swing Tiggy myself but for some reason Bob was swinging her for me. As per normal, she fired instantly and Bob climbed into FZF. I was not aware of it at the time, but he was not used to the light wartime propellers, and my prop had caught him on the finger. The Irish blood in my wife had not yet infused enough superstition into me, and we did not take heed. Bob had also had a mishap with his Pitts Special the weekend before. He had been flying so that the newspaper photographers could get some promotional shots for the show. On one of his flypasts he pulled away just to have his engine stop on him. At minimal height, he went for a landing ahead of him, his only alternative. It was all perfect, except for the fact that he touched down on top of a trench. What an ugly piece of fate.

We had now had our three warnings: firstly the Pitts, secondly the bad weather and thirdly his sore finger. However we proceeded to take off and resume the journey. As we progressed further, the cloud began to dissipate and as we approached Welkom we could see a huge cloud of dust masking the airfield.

We knew that this dusty sky, seemingly from a desert war film, was nothing more sinister than the dust thrown up by the ever-hopeful spectators. As we flew overhead, the ground below was covered with an ant-like procession of vehicles, all jockeying for good vantage points. As we glanced towards where the aircraft park should have been – there it was, empty! We were amazed to see that there was not an aircraft in sight. We proceeded to turn onto finals, with a dam below us, and approached over the cars.

On the ground we were met by a distraught group of airshow organisers. The bad weather on the Reef had prevented all the promised aircraft from arriving. The only other aircraft on the field was the Bucker Jungmann, also a biplane, but it was in the hangar. What had happened to it was that a wheel bearing had seized on landing and they had taken it off in an effort to get it fixed.

It was now clear that the air show belonged to Bob and I for probably the next hour or so. Neither of us was an intended air show participant but we were beholden to help the organisers with their unhappy crowd. We chatted and I suggested a bit of formation flying. Bob agreed and said that after that he would do a bit of an aerobatic sequence for them. I said that I would go out into the general flying area, brush up a bit, and then come in for a display when he was finished.

We took off together and opened the show with a few formation passes, and I then broke away to leave Bob to do his thing. As I left the field, I climbed up into the General Flying Area, and practiced a few manoeuvres. Periodically I looked back and I could see Bob's Tiger drawing shapes in the sky. When I could not see him any longer I flew back to the field and came in for my display. I proceeded to do a series of loops connected by stall turns at each end. As soon as the ground came as close as I had intended it to, I closed off my show with a last stall turn. At the top of the turn, as the aircraft turned around, I closed the throttle and changed my descent into a tight base leg and an approach to land. This I had found was always a very dramatic manoeuvre, while being totally safe.

As I turned over the dam toward the final approach, I looked down and saw a large white object in the water. At the time it was only an instant mental observation at not having seeing it on the earlier approach. I then transformed the turn into a steep sideslip onto finals and landed, all as planned. I taxied up feeling very relieved that it was over. Taking part in a show is always a worry, particularly when you are not prepared for it, hence my relief when it was over. Pleased with my flight, I taxied up to be greeted by a tear-streaked face as Jane came up to the cockpit side.

"What are you doing," she wailed, "did you not see Bob."

I replied that I had last seen him performing over the airfield, and that I was doing my routine as we had planned. I presumed that he was off flying somewhere.

"He is in the dam," she said, pointing.

I was shattered and as I shut down the engine I looked towards the dam. As I switched off the fuel and got out, an ambulance came wailing back from the dam. All I could think of was that poor Bob was in the best hands and I should go and see what I could do for 'FZF.

I ran to the shore and looked out across the water. I could not see any familiar Tiger shape. All that could be seen was a small white object, no larger than a pillow, breaking the glossy surface. This was, in fact, the tip of the rudder, which was all that was exposed. My adrenaline really started pumping. The chap next to me must have heard my sub-conscious comments and seen my concern. He said that he was part of the boat club and he would try to get us a boat. Soon there were also some members of the diving club offering assistance. On the way to the dam I took them past Tiggy. I showed them in detail what Tigers looked like, where attachment points were, handholds, and how the wings were braced. Being the eternal optimist, I was trying to prepare them for the retrieval of an almost complete aircraft!

At the boat club we boarded a small motorboat and headed for the sad little fin sticking out of the water. We soon got close and I was amazed at the colour of the water. In retrospect, when one thinks of the upset in the water it would obviously cause vast amounts of sediment to be raised. Contrary to my expectation of a soft landing in the water, the almost muddy liquid told another tale. I watched the divers working in the water as they secured a line to the tailwheel. They swam and dived in the water around where the poor aircraft was trapped. Soon both divers climbed back on board and declared that it was too difficult and muddy to do anything. I had a rather hasty debate and the captain voiced the opinion that all they could do was use the rope to pull her to the shore.

All I could visualise was the remaining bits being damaged as she was dragged through the mud to the shore. I vehemently said that that it was not an option. I then stripped and dived in myself. I must say that I am no great swimmer and I do not enjoy it much except in good coastal surf.

As I got into the water I was unprepared for the warmth and smell. The engine heat had caused so much warmth that the water was like a hot bath and the smell of avgas and oil floating on the water was soon complimented by an itchy skin as it started to take effect. I tried to submerge myself to get to the fuel tank area. The water was so unsettled that as soon as I was a few inches below the surface there was no visibility. I tried repeatedly but I could not get deep enough. All I could think about was getting entangled in broken flying wires.

Bob had got a message to me that he had lost his glasses when he had banged his head on the compass, and so, in all my naivety I visualised them waiting in the cockpit for me to reach down and grab them. Having to abandon the idea of simply swimming down to the cockpit, I had another idea. I thought that I would be able to simply pull myself down the length of the fuselage until I reached the cockpit. I knew the shape well enough to reach inside and try to find them. Even if I could not get into the cockpit on my first attempt I was sure that I would at least be able to assess some of the damage to the tank and wing structure, as I had outlined to the divers earlier.

My positive thoughts were just not working and, as simple as the task seemed, the execution proved impossible. I cannot remember anything that was so easy in planning and yet beyond my capability. I jumped in again and swam to the rudder. Grabbing at the rudder I gradually worked my way down the fuselage. I was amazed at the steep angle, it must have been around 45 degrees and as I progressed the pressure became significant. With the water completely dark at that depth, with no light getting through, I could not see a thing. Putting all my fears behind me, I tried time and time again. Each time I got as far as the back of the seat but could get no further and had to surface again. But to no avail, I had to admit defeat.

Back on board I tried to think of another solution, but the others wanted to drag the aircraft to the shore. All I could think of was the damage as it was dragged through the thick mud towards the waters edge, and the raft of souvenir hunters swarming over her. I imagined the thrill it would give them to wade in and collect bits, not to mention the front page of the papers the next day.

I resisted all their attempts once more and ended having a stand up scrap with them, threatening to remain in the water with her. In the end I won and after an exchange of ideas got the captain to agree to slowly tow her to the concrete launching ramp. There, hopefully, we would guide her slowly to dry land on her wheels. I explained that if we towed slowly, as she moved backwards, the wings would gently lift her higher in the water, clear of the obstructions below. In this way I hoped to minimise further damage.

Taking the slack in the line attached to the tailwheel, I waited with bated breath as he applied a little power. The engine revs gradually increased but there was no movement. I assumed that the propeller was stuck in the mud or vegetation below. I told him to move to one side and gently apply power to dislodge it. We then moved to the other side and repeated the attempt. We repeated this a few times and then tried a full steam pull. This time as we applied power a small movement was detectable and at last she was free. My hopes improved and I watched as she slowly rose from her muddy grave.

With deliberate, painstaking slowness, we headed for deeper water, and then turned towards the boat station. After what seemed like an eternity we saw the boathouses approaching. I had been monitoring our speed by looking at how high she was riding in the water, trying to go as slow as possible while still keeping her afloat. While holding a close vigil on our valuable cargo, I kept a watchful eye for anything that may have come detached.

When at last we reached the jetty, I jumped off with the line and got to the head of the ramp. By this stage the weather was improving and a number of aircraft had arrived. I watched them joining the circuit, sitting like a fool in my sodden underwear. I remember, for the one and only time ever, seeing the Staggerwing doing aerobatics over the field. The ramp was full of other aviators by the time we got there and so it was easy to get friends to help. We all grabbed the rope and slowly pulled her up the ramp. With bated breath I waited to see if she would roll smoothly up. I was horrified as the damaged aircraft surfaced. The eternal optimist in me, had expected a more or less complete aircraft to surface, gone were my thoughts of minor damage, she was looking really poorly.

Helping friends soon had her safely on dry land. Half the engine and propeller had been deeply buried in the mud and the one undercarriage leg was bent against the fuselage. I was amazed at the brutal strength of the water on impact; it was almost as if a solid object had been encountered. Being cold and miserable I went inside to dry off and put my clothes back on, while I left the others in charge of the sorry sight.

That evening, we had a rather sombre gathering at the hotel. Bob was back with us albeit a bit lost without his glasses, which could not be found. He had a large bump on his forehead, but was otherwise in good shape. Annie had been her usual self, looking after him and Brian had done his bit and arranged one of his company trucks to drive down the next day to take FZF home. I remember poor Bob being accosted by someone trying to buy her and trying to dissuade him from making a hasty decision.

The next day saw all the willing supporters climbing all over her and stripping FZF for her trip home. Soon she was standing on a splinted undercarriage, without wings, and with all the mud washed off. The oil and fuel tanks had been drained and washed out, the magnetos blown out, and soon we were ready to start the engine. This would be important to dry out all the moisture and to get oil to circulate, even though we could not expect her to run well.

Much to our relief, after some coaxing, she started and settled to a rather unsteady idle. The cylinders had taken strain as they presumably had sucked in volumes of water, damaging the head gaskets. The most important thing was saving any further damage by corrosion by heating the engine up. Soon she was loaded on the truck and we bid farewell to her on her last journey for some time.

Needless to say, Bob did not weaken to the offer of the sale and was to be seen working every spare moment over the next few years to get her back in the air again. Some years later the same willing helpers were at the new Baragwanath to welcome her home. Those willing hands helped Bob with the assembly and we were all soon rewarded by having both Bob and FZF back in the air with us again.

Take to the sky she did and in fact to this day, many years later Bob and FZF are still active participants in flying events, and hopefully for many years to come.

On yet another fateful day, we were off to an event early one morning, with the aircraft pushed out of the hangar, blissfully unaware of the scene to follow. Next to my hangar, at the old Bara, was a Procea, a low-wing composite machine, and alongside it was a Pacer (tailwheel Tripacer). I was preparing Tiggy when I saw one of the wives alone in the back of the idling Pacer. For some reason the pilot had got out. With the gentlest of movements the Pacer started to roll into the rotating propeller of the Procea, with the passenger leaning forward to try and stop the 'craft. Powerless, I was only aware of the mishap just before the impact, and I watched helplessly as the Procea's spinner exploded and the two aircraft became entangled.

We all collected together to survey the damage. The Pacer's spar had been sliced by the propeller and a few ribs were somewhat modified. As expected, neither aircraft was fit for flight so another seat swapping exercise took place before we took off. Needless to say it took much sweat and toil before the aircraft were back in the air again.

Two, rather less tragic spinner incidents centred around Tiggy. Tiger Moths have a large locking plate that prevents the propeller nuts from coming loose. It is held in place by a spring between it and the spinner. What seems to happen is that the constant spring force on the spigot, combined with the vibration, causes it to break.

The first time it happened to me, I was returning from the north, and was just coming up over the northern suburbs of Johannesburg. I was minding my own business, cruising along; when I was literally thumped back to reality with a loud bang as the whole aircraft did a little jig. Just a single bang and nothing else; I could not make out what it was. All the instruments were normal, no unusual flight pattern, no other unusual noise, and she kept going on undeterred. I assumed that I must have hit something. I cast my eyes around and saw a gaping hole in the left top wing. I considered diverting to Grand Central, but she was flying well and so I felt no real need. I carried on, keeping a close eye on the hole and landed safely back at Bara.

As soon as she stopped, I shut down and got out to do an inspection. Something had gone almost vertically through the wing and taken part of a wing rib with it. The broken rib was sticking out of the top of the wing. As I walked around I saw that I had lost my spinner and the large locking plate. I inspected the propeller and found that there was a bruise on the back of one of the wooden blades. The only explanation was that as it had come loose, the blade had given it a huge smack, sending it through the wing, making the thump that I had felt.

I was extremely lucky. Firstly the propeller had not been severely damaged, and if the strike had been closer to its tip, things would have been very different. Secondly, the left propeller blade travels down, so it must have been struck by the upcoming blade on my right. The plate must have then crossed in front of me, between the fuel tank and front windscreen, to strike the left top wing as it had. Quite a sobering thought. I replaced the plate, spinner and spinner plate and repaired the wing and all was well again.

Some years later I was flying with a good flying friend, Graham, returning once again to Baragwanath. As I turned onto base leg, we saw the spinner flash past. I yelled over the Gosport for Graham to keep an eye on it as I pulled into a turn to try to follow it. I proceeded to follow it in a spiral also keeping an eye all around. True to his persistent self, he kept his eye on it and we both saw it splash into a small dam. Making a mental note of the area, we returned to land at Bara. Hastily we jumped into my car and followed our mental map to the dam, remembering the point of impact. We came to the edge of the small dam and we agreed on where it had landed. We removed our shoes and plodded through the mud to the spot. To my amazement he proudly reached into the water and held my spinner aloft. I was relieved, as this was my last spinner.

As a result I had to adopt a new approach. Luckily this time the plate had remained behind and so no damage was caused. I replaced the spring with a piece of plastic tube as it accommodated the distance without causing a constant strain on the central spigot. Whatever the sceptics think, some 25 years later I have had no more spinner problems and I still use the same spinner that we pulled out of the dam, still with the plastic pipe and still 'going strong'.

Chapter 21

We were always supporters of the air-show circuit, and at the height of it there was a small air circus going. The 'Pomp and Jive Air Force' was the name coined by the mainstay of the aviators at Baragwanath Airfield. One of the acts in the 'Air Circus,' that had been an old favourite in the past, was 'Snoopy'. Although we had always flown in and often done some formation flying, I had not been actively involved in the show acts, and so my time had now come. I was to be involved in recreating the Snoopy act as well as a balloon-busting act for an air show in Pietersburg.

The balloon act involved a wing walker and Dave, one of the enthusiastic pilots, was 'volunteered' for the job. As I had not taken anybody on the wing anywhere near the ground before, and Dave had not done any wing walking at all, we embarked on some practice. Both of us were very cautious and so it all started with quite a serious briefing. I showed him safe footholds and where not to stand, and then we went to Tiggy to try it out.

Tiggy at Baragwanath

With memories of a Tiger dropping into the trees, I opted for Dave keeping on the walkway rather than on the wing itself. I was quite happy to do these strange things, but only if I could keep control of the odds against me by being cautious. My mind always reminded me of the saying: "There are old pilots and there are bold pilots, but no old, bold pilots."

'Daring Dave', as he became known, was required to stand on the aircraft and shoot at a row of balloons with a revolver in one hand, while holding the nearby strut with his other hand. While all this was taking place I would fly the aircraft low over the 'Snoopy Kennel'. The balloons were attached to the house with short strings and as soon as I lined the aircraft up he would shoot at the balloons. Most of the time, as soon as the puff of smoke passed me, I would see the one of them pop, and I would zoom up for the next pass. After the weekends practise, his shooting got quite good and I was happy flying with him on the wing. We were ready for the show.

The following weekend we got ready to go. I had recently purchased a Piper Tripacer from a friend, Rod, and he offered to fly up with us. Tony, my brother, was with me in the Tiger and the rest of my family went in the rather full Tripacer with Rod. Dave was with Rod in the front and Jane in the back. We flew together all the way until we were within sight of Pietersburg. With the limited range of the Tiger one tends to become rather particular and precise as to ones whereabouts, and so it was a bit strange when the Tripacer drifted away from me. They were a bit faster and I again checked my map reading in case I was wrong. I saw nothing amiss and so I carried on, with 'The Brick', as she was known, supposedly ahead of me.

I landed and taxied up, looking for Rod, but I seemed to have missed him. Once I had parked Tiggy, I asked around but nobody had seen them come in. As sure as I was that they must be there they were not to be found. Soon the 'chirp' of tyres announced their arrival and I followed them as they taxied up. They had got lost and had flown well past Pietersburg before realising their mistake. As mentioned earlier Jane suffers terribly with motion sickness, and today was the worst yet. She fell out of the back door as soon as the aircraft came to rest and as I approached them I saw her hugging the ground.

Once we had all got ourselves together, the show was ready to begin. We watched the glider being towed up to open the show. Dave and I were next, so we taxied to the holding point and got ready. I took off and as soon as I was safely aloft, Dave got out onto the wing and braced himself. As I flew alongside the runway, Dave levelled his revolver at one of the balloons attached to the

Snoopy Kennel. On each pass as soon as I saw the puff of smoke I would pull up for another pass. On almost every pass I would see the balloon burst as the revolver barked. After his last shot he got in and we landed. We taxied up to the cheers and whistles of the appreciative crowd. With the inner warmth it gave us, we knew that our first act was a success. I parked and we got out to watch the next few commercial aviation slots and flypasts.

Next up was the Snoopy bit. I took off on my own while the crew on the ground buzzed around the kennel getting ready. When they indicated that they were ready, I turned and zoomed at the Snoopy figure atop the kennel to the sound of 'my' rapid machine gun fire added over the public address system. As I turned, I could see Snoopy waving his fist and dragging along his big cannon. With only my wooden floorboards to protect me from it, I made another low pass. As I approached I saw Snoopy bending down over the cannon getting ready to fire. I passed low over the white figure and with my hand outside dropped my bomb over the side of the fuselage. Looking back I saw the explosion and almost at the same time heard the sound of his big gun having a go at me. Dust and smoke poured out of the muzzle as I turned for the last pass. I saw Snoopy waving a white flag in surrender. I had won. I came in to land and for the second time that day taxied up past the cheering crowd.

This was the usual type of participation in the air shows. Obviously we were not using anything other than blanks and pyrotechnics but the effect was good and the spectators loved it. Dave was our pyromaniac and as he got more into his pyrotechnics, the displays got even better. I remember a show at Grand Central where the grass caught fire (our occupational hazard) and the huge dedicated aircraft fire engine appeared to put it out. To the organiser's embarrassment, all that emerged from its automatic systems was a pitiful trickle, and we all ended up beating the fire out ourselves.

Often if there were a few other Tigers around we would put up a formation as well. More recently, Tigers have had to take the back seat as more formal teams have got together and their precision displays have rather stolen the limelight that we enjoyed. This changed the airshow scene rather drastically because soon we were to see Harvards, Zlins, Pitts Specials and other aerobatic machines in more formal teams expecting payment for their displays. The era of the ex SAAF Harvards was soon to be followed by a series of ex military jet aircraft. The costs of running these beasts demanded that they got a cut of the action and so the traditional circuit that we had supported for many years took on a commercial aspect. Soon pilots got so used to being paid that within a short space of time there would not be a show without a sizeable amount allocated for the display teams.

Having been through the transition to hard commercialisation, we longed for the old, less formal events. The Experimental Aircraft Association provided what we were looking for as it has always held a number of events each year. As a result, the pilots that in the past made up our old air shows were naturally attracted to the EAA events.

The next EAA convention was at a small place called Allemanskraal. I understand that the usual gathering was there but with Jane just having produced our first son we gave it a miss. For the following year, as the whole EAA concept had strengthened, the possibility of having the Annual convention nearer the coast began to take hold. This idea was a winner, and the venue chosen for 1981 was Margate, the hub of the Natal South Coast. The event was well attended and the venue was used for quite some years until the local authorities used us for their own gain to the extent that it was not worth being there.

At an evening EAA meeting, just prior to the first Margate Convention, I was chatting to a friend who was into filmmaking. I suggested filming the impending journey to the coast. Surely the event together with flying down in the Tiger Moth would be a good subject for an SABC (South African Broadcasting Corporation, the local Television Company) documentary. Having been involved in a few films with the old cars I had an idea of what was a saleable subject. I outlined my thoughts and he presented it to them with success. Not only was it accepted but he got a budget for a whole film crew as well.

We got together to discuss the details. The only fuel available was at Petermaritzburg, beyond the range of a Tiger. The solution was to stop at Warden and top up there from a drum and then meet the film crew at Ladysmith. Thereafter it would be another refuelling stop at a glider field at Estcourt and on to Margate. Bobby, a new member who had just acquired a Tiger, agreed to fly down with us in his Tiger and so I ordered two drums of fuel for delivery to Ladysmith. We chose Warden and Estcourt as they had small, accessible airfields where we would not have to waste valuable fuel flying circuits. We would need top-ups at both stops. The second stop was easy as I had a friend that lived close to the Estcourt field, and he would organise some fuel for us there. I would have to arrange for some fuel at Warden.

Richard, my film contact, had got things going beyond my expectations. I was thinking of him with a camera and a few films, but never visualised a Combi with a whole film crew. He offered to get them to get hold of the drums prior to our arrival and help us when we got there. That would also enable them to get some footage as we arrived and departed. It all sounded wonderful but as with all great plans the reality is always slightly different.

We duly met at Bara in the early morning, and Richard proceeded to unload his car. He took out the largest camera I had seen, as well as extra batteries and reels of film. As the pile next to his car grew I looked in dismay. Together with our minimal luggage and the oil that was a compulsory cargo on a long trip, his equipment made the whole thing unmanageable. With a little help from Bobby we managed to spread the load out between the two aircraft. As the usual grade of oil is often not available, each of us had to carry at least 10 litres. In more recent times the piston ring mods have cut oil consumption down to amazingly low proportions, making life much easier.

We loaded up and when we could fit no more in, the time came to get going. I took off and was immediately aware of the extra load as I had to use the trim fully forward, an area that I had never used before. To add to my anxiety his camera seriously hampered my forward view as he filmed. In the interest of the exercise I decided to only comment if it became a real safety hazard. A Tiger pilot has to get used to his view being seriously restricted by the helmeted head in front of him. This is often reduced even further when the head in question moves from side to side to get a better view. This normally happens at the most crucial stage of flying.

I settled into a slow but steady climb keeping south of Rand Airport with Bobby flying alongside me. It was a lovely fresh morning and we settled in to the prospect of a long, formation flight. Richard, my passenger was exercising his full viewing rights, but with the addition of this large camera that belonged in a film studio. Nevertheless, after an hour I began to get used to the new handicap and got on with the task at hand, namely getting from A to B. My thoughts wandered as we flew on and I tried to anticipate all that was in store for us.

I had arranged to meet a friend at Warden to get us some fuel. He was driving down and would take some containers so that we could top up. It was a bit difficult because at the time fuel restrictions were in place and it was illegal to transport fuel in containers. The plan was for him to fill up and siphon from his car into the containers at the field and we could refuel that way. I looked down at the cars below us and was thinking how far he was along that very road. We had anticipated the timing so that we would hopefully arrive together. Bobby was keeping his position on my side as the landscape slipped behind us. As we came alongside the solitary hill to the east of the road, I knew that our first stop was approaching and soon the town was identifiable.

As I got my thoughts focussed on landing at the field, I was made well aware of my loading situation. I was descending and as soon as the speed reduced I was well aware of the weight in the luggage locker. The tail became very heavy and needed a good deal of forward stick. As a result I kept a fair amount of power on as I descended to keep a good airflow over the tail feathers. As I throttled back she almost immediately went into a three-point configuration and a super landing without any floating. I breathed a sigh of relief and dared not think of what might have happened in more difficult conditions. Bobby who had kept me company all the way landed and taxied up.

As I shut her down, I was happy that I had used up some of the oil and would be transferring a good 3 to 4 litres from my locker to the engine. In addition to that weight reduction, I would also be flying at a lower altitude so from that point on things would improve. We did not wait long before, true to form, my friend drove up and parked next to us to start topping us up.

No sooner had we got down to siphoning from his car, when we heard another vehicle approaching. It turned out to be the local police officer who had seen the goings on from afar and had come to see what it was all about. No doubt the landing of two aircraft, let alone Tiger Moths, was probably worthy of front-page news in the local rag. We were immediately concerned that his interests were not purely platonic, particularly with the banning of petrol transfer due to fuel restrictions, so we resigned ourselves to waiting patiently until he had disappeared.

He asked us where we were off to and we told him. With that he disappeared and we got on with the refuelling. To our horror he had just gone to collect the rest of his family and he reappeared with his whole entourage while I was standing on top of the aircraft filling the tank. I clambered down, hoping that he had not seen too much, and spent anxious moments answering a barrage of questions about the aircraft and what was happening in Margate. He must have been aware of us being edgy and looking at our watches, and he suddenly packed up, wished us well, and left. None too soon as we were getting a bit worried about the remaining distance to cover.

As we saw the dust disappear behind him, we resumed our operation, and soon we were ready to go and brave the skies once more. Passing over

Harrismith Airfield, we made a mental note of our retreat path. We then flew alongside the flat-topped Harrismith Mountain at 8000 feet and looked at the huge dam that few people realise adorns it. Bobby and I flew in a loose formation and soon the huge shapes ahead turned into the notorious Drakensberg Mountain Range.

As we approached the Drakensberg our hearts sank. Ahead of us was the most unwelcome sight. As if posing for an ethereal artist sitting on his stool in front of a canvas, we saw a huge bank of cloud covering the lower reaches and blocking our path. We were committed to land and refuel at Ladysmith to continue our journey, and the only other airfield nearby was Harrismith, that we had just passed. The die was cast. Unable to get into Ladysmith, we had no option but to go back to Harrismith. Once down I thought that we could communicate by telephone and get the film crew to bring at least one drum of fuel to us. Fate might even be kind to us and we could possibly even continue over the 'Berg and get through. With full tanks we could at least venture a bit further to see what lay ahead, while still keeping an eye out behind us in case it all closed in.

With such a simple thought I led the landing exercise and taxied up onto the hard standing. Switching off, we removed our helmets and got out. After a welcome stretch our minds started to work and I looked for a 'phone. Up there it seemed so simple, but on the ground no phone could be found. A couple of houses were visible outside the perimeter and as I looked longingly towards them I spied a derelict telephone box. The familiar red-framed, glassed cubicle was rather faded and covered by foliage, but nonetheless I strode towards it. To my joy it all looked in order and when fed with a coin and the Ladysmith number, dialling tones emerged.

My joy was soon to turn to disappointment as I realised that the simple matter of a connection was not happening. Some hours later, I had spent an enormous amount of money feeding the machine and we had lost the greater part of the day, but in the end I had managed to get hold of the film crew. An hour later, the Kombi arrived with its valuable cargo of fuel and pump. As we refuelled, the plan started to gel. It was no longer possible to get through to the coast and so we elected to spend the night there. While we refuelled, some of the crew went into town to see if we could get in at the Holiday Inn. Shortly after we were finished and secured for the night they arrived back to confirm that we all had beds for the night.

The next morning found us, after a good night's rest and a good breakfast, in the early morning mist, untying our machines and getting ready to go. I well remember how cold it was and trying to swing the prop with enough impetus to get her started. Richard, at that stage had forgotten his cameramanship and was trying to keep warm in the front cockpit, away from the freezing breeze.

We eventually got both machines started and were ready to go. With the vista of the wide grass runway unfolding ahead, the temptation got the better of us and we gave the locals a formation take-off. Shivering we set course over the 'Berg. By our calculation we now had enough range to get to Escourt. The Kombi had left as soon as they had dropped us off and so had a good hour's start ahead. They would meet us at Estcourt with the remnants in the drum.

Our shivers slowly gave way to a sense of delight as we passed over the foothills of the 'Berg and beheld the wonderful scenery. We flew down van Reenens Pass, looking down at the long lines of weekend traffic below and wondering where the Kombi was and if they could see us. Not wanting to lose time, we tracked directly to Estcourt and were soon lining up to join the circuit with the dam alongside us. Keeping a close vigil on the gliders, we slotted in to the circuit and landed.

We met the Kombi and after a quick refuel from the drum we were ready to go. The weather had made up for the previous day and was superb. As we climbed up, the air was clear and the view was spectacular. The rolling carpet of the 'valley of 1000 hills' slipped beneath us and the green countryside that we were used to, slowly gave way to an irregular wavy line across our path. This was, after all, my first flight from the highveldt to the coast. A feeling of elation grew, firstly seeing the coastline appear as the rollers slowly became visible and secondly, knowing that the weather was safely behind us.

We crossed the beach and turned down the coast for Margate. We flew along the yellow sand, looking at the bathers in the warm Mozambique Current and passed over a number of the small coastal hamlets. We then flew over the large town of Port Shepstone and soon Margate. As we approached the airfield we could see a huge amount of activity. We flew proudly along the runway in formation and broke to join downwind. I throttled back and let Bobby pull ahead of me. I had a great feeling of belonging as I looked down at the variety of aircraft below me on the apron. Soon I was aware of the effect of the dense coastal air on the flying surfaces and I prepared to land behind the other Tiger.

As my speed dropped off on final approach, I looked out the open door in typical Tiger fashion. I was very grateful that we were vintage aircraft as there was a long line of modern machines parked just off the taxiway almost to the threshold. After the landing roll, I turned off onto the apron, to taxi past the Spitfire and the Air Force Harvards toward the parking area for light vintage aircraft.

We shut down and removed our helmets and shook our heads. We ran our fingers through our hair as if to chase away the huge beast holding onto our heads. The tingling that the helmets invariably bring gradually went away. Once out of our machines, the flying enthusiasts that had congregated from far and wide greeted us. I always feel that a yardstick of a good friendship is the ability to meet after a long period, and within minutes feel as if you had always been together.

The turnout of aircraft was something never before seen in SA, and it showed the interest in the coastal venue that we aviation enthusiasts were to enjoy for many years to come. Sadly the venue was ultimately to be devoured by the money beast, leading on to a quest for a replacement. Margate was to go down in the history books as our most successful venue. There are still those of us who would like to resurrect it for the annual convention.

That afternoon we were all enthused by the array of aircraft and wanted a bit of formation flying. Shades of the past with Uncle A and 'Penny' tied together came to mind and we decided to give it a go. We scratched all around the airfield for a long suitable tape, but all we could find to tie our two machines together was the plastic, red and white striped barrier tape. It looked a bit flimsy but we would give it a try anyway. We spoke to the controller and formulated our plan. We would taxi down to the threshold and wait for him to advise us of a break in traffic and we would give it a go.

We taxied down and prepared ourselves. The holding area is a large circular, tarred area, big enough for both of us to park and still leave enough space for another aircraft to pass. I tied the tape to the interplane struts and paced out backwards to see how much slack we had. Happy with the arrangement we waited for our cue. Soon enough we were given the go ahead we started up and taxied into position.

We opened up together and as we picked up speed, I could see the bunting trailing behind us. It was all looking good, but as soon as we got near the lift off speed the tape broke. We continued the circuit and landed for another attempt. We persevered a number of times and as the tape got progressively shorter we even managed to just get airborne before it broke again. The tape just was not strong enough to withstand anything over about 50 m.p.h. Unfortunately we had to admit defeat to the plastic tape.

The next day we arrived for the compulsory briefing, somewhat refreshed after a good sleep. At the briefing we were advised that some aviators had displayed their highveldt ignorance of coastal conditions resulting in a visit from a few locals. They were fishermen who were very quick to point out that an offshore breeze means kite fishing to them. The early rising pilots had been unaware of the kites being used to take the fishing lines out to sea. As a result aviators had caused the loss of 5 kites before 9 o' clock in the morning! Being keen and stimulated by the thick coastal conditions, the low flying culprits had been below the kites and had severed the lines without even seeing the kites themselves.

The rest of the briefing covered the usual attention required in crowded skies, flying over crowd line and other safety issues and we soon dispersed. Bobby and I spent some time looking at the huge Dragon Rapide, with simultaneous thoughts of formation flying. A Rapide is a De Havilland biplane made just before the war. Like tigers, it is fabric covered, but that is about where the similarity ends. Designed to carry 8 passengers in a cabin separated from the cockpit, and powered by two six-cylinder engines, it stood proudly matriarchal over the Tigers. We chatted about how fabulous the three craft would look in formation.

I approached John, the owner of the Rapide, and put forward our suggestion. Having met him often at previous air shows, I was confident that he would agree. I was staggered at his rejection of the idea. He insisted that the co-ordination would be difficult and not worth the effort. The mental picture of the three-ship De Havilland formation was fixed in our minds and we were not to be deterred and formulated a plan. John had been doing some flipping in the Rapide and we decided that the next time up we would be there too. We primed the film crew, and Richard got a cameraman and our local aviation historian onto the next flip. Everyone was now in position and ready, and all we needed was the Rapide to move for it all to happen. We even had another cameraman set up to shoot the flight from the ground.

Bobby and I sat near our Tigers waiting for a sign of movement. It happened. We saw activity around the Rapide increase and we were galvanised into action. With military timing we taxied behind the Rapide, ready for an immediate take-off. John sat way up in the nose and did not suspect a thing, we were presumably well behind and not easy for him to see. He stopped at the threshold to do his runup and presumably could then see the two of us. "Did he suspect anything?" Was going through our minds as we saw him turn onto the runway. We tucked in, one each side as he opened up and we followed suit. As I pushed my throttle fully open, I could see the historian Dave who knew what was happening, poised immediately behind John. The Rapide accelerated rapidly and was drawing away from us and we tried hard to catch him. When we were about to give up the Rapide slowed down, much to our surprise and joy. I later learned that Dave gently tapped John's shoulder and asked him to slow down for us. Amazingly he obliged and allowed us to come in close and the trio continued a flypast.

It was the most amazing success. Once it was all happening, John had realised the amount of effort we had put into it and given us the chance to prove our safety and airmanship. He continued to lead us for a few flypasts until we broke off, much to the delight of those on the ground, the camera crew, and most of all, us. We had footage from inside the Rapide, my Tiggy and from the ground and the compliments when we landed were terrific.

By this stage John had entirely softened his approach to us, having recognised our keenness and the fact that we were able to fly a safe formation. The next appearance was the following day, with another variation. I had offered to take up some parachutists for a drop and someone had suggested dropping them all as a trio. We thus ended up in a similar formation while we climbed for height, but this time all with parachutists on board. After all it is not often that your passengers don't land with you at the end of the flight!

In the interests of safety we had agreed that when the Tigers were ready, the Rapide would gently pull away and leave us to drop our parachutists in a loose formation. Dropping a parachutist is not as simple as it sounds. When they climb up out of the front cockpit, the pilot has to use a very significant amount of forward stick to compensate for the drag of the body sticking up out of the cockpit.

Doing that at the best of time was not easy, but being in formation, we bore it in mind and we were careful not to be too close to each other. The two parachutists looked at each other as they stood on our wings, and tried to time it so that they jumped off together. Even though they tried to get a simultaneous drop it was not as smooth as we would have liked and we watched as the other parachutists jumped out of the Rapide just ahead of us. My wife, Jane and our young son Courtney were quite fortunate as they were in the Rapide with a view to die for! I was thinking of them as we flew and visualised them watching the chap leaving Tiggy. Even though we felt that the formation drop was a bit cautious and loose, those on the ground felt that it was a very worthwhile display, and we taxied up to a cheering crowd.

The rest of the weekend was superb. We stayed at a high-rise hotel in Margate with easy access to the beach. Those of us from the Transvaal highveldt, being over 200 miles from the coast, really enjoyed the seaside. It was super to be able to combine a flying holiday with all the beach activities. With the car available, Jane and Courtney could intersperse their airfield and beach visits to the utmost benefit.

The weekend ended as a huge success and with sadness we bid our farewells for another year and started our various journeys homewards. Other than being a huge success from a flying and enjoyment point of view, we had over 5 hours of professional video to take back for editing. All this, coupled with the huge safety standards that had been maintained, gave us great memories to cherish. We flew home uneventfully, our remaining drum of fuel was waiting for us at Ladysmith, and all was well. Richard was so pleased with the footage that he decided to expand the film to include some projects under construction in homes and garages. The result was a magnificent 60-minute film that was shown on SABC TV and I'm sure that many copies still exist as memories of that very first Margate.

Chapter 22

The next time that I took Tiggy down to Margate we were again caught by the weather. We were to fly two Tigers down, the other piloted by John, an ex-military chap who had joined our recreational flying fraternity. As before we had planned a similar refuel at Warden, but this time we each carried a drum in the front seat. All went well until we had just got past Harrismith. Fuel pumps had been installed at Ladysmith and so that was our next intended stop. We were flying in loose formation within sight of the national road to Durban and we became aware of a gradually descending ceiling as we progressed. We were approaching van Reenens Pass that would lead us over the escarpment to the lower ground beyond the mountains. As the ceiling got progressively lower, we were ever hopeful that the ground and cloud would not meet and that we would be able to get over the pass to reach the valleys stretching to the sea. As always, I kept a good watch behind me to avoid our retreat being closed up on us.

The closer we got to the ridge, the darker and gloomier it got, until I simply saw the national road disappearing into the cloud mass. I knew exactly where we were and how close we were to the ridge. I was talking to Bobby in the Staggerwing above us. He reported that the cloud mass was localised around the escarpment, as usual, and that he was in clear air and could clearly see the Valley of a Thousand Hills beyond. With sufficient fuel he was steaming on. We however were committed to refuel fairly shortly and so had limited options. Bobby also felt that it was likely to burn off as the day progressed. With all this in mind we turned around and flew back along the road to Harrismith.

Out of the corner of my eye, I caught sight of a large field that had been recently cut. The huge rolls of grass were still scattered over the field. This was an ideal opportunity as one could easily see that there were no termite mounds. I indicated to John on the radio that I would do a precautionary landing if it looked reasonable and sit out the weather for a bit. I carried out an inspection pass and eyed out a good landing area. With all my checks done, I nestled into my seat and prepared to land.

Nothing could prepare me for the doubt that came into my mind as I settled onto finals. As you cannot see directly ahead in a Tiger on finals, I wondered if perchance I had lined up incorrectly and was heading for one of the giant grass rolls. I strained out of each side of the cockpit like never before to see ahead, but all seemed well. After a super smooth landing I taxied to the side of my chosen path and watched to see if John would follow suit. True to form, I watched him line up and land. As we taxied to the edge of the field I saw a vehicle rushing towards us.

Coming to an abrupt halt, a perturbed farmer got out with horrific visions from the big screen. He was having tea on his porch when he saw us disappear overhead and visualised a couple of aircraft crashing into his field. Much to his amazement he saw two normal looking guys standing next to a couple of antiquated flying machines. We greeted each other and I explained that we were en route to Margate and were caught by the weather. We would only use his field for the next hour if possible while we waited for a gap. He was as happy as the proverbial tick and went rushing off for his camera. We discussed the fact that if we went back as far as Harrismith, we would not be able to get back to Ladysmith without extra fuel. It was thus prudent to wait for a period in the hope of continuing our journey if the weather lifted.

By the time the farmer got back, we had isolated a few grass rolls that would be better moved to offer a clearer runway, and we were walking towards them. When we got close to them their size was amazing. From the air they looked much smaller and I thought that we would be able to roll them but even with us pushing and nudging them with his vehicle they were impossible to move.

We sat and watched the clouds do nothing. Not any sign of movement. We gradually realised that our optimism was not well founded and that reaching Ladysmith that day was a myth. We got ready and thanked our host and I started my takeoff roll. I saw a bit of a hump in the ground close to where I was to lift off. I realised that unless I could lift off before it I would be wise to hold her on the ground until I was well clear. The take off went well and I turned back to see John's takeoff. He appeared not to have observed the hump and as I watched he was catapulted up into the air, rather like an aircraft carrier takeoff.

The rest was uneventful and we stayed the night in the Holiday Inn. As comfortable as it was, we would be far happier to have reached Margate. The next morning we awoke to see the most beautiful sight as the sun illuminated the mountain. We went down and enjoyed a good breakfast only to be greeted by a horrific sight as we left the dining room. A huge blanket of cloud had come in to cover the mountain. It would have been an artist's dream, but we were aviators and to us it was horrid. This spurred us into action and we were soon on our way to the field.

Fortunately we had refuelled the night before with car fuel from the local garage and so we could quickly get airborne. I pulled the prop through to prime her and again was amazed at how the oil had thickened in the cold. Eventually she fired and we set off on our way. We realised just how lucky we were not to have lost any more time. As we headed for the coast the cloud was already covering all the high points around us, but we could see that it was clear beyond. As we progressed, the weather lifted and we were able to enjoy another great flying Margate weekend. By this stage we had assessed the area and rented a super house right on the beach. Again Jane, Courtney and Patrick (my youngest son), came down by road to join the wonderful family weekend.

I only ever had one irritating mechanical problem over all the EAA conventions, and it attacked at the culmination of a series of Tiger Moth aerobatic contests.

The contest, open only to Tiger Moths, was to be held in the UK at the annual De Havilland gathering at Woburn Abbey. A participant from each country was invited, and so each country was to hold a series of competitions to choose their representative. The contest was intended for the amateur pilot and so no commercial or official display pilots were eligible. The event was to be sponsored by a long-standing friend of my family, the Hon. Patrick Lindsay. This, together with all I had heard about the Woburn gathering, was a tremendous motivation for me.

When I heard about the series of contests in SA to choose our participant, I was overjoyed as I thought this was just for me. The events to be held were advertised in our local Tiger Moth Club and we had a good gathering at the first meeting. All was well until we were addressed by one of our Springbok Aerobatic pilots. The Tiger pilots, who had initially shown interest, all of a sudden had a change of tune. I tried to speak to them but to no avail. "There is no point in competing, you have just seen the winner," was their reply. I tried hard to reason that their involvement was just to lead us along the way and that a Springbok Aerobatic Pilot was in no way a contender for an amateur competition. They felt that they would not take part, as all their efforts would be in vain.

Even though I did not share their concern, and I wanted to have fun, I put in all I could and gave my support to the event. In fact Alan proposed that two candidates should be put forward who would each agree to pay half the costs. I supported it and felt that in that way at least the winning would be spread out a bit and hopefully get in a few more interested pilots.

With the first contest, my confidence was questioned and I began to realise that I was possibly wrong. Throughout the competition there were only four contestants. Two of them had a number of World Aerobatic Contests to their name, and the rest was left to us two amateurs. I maintained a consistent third place in the contests behind the two national pilots and maintained my view that the intended amateur status would be upheld.

My mechanical problem came at the final contest to be held at the annual Margate EAA Convention, just to crown it all. I had flown Tiggy down from Baragwanath and, just as I was on the last leg flying down the coast, I heard a bang and the engine started making a strange noise together with a distinct loss of power. My instinctive reaction was to glance at the oil pressure gauge, just to see that it was normal. As drilled into us during training, the important thing is to keep flying and look for landing alternatives. As I looked around, I throttled back slightly to get the carburettor heat on, and she seemed a lot happier.

I was a good 30 minutes from my destination, had just passed a small airfield at Hibberdene, and was coming up to Port Shepstone, a rather large town. I had to think smartly about turning back and quickly assess the merits of continuing. As I opened up again, to try to gain as much height as I could, the engine again went rough and delivered less power. After a short time I reasoned that it was not carburettor ice and that I could continue at a low power setting and take stock of the situation.

As I approached Port Shepstone, the impossibility of a smooth precautionary landing was obvious. The development on the coast was intense and no open areas were visible. The only two options in the case of engine failure were the beach, and the sugar cane fields promising some safety, but with guaranteed damage.

With this in mind, still with oil pressure and an engine that was just keeping me up, but unable to climb, I continued keeping sight of my two options. Rather gingerly I approached the town and instantly I seemed to have lost height. The psychological effect of a poor motor made me feel so low, but my altimeter told me otherwise. I diverted slightly towards the beach, giving me a bit more height over the densely populated area and bringing me closer to one of my emergency options. With my wits sharpened to the maximum, and waiting for a total power cut, I passed Port Shepstone and saw Margate get closer, bit-by-bit.

Time stood still as I looked at the area where I knew the airfield was located. After what seemed like an eternity, the town and the airfield were visible. The field is only 400 feet above sea level and so, almost instantly, the height seemed to fall away as I approached. I had already been cleared for a long final and so there seemed to be no need to call an emergency. I came in and made a very welcome landing. As I taxied up, I tried different throttle positions to try to isolate the problem. Once parked, I opened the cowling and saw that one spark plug had lost its inner. It seemed a simple problem and explained the weird noises coming from the front.

I fitted the insert back and screwed on the locating ring. Hopefully, I started the engine and did a run-up, only to find that the weird problem persisted. Each time that I opened up to anywhere near full power, the backfiring and popping started. That evening, by the time we went to the flat, I had diagnosed a possible carburettor problem and had removed it for a closer inspection that night. As is so often the case, when I stripped it, no obvious fault was evident.

The following day I was fitting the carburettor back while I had the odd look up at the Tigers and other aircraft practising above me. With everything assembled I held thumbs while I waited for Tiggy to warm up while she idled. Being very positive I increased power, but as soon as I got anywhere near cruise power the banging persisted. The carburettor was off again and again the exercise of stripping and cleaning yielded nothing. I carefully checked all the jets, needle valve and passages but found nothing, just like the previous night. I installed it all and tried again. A repeat of the earlier exercise, again without any evident improvement.

This persisted into the afternoon, by which time I was thoroughly cheesed off to say the least. Used to flying at 5 500 feet, I had lost the opportunity to practice at the lower altitude, and did not even have a serviceable aeroplane. My objective had to change from practising at sea level before the contest, to simply competing at all. The next day was the competition and only the allocated flights were allowed after the designated start time. My back was against the wall, but I was determined to give my best. The evening light was slowly advancing making the possibility of flight difficult. All I wanted to do was get her serviceable for the next day. I was cross as I got in and taxied down to the end of the runway to do a full power runup.

I lined up and decided that if the engine took reasonable power I would attempt to get into the air. As I opened up and got to full power the popping persisted but I was so desperate that I wanted to see what would happen if I continued the takeoff run. After all there was plenty of length to abort the take-off. I got sufficient power and decided to continue. As if on command, as I lifted off and started to climb, the popping stopped, the engine note settled and soon the steady purr was back and the problem was never encountered again. How the problem occurred, and what the loose plug insert had to do with it, will always be a mystery. Suffice to say that everything seemed to be in order, and I would be able to compete after all, even if I did miss out on the practise.

The next day was perfect and I flew to the best of my ability. By the evening the results were out and despite no coastal practise I had maintained my slot in 3rd place behind the two National Springbok pilots and I was really pleased. I was sure that I would be the chap sent over or possibly together with one of the others as Alan had suggested at the initial meeting. One can imagine my horror as they announced later at the prize giving that the National Open Class Champion Springbok was chosen to be going over. I was devastated. To rub a bit of salt in, compared to me battling with my problems, they had not even brought a machine down but had merely organised to 'borrow' one down there. My efforts at flying down were of no help to me at all. I was so utterly disappointed that I left the evening's event and went back to the flat.

The double tragedy was that, not long after the overseas competition, Patrick Lindsay, the sponsor, died and I was never to see him again. The event went off well to all accounts and was a walk over for SA. The next morning we all had to leave for home and it rather felt that there had not been a convention at all. I have a memento that hangs on the wall, a bronze plaque that reads 'International Tiger Moth Aerobatic Contest, South African Trials, third place.'

Chapter 23

Being on the fringe of aerobatics, I always wanted to get more involved in the sport, added to the fact that I have always been a sucker for a project. We were chatting and reminiscing one evening at old Bara, when the talk got around to the old Zlin 326 that Nick used to campaign. The aircraft had been in the process of having a modern engine fitted after a series of forced landings. Just when the project was going well, Neil Williams had his mishap in the UK, putting all the Zlins back a bit.

He was one of the most experienced world-class aerobatic pilots and was flying a similar Zlin at the time. He heard an unusual noise and immediately felt and recognised what had happened. His main spar had failed and the wings were in the process of folding upwards. With the most amazing presence of mind he rolled the aircraft and flew back to the field inverted. He executed an inverted approach and rolled out at the beginning of the runway. His judgement was so fine, that a path was cut in the grass as he rolled around the wingtip. As he expected, the wing collapsed as soon as the positive aerodynamic load was applied. The result was twofold; he had firstly saved his skin and secondly brought back a failure so that a remedy could be found for the spate of spar failures.

As a result of the new modification required, the rebuild had been halted while the structural repairs were being incorporated. By the time they were complete, the level of interest had waned and the project came to a bit of a halt. To me this sounded like a golden opportunity and in a short space of time a preliminary deal had been sorted out. I was to complete the rebuild in exchange for a one-quarter share. As we discussed it, and the outstanding work was itemised, I became very excited and made an arrangement to see the aircraft on the weekend. We drove out to the East Rand, charged with enthusiasm. I was led into the garage and cast my eyes on the craft that I had not seen for some years. As I took a close look and envisaged all the work to be done, my enthusiasm strengthened and I was even more committed than before. During the following week I towed the fuselage on its main wheels behind my truck to the industrial premises I was using for my fabrication business in Wynberg.

Having the aircraft at my factory was a real bonus as there was always a bit of slack time that I could utilise. In addition, the ability to include shopping sprees in my everyday business, was another benefit. I also had a great assistant in my driver, Nene. He had been with the family for years before leaving to get his heavy-duty driving licence. We never thought that he would come back, until one day he pitched up in Wynberg, knowing that I was running a factory, looking for a driving job. I immediately employed him and he was my most valuable asset until his unfortunate and untimely demise at the hands of criminals outside one of the hostels. He was a dab hand at doing things and was very reliable and adaptable. With all our spare time now occupied, there was a weekly discernible difference and soon an aircraft was being born.

Once the fuselage was recovered and all the instruments and controls were fitted, the next major steps were retraction tests and engine runs. Once all the damage from the wheels-up forced landing was repaired, I made a stand to carry out the undercarriage retraction tests. With the aircraft jacked up securely on the stand, I connected the battery and got ready.

The Zlin 326 is a tandem, two seat, low wing aircraft with retractable main wheels. The wheels and retracting mechanism are contained within the wing stubs on the fuselage centre section. This means that, unlike many retractable aircraft, the fuselage can stand on its wheels without the wings being fitted. As a result, I was able to carry out the retraction tests and the engine runs at the factory. As I gingerly selected 'up', my excitement was enormous. I recalled the many occasions when I had seen Nick flying the Zlins and I visualised the retraction after takeoff. The sight of the wheels slowly folding backwards into the wells was very gratifying. After a few cycles the whole system could be considered serviceable with one remaining test with the wings on. The accent then moved to the engine preparation and testing.

Each time I started the engine it would mysteriously stall within a very short space of time. The problem was obviously a bit complex and I gave it quite a bit of thought before I realised the complexity of the problem. What was happening was that the variable pitch propeller was going immediately to full coarse pitch and stalling the engine. After some searching, I ascertained that the propeller constant speed unit was not fitted to the normal position for a Lycoming engine. Because of the need for a scavenge oil pump, the normal position could not be used and the accessory drive was used instead. Suffice to say that it meant that the unit was being driven at way above its normal speed, and the propeller was going into a coarse setting and stalling the engine as soon as the oil pressure came up enough. The solution was obviously going to be complex and after consulting a raft of aircraft engineers, was told that the situation was impossible.

Undaunted, I stripped the constant speed unit, a real no-no, to understand how it works. A solution was soon evident, and after a few iterations of spring setting and changing gear positions, I had beaten the odds. I had a constant speed propeller that did just what it was supposed to do. Because of my changes and the different speeds, the pitch control was very sensitive, but it worked perfectly. It all sounds so easy but without fail every person I consulted said that it was not possible, leaving me very despondent, until the day they were all proved wrong. I must say that I was keen to see how it reacted over an extended period, running 50% above its design speed.

With this breakthrough, we were all set and soon the day dawned to take her to Bara. I did not want to repeat the road tow as the distance was so much greater than the previous one and so I ordered a crane truck from my usual supplier at work. At the appointed time it arrived, and very gently and easily we lifted the fuselage onto the back of the truck. All my space calculations worked out and soon we were on the road. At Baragwanath, we reversed the process and proudly pushed the fuselage into the hangar. The next step was to be the final assembly and rigging.

We had a time constraint as our trusty airfield was to be demolished and incorporated into a new exhibition centre. We had obtained some land to the south and were going to move the complete airfield out there. As the new field was not yet ready for occupation we had some time at hand. As soon as it was ready, the first few hangars would be vacated and moved to the new location. As each set of hangars were vacated they would in turn be moved and so, having chosen the last row for the Zlin, we had as much time as possible.

When I offered the newly painted wings up, the attachments looked a little strange even though they all worked out when I checked the individual dimensions. That was when all the doubting Thomasses arrived. Isn't it fascinating, when one is busy with a job, very few people will lend a hand, but how often people will come along to tell you either how to do it, or why it won't work.. I was told it was all wrong, all the bits were welded on wrong and so on. I resisted and persevered and at last the penny dropped. The geometry determined that the wings should not be offered up directly, but with the front fitting inserted with the wingtip well forward. The wing could then be swung backwards into place and the other bolts fitted.

Well, it worked out a treat and they slid quietly into position, much to the consternation of the sceptics. With the wings and tail assembled, I then carried out a further series of retraction tests to ensure that there was no chance of any fouling with the wing or fittings.

As so often happens in life, we were now running short of time at Bara and she had not yet flown. An added complication was that no pilots in the country were current on that aircraft. In the nick of time, one of the owners Piet came forward with a suggestion. He was the only one around who had flown the Zlin, albeit 10 years earlier and with the old engine, and would fly her to the new airfield keeping the wheels down for extra safety. That certainly would solve our 'transport' problem. At the designated time, we all met at the 'drome and got ULA ready to go on her first flight since Neil Williams' debacle. I was a bit on the nervous side, being pushed towards a cross country as a first flight, but anyway it was out of my hands. I remember seeing her taxi down to the holding area for the run up. As we watched, after a successful run up and variable pitch propeller check, she entered the runway and began her roll as the last aircraft to leave the old Bara.

Tail up and soon light was visible under her wheels. My ears were listening hard for any change in the engine tone. All I could hear was the expected pitch change as Piet coarsened the prop when he was well clear of the runway. All I could think about were my changes to that constant speed unit, and how it would react to flight. With relief, we saw Piet circle over the field before waggling his wings and setting course for our new home. Tiggy was already there and had been the first aircraft there by a couple of weeks, proudly occupying Hangar no 1, while my trusted driver Nene had helped with much of the equipment moving for the club. I had thus been the prime mover in the first and last aircraft to leave the old for the new.

We arrived at Syferfontein (as the farm was known) to find Piet all safe and sound and happy as a tick. "How was the flight, and how was the prop." came automatically out of my mouth. "All that was fine," he said, "but you better look at the fuel system because I had to have the electric fuel pump on all the way here." I was driven to action and the cowlings were soon on the grass. Once she had cooled off enough to unbolt the pump, all was evident. The diaphragm had suffered from dryness and had stiffened and cracked during the flight. With that rectified, together with a few other minor bits and pieces, we were ready for more tests.

By this stage the paperwork was in order and we could do a proper test flight. I watched in anticipation as she left the ground for the second time. As if by clockwork, I saw the wheels fold neatly back into the wings and she climbed swiftly out for the second time in recent years. After a textbook circuit Piet, brought her in for a landing and taxied up with a big grin on his face. When he got out we congratulated each other at having another machine in the air and put her to rest for another week.

The following week, Piet was overseas and Brian then came out with an interesting idea. "Piet has flown her here, you rebuilt her and I have an open rating, so lets go for a circuit." Still with a look of amazement on my face, I got into the rear cockpit, with Brian in front of me. After going through all the checks and a run-up, we lined up on the runway. As he opened up and we gathered speed, I could not get over how noisy she was. The noise added to the impression of speed as we accelerated down the runway and climbed steeply away. I saw Brian's hand going for the undercarriage switch and, as he flipped it, my eyes went to the telltale stalks on the wings. On cue I watched as both indicators disappeared into the wings until their tops were flush with the top surface, showing that the wheels were safely stowed. As I looked at the panel, I saw that both green lights were glowing and a feeling of pride welled up inside me.

After flying around and getting to know her, he selected undercarriage down and I watched the green lights go out. My eyes turned to the wings, and as if by magic the two stalks appeared to show their red and white candy stripes. We joined the circuit, and by the time Brian turned onto finals for runway 31, he had established a steady rate of descent. Over the fence, he eased back the stick. Both of us were caught by surprise as the left wing dropped out from under us and we landed on two points (one wheel and one wing tip!). Brian held her steady and averted any further mishap. As we taxied up, my thoughts (and I'm sure Brian's) were on the wing tip. When we were out of the aircraft we both inspected the tip and were quite relieved to see how lucky we had been. The paint was barely scratched.

A very lucky escape, but it was a really good lesson on the dreaded stall/spin problem. What had happened was that in the original form, two angles were fitted to the inboard leading edges to precipitate a gentle stall from the inboard section of the wing. These had been removed for competition to give a very sharp, clean break into the stall, as we found out, nearly to our detriment. Despite that and the noise element she seemed a real joy to fly and I was itching to have my turn.

My next step was to get the conversion sorted out. I was itching to have a go myself, and had been in touch with DCA and a willing instructor, as to how to get my conversion. The problem lay in the fact that no SA instructor was current on a Zlin 326. With that in mind, DCA ruled that it would be acceptable for me to be shown the ropes by someone familiar with her and an instructor to give me a check out. After I could prove my competence to him, the instructor could sign me out. With only two pilots current on her, the obvious conclusion was to familiarise myself with the aircraft under Brian's 'instruction' and when we both felt that I was up to it, call on the instructor and show him what I could do. I would then take the instructor for a few circuits, and if he was satisfied that I was competent, he could sign me out, according to DCA.

This was quite a step away from Tiggy and a big challenge for me. On the one hand, I had a huge advantage being familiar with the mechanics, but on the other, it would be my first time with retractable undercarriage, variable pitch propeller and flaps. To cap it all, even the speed ranges were in another dimension. My overall impression was of speed, noise and frantic activity in the cockpit, keeping it all going well. My thoughts drifted to the old WW II stories and I felt like a rookie pilot being sent on his first Spitfire solo after a few hours in Tigers, but at least I had someone with me.

I seemed to be bridging the gap between the two World Wars. Tiggy typified the First War fighter/trainer aircraft. The speed range was low, the open cockpit was simple with no flaps or other marvels of science. The Zlin, on the other hand, had retractable gear, flaps, a constant speed (variable pitch) propeller as well as an electric fuel pump and an assortment of switches and levers to keep the pilot occupied. The speed at which it flew and the speed at which things happened was a revelation. The aircraft felt more like what I would expect of a World War 2 fighter than anything else that I was used to in the past.

After some circuits with Brian, he felt I was ready and I contacted the instructor. The day arrived and I took the instructor up to check me out. After a couple of circuits I was pronounced safe for a solo circuit, and all that remained was a trip to Pretoria for a stamp on my licence. That done, I was to spend many memorable hours in her, some more than others.

One such occasion was my first cross-country in her. The EAA Convention was approaching and nobody had done a long cross-country flight, particularly with the new engine. It seemed the ideal occasion for a good cross-country. When I started the rebuild she had already been fitted with a Lycoming 200 hp engine and constant speed propeller. We had no idea of the fuel or oil consumption and so I filled the tanks to the brim. In addition, the situation at Ladysmith had changed and there was no longer any fuel, so I strapped two 5-

gallon jerry cans in the front seat. My wife and sons had gone down a few days earlier and so, in addition, I had some extras for them. As well as the jerry cans, there was a bundle of underclothes for Jane and a metre long sailing boat that I had found and resurrected for Courtney and Patrick.

She cruised along beautifully and I was very impressed at the ground speed I was achieving. After some time I was aware that fluid was contaminating the screen and upsetting my vision. I realised that it was some form of oil leak but I had no means of determining the extent of the leak, or which oil circuit it was. As long as I had oil pressure, I knew that I could safely carry on. Rather relieved, I landed at Ladysmith, got out and looked at the nose of the Zlin. It was clear that oil was being flung out of the propeller boss seals and back onto the screen. I contacted Brian in Johannesburg and asked him if he could possibly bring a set of seals with them when they came down the following day.

Looking at the oil level, it seemed that very little had been lost and that I should just carry on while keeping a close eye on things. The two jerry cans of extra fuel were adequate to get me to Margate and so once the fuel and oil was topped up, I cleaned the screen. I then went over to the hotel adjoining the field and got a toasted sandwich. Stretched, refreshed and fed, I climbed into the cockpit, strapped myself in, got ready to go, and fired up. I took off and as I was climbing out, I could see in the distance that the weather was closing in. As I peered ahead, trying to assess the weather, my thoughts rambled and I had a rather macabre thought. Imagine the wreck alongside a small village and the people looking for the owners of the ladies garments and the toy boat! As far as the eye could see, the ceiling was descending all the way to the coast.

Rather than carry on crossing the series of hills and valleys, I chose to fly towards the coast and down the first large valley that came along, thereby attempting to maintain a constant clearance below the clouds as the ground dropped away to the sea. It worked out well and I had lots of clear air above and below me, without even having to descend into the valley. The weather did not deteriorate further, but nonetheless I was relieved to see the surf slip below my wings as I turned south, down the coast. My elation was short lived as I began to realise that I was encountering a severe headwind and to aggravate matters more, the screen was again covered with the film of oil.

My progress down the coast was decidedly slow and became a matter of concern. Having flown down the valley, I was not completely sure where I was and when I attempted to pinpoint a few landmarks, I could not believe that I had not progressed further. The visibility through the screen was now becoming very difficult as the moisture was adding to the complication. To check myself, and also because I could no longer see straight ahead through the murky screen, I flew low past the railway stations to try and read the stations' names. After passing a few I got proficient and deciphered one of them.

To my horror, the sign showed that I was far from Margate. Looking to either side of me, I checked the fuel contents gauges and saw that I was still up with a sporting chance, even though it was looking a bit grim. I did have a safety net because there were two airstrips to fly over before reaching Margate.

At long last, the town of Margate came slowly towards me. Knowing the position of the field I set myself up on a long final approach. The wind was so strong that it seemed forever before I was on short finals. Unable to see anything other than a murky haze ahead, I put my cheek right up against the canopy in an endeavour to see enough to keep straight. Only when I prepared to throttle back did I realise how strong the wind was, I kept some power on and carried out a wheel landing (i.e. keeping the speed up and landing on the 2 main wheels). The aircraft was moving at walking pace as I touched down, with the wind speed almost matching my landing speed. I got out and realised what a fine line I had been cutting, even though I had not been compromising safety. I had at all times kept alternates available. We later found out that she did not appreciate a completely full oil tank and as soon as the level lowered a bit, the oil loss stopped and the problem never arose again.

As always, the weekend was a roaring success, with a comprehensive array of aircraft types on show. The aerobatic displays by the Air Force, private teams, and individuals were supported by a variety of other routines. One old favourite that was coming back on the scene was Scully's old man act. His intimate knowledge of the local terrain, and his uncanny ability with aircraft, put him in a position to use it to the full in his J3 Piper Cub.

The act starts with the announcement that an old war veteran had been seen at the show and would any pilot be keen to take him for a flip. In due course the announcer says that he is now going to have a ride in a J3 Cub. With that, the most wrinkled old man that you have ever seen appears, waiting for his ride. The J3 taxies up and he is helped into the back seat and strapped in. The J3 taxies out to line up and begins to roll. No sooner is the engine at full revs than the throttle closes and the aircraft comes to a stop and the 'pilot' gets out and goes to the tail. The announcer says that there is apparently a problem and as the 'pilot' starts to examine the tailwheel, the aircraft takes power and hurtles down the runway in a haphazard manner. It takes off and carries out a swift turn back to the field. The 'craft flies low over the runway in a series of uncontrolled lurches and plunges, and we can see that both of the occupant's legs are out of the open door, and then it all seemingly disappears below ground level.

The J3 Piper Cub is the perfect machine for the act as the pilot sits in the back seat, not quite what you would expect, and it has all the low speed characteristics that are required. You can imagine the carrying on, the announcer fuelling the crowds' anxiety, the fire truck and sundry bodies rushing hither and yon. Scully plays up to it all even using a huge valley next to the runway to make the aircraft disappear from view as if it plunges into oblivion. Amidst sighs of relief, the aircraft pops up again further along the escarpment edge, and Scully in his old clothes and mask, continues the series of hairy flying manoeuvres. He then ends off in a spin, the motor cuts and he pulls out into an engine-off loop. He ends it all in a rapid turn and lands in front of a breathless, relieved crowd.

Although old and corny there are always people taken in and the flying is such that we all wait and enjoy it, even for the umpteenth time. No air show is complete without an old man act.

Another interesting experience was also on the way to Margate. I had flown down in my newly acquired Tri-pacer and we all were eagerly awaiting Piet in the Zlin. We had experienced a couple of blockages in the injectors and so part of our toolkit was a socket to permit the nozzles to be removed, stripped and cleaned. Needless to say, the tool had been left behind and we got a message that without it Piet was stranded and was going to overnight at Escourt with a probable blocked injector.

Dawn the following day found us at the Margate field preparing to depart with Bob in his company Centurion, suitably armed with a liberal supply of tools. As we were getting ready to go in the darkness of the dawn, a little female voice said. "What is going on here?" And with that I turned around to find the only other person likely to be around at that hour, another Tiger owner, Pat. Camping on the field, she had been woken by the goings on and wanted to be part of it all. Later that day I was to be quite glad that she was there, but I was not to know it at the time. "Is there a seat for me?" she said in her beguiling female voice. Needless to say, takeoff found the two of us in the rearmost seats of the 210.

We duly arrived at Escourt, and as we joined overhead I could see the Zlin parked on the apron. We landed and soon I was up to my eyes in the Zlin engine. After stripping and some fettling, even without the proper tool, I managed to clear the injector and she was ready for flight. There was no sign of

Piet and so Brian suggested me flying her down to Margate while they waited for Piet. I resisted because there were no maps as presumably Piet had them with him. There were also none in the 210 as they had used their ADF and VOR radio navigation aids. My objections were heard and overruled. I was not at all happy with the prospect of nearly 200 kilometers without a map, but the others bravely insisted that it was easy, "Margate is just over there" they chorused, pointing, "just climb up and you can virtually see the coast from here." Pat, who claimed to know the area well, eagerly supported this. "I will come with you." And with that my objections seemed to flounder. I got her into the rear seat, climbed in the front and got going.

Without maps, and with an engine that had just blocked an injector, I climbed as fast as I could to get as much height insurance as possible both from the point of view of visibility and gliding. Pat was soon keeping a running commentary referring to a string of landmarks, and that at least kept a positive side going and I soon appreciated having her with me. I flew along keeping the huge Drakensberg Mountains to my right, and I knew that as long they gradually receded, we were on the right track. All the way I expected to see the 210 pass us but we never did. That alone was a bit of a worry, were we on the right track? After an hour and with a bit of straining (or was it imagination) I began to see the coastline approaching. Soon I could make out the Margate environment and then the field itself came into view.

Once we had thankfully landed, we saw the 210 surrounded by a bunch of individuals waiting for us. They had been scouring the sky to find us but had not expected us to be flying so high and when they saw us they were at 9 500 feet and we were so much higher than them that they just continued. Among the crowd was Jane who, bless her, was horrified to see Pat get out of the Zlin. Yet again, the 'airfield girls' had succeeded in ruffling the feathers of our very beloved homemakers. Again I tried in vain to explain the circumstances but soon I had to get prepared for my competition flight in the Zlin and that took up my immediate attention.

The pressure of the morning thus far was not conducive to a good flight, and in addition I had not practised at the coast. I climbed up to the correct height and entered the aerobatic box. My strong recall is a constant battle to keep my airspeed to acceptable limits just like the previous year. The aircraft was so sleek, with so much power and penetration that I had quite a battle keeping on top of the situation. Rather relieved I landed to what was proving to be a long day. Ironically, that was the last blockage that we ever had. Fate always decrees that it will happen at the most inconvenient time, but when it is all over one is always relieved that it ends well.

Another weekend away and another aerobatic contest with the Zlin found Jane and I preparing to leave for a private strip near Ermelo with the usual group of enthusiasts. We left Bara and were flying alongside the ridge to the south of Johannesburg City to avoid the Rand/Jan Smuts area. With Jane in the seat behind me on her first flight in the Zlin, I looked disapprovingly at the weather. As is so often the case, we were not destined to be very lucky with the weather, and as we flew on the clouds got lower and lower. Rather relieved, we landed at Peter's strip and were greeted by a group of concerned people. One of the wives had recently got her licence and was flying down on her own. Had we seen her on the way? Rather reluctantly we had to say that we had not seen her.

Some time later even the most optimistic of the boffins agreed that her aircraft could no longer be in the air. The tanks would definitely be dry and she must be down somewhere. Without the wonderful cell phones that we have today there was no means of communication, and all we had to do was wait with the anxious husband for some news.

As all the prophecies of doom and gloom were being forecast we heard the drone of an approaching aircraft. We looked to the heavens to see a lone 172 battling through the pea soup above us. As we watched, the 'craft turned onto finals and we soon heard the gentle squeak of tyres announcing her arrival. As a very relieved pilotess got out, the story unfolded. Being unaccustomed to the use of a Directional Gyro, she had not understood the way the wandering of the gyro needs regular resetting. As it did she simply drifted off course in sympathy, unable to make head or tails of the situation. Rather wisely, she decided to land at an airfield that she saw approaching. Friendly souls then informed her that she was at Witbank, miles off course. They explained what had happened with the wandering and soon she was on her way again, this time in the right direction. After an uneventful flight she landed on Peter's farm to join us, once more proving that a good fright is worth ten hours dual.

Peter was a super host and a most amazing person. He said that all the accommodation was arranged, and, as we arrived I was given a set of keys to a vehicle and directions to a house to share with another couple. He was such a major force in the local farming community that he simply asked the locals to go on holiday for that weekend so that we could use their houses. It was an amazing feeling opening a front door to 'your' house for the weekend when you don't even know the owner. Thanks to his organisation we were all extremely comfortable despite the cold gloomy conditions.

The conditions did not improve and so the weekend was a bit of a disaster from the competition point of view, as the whole contest had to be postponed, but we all had a good social time. We congregated in the dining area where Peter laid on a good supply of videos, food and refreshments. New acquaintances were made and existing friendships strengthened. By the time we had to leave the weather improved and we all had an uneventful trip home.

Chapter 24

My mechanical engineering study at university encompassed a wide range of disciplines from pure mathematical design, through manufacture, to maintenance of existing equipment. I thoroughly enjoyed the challenge of the mechanics of design but as I was no mathematical genius I did not enjoy that side as much. I could already see a greater interest in the manufacture and maintenance side of things developing.

My favourite class was a particular design workshop that necessitated solving problems that occurred in design, rather than accentuating on the pure mathematical design itself. Rather than working out the sizes and strength of the components we were involved in getting solutions to existing ideas and designs. We were often very involved in mechanisms involving linkages rollers, cams, and levers. This required a particular type of mechanical understanding, lateral thinking and problem solving, which I really enjoyed.

This was not strange as my whole love of mechanics was driven by my hands-on experiences with the cars and aircraft. My father had passed on a particular appreciation by never giving me anything that was useable without having to be repaired or rebuilt. As a result the skills that I did have, once I was finished training, was the envy of all around me. In retrospect I can see it now, but at the time it was such part of my life that I assumed it to be normal.

I started my working career in production and I found the challenge of manufacture and optimising the design very satisfying. The natural progression guided me into a supervisory role that soon led into true management. After years of working in manufacture I got more involved in maintenance, which in turn led me into authoring and production of technical documentation.

Throughout my working career there was an aviation thread that used to surface periodically, and so it was not unexpected when my documentation career ended up in aviation. While working for a documentation company, I was requested to consider the possibilities of updating existing helicopter maintenance manuals to incorporate an updated version with larger engines. I figured that it was just up my street and so I went 'all out' to get the contract for the company. There was an incredible amount of work required due to the extensive nature of the upgrade and the impact it had on the manuals. To get the job and ensure that it could all be set and printed timeously, I even had to get a meeting together at Atlas Aircraft to show the typesetting and printing department what was involved. I knew that I could do my share, I just had to make sure that they could do theirs.

We completed the contract in time and the client was so pleased that I immediately got another helicopter project to start up from scratch. I was immensely happy and the documentation was progressing well when the dreaded threat of politics reared its head. The contract for the helicopter was shelved and the documentation stopped. I was without a job.

I spent some time in another documentation company without a great deal of success and found myself the owner of a motor vehicle fitment centre. Rather too late I discovered what had remained hidden during the sale. The location was at a shopping centre. Without a commercial area close enough to support me I was left with a client base made up of young or retired people. Without a good client base, even though all my efforts got me awards from the franchise group, I could not get the turnover to succeed. I was faced with a gloomy future, unless I found a bag of lucky white rabbits.

At that point fate came in to play, ending up in quite a career change. One of my workmen apparently had omitted to tighten the wheel nuts after fitting tyres on a vehicle destined for Durban, 500 kms. away. The client phoned me on arrival to say that the wheel was damaged as a result of loose nuts and he would see me on his return. The only person that I could think of to repair the fancy mag wheel was Peter, an old friend of mine. I had flown with him many times when we both had Tigers in the 60's, and he had subsequently chosen to be a commercial pilot. All these years later he had loads of experience and was operating a small machine shop outside of his flying career. He repaired the wheel, much to my relief and the customer's delight, and during my visits to him I had some interesting conversations.

He had made contact with a crowd operating a cargo Boeing 707 into Europe and was in the process of getting his conversion. We talked about my career having fallen apart and the life of a commercial pilot in a cargo operation. That night I had a vivid dream of being a flight engineer on a cargo aircraft. The next day I woke and continued to see myself as a flight engineer. The dream I had had the night before was incredibly detailed and specific. This was very unusual as I only remember dreams in a vague way, if at all. The amount of recollection I had was amazing. The more I thought about it, the more feasible the whole idea seemed. As soon as I had the fitment centre going for the day, I was off to see Peter to put my ideas across.

Peter was as always very interested and supportive. Surely with my technical background I could go directly into training as a flight engineer? I did not even entertain the idea of being a pilot at all. He gave me a huge file to copy and we contacted the Division of Civil Aviation. They said that if I passed the technical subjects they would be prepared to reduce the 12-month working period to 6 months in view of my experience. Peter said that I could easily do a course and be a loadmaster for that interim period.

With this as a new perspective on earning a living, I started to study the notes and to spend any available time helping with the 707 whenever needed. Cargo flights always seemed to go at night and so it was usually convenient to help them. Over the next few months I was to get to know the crew, the operation, and the aircraft quite well.

One of the occasions when I was called on to help offloading the 707 was the evening they were expected back from Germany carrying a cargo of 55 heifers. We were due to go to an Octoberfes evening at the Country Club and as per normal the flight was due in late at night. I had arranged to keep in contact from the club so that I could leave in time to meet them at Jan Smuts Airport. I had arranged that someone in our party would give Jane a lift home, leaving me free to help out with the offloading. I got confirmation that the flight was due in at 0100 and so left around midnight for the airport.

I was greeted at the apron by the sight that was now becoming so familiar. As I walked up from my car all the support vehicles stood in silent vigil, looking like a midnight forest scene from a horror movie. The vehicles had arms and platforms extending into the cold, still, misty night like long distorted tentacles. In between these shapes were what looked like an array of picket fences, adding to the atmosphere. Mark had fabricated a series of wooden pens to contain the creatures, and to herd them into the trucks as they arrived.

Nothing moved. As I got closer the shapes took on more recognisable forms, with operators resting in their warm protected cabins waiting for something to happen. As I walked past I could see the way different people wiled away their time. In the dim light of his little world one chap was reading, while others were dozing or drinking countless cups of coffee to keep awake. Other groups had squeezed into single control cabins and were into chatting or card games.

The hypnotic silence, only gently broken by the background humming of the machines was soon shattered by the sound of a Boeing 707 on finals. The harsh, hollow crackling of the engines at full reverse thrust soon followed, and the culprit appeared out of the mist into the apron lights. The beast followed the directions of the waving batons and as it came to a halt its nose dropped in salute. The drowsiness of the previous scene immediately disappeared, to be replaced by urgent action.

The stairway arrived at the doorway almost as the door opened. The door opened inwards, went through its motions to get through the opening and was and allowed to gently rest on the fuselage side. I could not wait to get up and see inside. I eagerly clambered up the stairs with the others and greeted the crew. Looking into the eerie glow of the cockpit, seeing the pilots at their stations tidying up, conjured up visions of long distance flight. I turned around and squeezed past the 10 g restraining net to see the cargo. What greeted my eyes was a shock to my system. I assumed that I would see a load of young bulls that I expected the heifers to be. What I saw was a collection of bulls larger than any cattle I had ever seen before. Lightweight pens penned them all off into small groups and the floor was covered in wood shavings on plastic sheeting, to absorb the moisture and protect it.

The pens separated the animals and prevented a mass movement from one end of the hold to the other, with the obvious disaster that a drastic centre of gravity change would cause. The hydraulic cargo door opened and as it lifted up into the night the scissor truck positioned its platform. The pens were easily dismantled and soon we were herding the heifers into the pen constructed around the platform perimeter. The animals were totally intimidating. They were so huge and strong that as much as we each tried, we were aware that we had little persuasive power to keep them under control.

Moving the beasts was no mean feat; they were just pushing us aside as they tried to break through the wooden railings. We had to support them as the heifers leaned against them. I visualised the airport festooned with these animals running around having broken through Mark's fences. With a few on the platform it was lowered and we had to drive them into the trucks positioned on the ground. They were pushing us aside as we held their horns and tried to drive each one like some huge motorbike. All the time we had to maintain our guard to avoid being speared by the huge handlebars.

By the early hours of the morning, because the cargo aircraft had no air conditioning in the cargo hold, the cattle were showing signs of heat stress. Even though we were gradually winning, we had to ensure that they did not suffer. I thought hard to find a solution to the excessive heat building up in the cargo hold, even with all the doors open. Suddenly I thought about the fire truck and rushed off to find the firemen. Once I got them to the aircraft I explained my idea.

If they could get their hose through the cargo door they would be able to spray along the length of the cargo hold, thereby cooling down the animals. The crew all accepted it as a feasible concept and agreed that provided the area was not drenched, the effect on the aircraft was negligible. The floor was covered with plastic under the sawdust to absorb any moisture and the sawdust over the entire area would absorb the spray. All went according to my plan and the animals seemed to be less stressed after their cooling down.

We continued the unloading and it was only when the sky began to lighten did we realise that we had been going all night. It was only at 0630 the next morning that we could call the job complete. All the heifers, barring one that had died on the flight, were safely tucked away in the three cattle trucks that had come to fetch them. I drove home rather wearily but happy at a job well done. Over the next few days my car took on a distinctly cattle smell, and every time I had been driving, I was left with a pungent reminder on my hands.

Chapter 25

The cattle flight was my first direct involvement with large aircraft and the loading techniques. The next few weeks gave me a much closer involvement with the company and a deeper insight into large aircraft operations. Peter's idea was a bit hectic while I was still managing my fitment centre. Fortunately I had a good manager who held the fort and enabled it all to happen.

I was finding all this new knowledge and experience very interesting and stimulating. I went through the loadmaster's course, passed and waited for my number to come up for me to become a crewmember. Despite the ongoing demand, I was never called up. At each flight I would wait eagerly for my turn, but in vain. In due course Peter came up with another idea. Perhaps I was better suited to pursue a career as a commercial pilot. His feeling was that the demand for flight engineers was well filled as they were being phased out on the more modern airliners. As a result there were numerous flight engineers in the market place. There was a greater demand for commercial pilots, and he had confidence that I would succeed.

This new advice really got my mind going, and I tried to imagine the future. I started looking for a suitable flying school and settled on one at Rand Airport. I attended the classes, studied hard, kept in with the company, and still managed the fitment centre. After three hectic months I got my reward, I had passed all my subjects. The next step was to get my night flying, instrument flying and commercial licence preparation behind me. I kept my Stinson at Rand outside the flying club and used her for the flying training. Other than the dual hours spent in the Stinson that I had bought, I spent hours on my own above the brightly lit Johannesburg and suburbs clocking up sufficient night flying hours.

The requirement for a Commercial Pilots Licence test requires it to be carried out on an aircraft with a variable speed propeller and retractable undercarriage and so I hired a retractable Cherokee Arrow for the last few hours. I carried out my final preparation lesson on it and flew it solo for the first time across to Lanseria for my test. My instructor suggested that I try to get to know it as much as possible on the way over so that I could cope with any situations that the testing officer may throw at me. Much to my surprise I passed the flight test and flew back home proudly to announce my success. It was 30 years and three weeks earlier that I had been issued with my Private Pilots Licence.

Armed with my fresh Commercial Licence, I was just in time to attend the 707 technical course. I found the course very interesting and it certainly gave me a good insight into large aircraft. Already having an engineering training, I soaked up all the information like a sponge. So many of my unasked questions were answered before they were even formed. Our next bit of training took us to the Boeing 707 simulator at Jan Smuts.

Even though it was very old, had no visuals, and demanded a huge computer backup, it performed well and we spent a number of hours there. All the landings were totally blind, relying on the radio altimeter height being called out. Despite that, it was a most wonderful tool and was sorely missed when it was sold. A huge range of emergencies could be simulated that could not be performed safely on the aircraft. I spent many hours watching the others going through their paces, often acting in the capacity of Flight Engineer. In due course my turn came.

On one of the training sorties, we were short of a captain and so I was called up to fill in while the First Officer was being checked out. An emergency was declared and we had to fit our oxygen masks. I had mine on and was flying when I became aware that it was not set correctly and I could not breathe properly. Unwisely, realising that it was only a simulated emergency for the test, I opted to lift the side of my mask to breathe. That way I figured that I would not upset his test. I was flying an emergency go around and thought I was doing well until the world started to spin. With a cool "I've got her" he took over while I tried to recover. Being unable to breathe properly, I had suffered hypoxia, and had made myself look like an absolute fool. Fortunately it only added an extra dimension to his simulated emergency and he passed his test.

We then did the full performance course. Even though it would have been better placed before the simulator, bookings had not permitted that to happen. The next event looming ahead was the actual flying. I could not wait, even though I was only an observer on this flight.

We took off from Jan Smuts and made our way to the Magalisberg area where we to do our general flying. The area was so familiar to me and I was absolutely amazed at the gentle characteristics of this huge bird all through the speed range. I now could see why the 707 became, not only a household name among passengers, but also a favourite among pilots. Steep turns and slow flying, even up to stick shake, was executed with the most amazing ease and gentleness. In due course we returned to Jan Smuts for some circuit work.

Circuit training under these circumstances was a new experience. I remember looking down on Brakpan-Benoni airfield as we sped overhead on our downwind leg. Crossing over at little over a 1000feet in such a monster left me with a feeling of awe, making me think back to the early Bara days with the 707 flying past at low level at the air show. After both pilots had satisfied the instructor, we came to a full stop and taxied back to the freight apron to park. This was a most amazing experience for me as it was the first time that I had been in the cockpit of a huge jet during the take off and landing. Having just gained enough knowledge to follow through a few of the basic actions, gave the whole exercise a degree of meaning and usefulness.

Shortly after this, things seemed to deteriorate and the owner of the aircraft took it back and the company closed its doors. Peter, with his enormous drive found another freight company and continued with them. Even though I continued helping whenever required, I was unable to get any further with them. I was given a few promises but they all died soon after conception.

One Sunday we were playing tennis when I received a frantic call from Peter. I had to drop everything and go and help him. To my surprise I arrived to find him engrossed in papers. He explained that he had to design some tanks to transport fuel in bulk. I sat down and worked out the basic design, with each one mounted on an aircraft pallet. I also suggested how the tanks would be vented, filled and emptied. When I left that afternoon he had enough of a preliminary design to prepare the quote the next day.

Unbeknown to me at the time, the tanks and fuel supply were to play a role in my career even though it was some time in the making. As with so many of my attempts, the cargo operation gradually died a natural death and my only benefit lay in a slow accumulation of knowledge and experience.

During the day I would manage my ailing fitment centre while I was looking for a buyer and continue my training. I found my Stinson to be a most suitable night flying and instrument training platform. Even though the instruments were rather antiquated, and not mounted in the modern 'tee' layout, they proved out to be very reliable. Going to Margate on one occasion, I took an instructor with me to do some instrument work on the way. Little did I know what a valuable lesson was in store for me.

All was well on the way down, but true to form we awoke to disastrous weather on the day of our departure. We were told by the controller to proceed low level up the coast, on the seaward side, past the main Durban airport, to Virginia and then turn inland. With all the positive feelings, and having the super duper instructor next to me I happily set forth. We had a good, very interesting trip up the coast to Virginia, at 500 feet out at sea passing the collection of Jumbos and other huge hardware, as instructed. We looked at the weather, then at each other, as I turned inland.

"Do I climb or do you think our flight stops here?" I asked my instrument rated instructor.

As I tend to be a belt and braces type I asked the question three times and each time he vowed that we should continue. I settled myself comfortably, started to go into a mental instrument mode and began my climb, waiting for the clouds to engulf me. Before I got to 2000 feet I was in thin cloud and I continued at a steady, slow climb inland, knowing that I had to climb to over 8000 feet to keep well clear of high ground.

I was amazed at how thick the clouds were. Deon took over the radio, which was one thing less for me to worry about. I continued my climb for 20 minutes and lo and behold we popped out the top at 10500 feet. By this stage I had put my trust entirely on his expertise, knowing that I was under his instruction. We were soon within range of the Ladysmith beacon and so tuned in the old-style ADF, listening for the identification. We realised that we had had quite heavy headwinds, as had been forecast, and we were considering putting in for fuel at Harrismith. Under normal conditions we would have the range but it was not worth pushing the odds in view of the headwind. In addition the concentration was taking its toll and a break would be most welcome. The vista above the clouds was awesome; the cloud tops were as flat as could be for as far as we could see.

I had done my homework and as well as the Met Report I had also phoned Harrismith to make sure the weather was clear there. It was imperative to ascertain that we could descend safely. I started a gradual descent through the clouds and soon we were breaking through, well clear of the high ground. We landed and taxied up to the fuel bay.

As I checked my mags and shut down Deon said, "Boy I'm glad that that is over."

"What on earth are you on about," I said, "you are supposed to be a fundi at this stuff!"

He then went on to say that he had never flown in such thick cloud, that he had no idea how to fly on 'those old instruments' and that all he used in bad weather was his wing leveller (a simple form of automatic pilot fitted to many modern 'planes). I nearly attacked him I was so cross! Only then did I realise how he had pushed me into a situation that I could barely cope with, and how closely I had been courting fate putting all my faith in him.

The rest of the flight went well, all very visual, and in complete silence. Needles to say, that was the last time I relied on such a so-called instructor. The lesson is clear to all. Those of us who got through such experiences are indeed very lucky. Don't take everyone at his or her word.

Later on when I did get my instrument rating I was all too aware of the danger and the words of my examiner will always remain in my mind.

"This rating is the most dangerous thing you will ever have in your life. TREAT IT WITH THE UTMOST RESPECT". Never was a truer word said.

My final Margate memory was during the hours of darkness. I had at that stage got my Commercial licence and night rating and wanted to do some night work. We did not have lights at Bara and I was not often at lit airfields so it was a good opportunity for some practice. I had been doing a bit of general flying and was returning when I heard two aircraft calling the tower. As I listened I recognised the early registration and wondered what was going on. En route winds and weather had hampered them. Throwing caution and good judgement to the wind they had continued, one following the other in a 'blind leading the blind' fashion, when the leader lost his source of light. He had a GPS and was using this both to navigate and illuminate his panel when he ran out of GPS battery. They called approaching from the North, but could not see anything. I called the tower and offered to circle overhead to give them lights to lead them in and also to be out of their way.

At last I was told that they were safe on the ground and that I could come in and land. All was well although I am sure that their night flying preparation in the future will be a little more comprehensive. Sadly this was the last convention at Margate and it will have lasting memories of being the best location and perhaps one day the politics may be sorted out to facilitate it being used again.

Chapter 26

During the period when my fitment centre was going through its death throes, and while I was getting my commercial pilots licence, I visited Rand on many occasions. I had a firm conviction that flying would provide me with a reliable source of income (how wrong I was), but equally realised that it would not be as immediate as I would have hoped. In the interim I was working on motorcars, or any other work that I could pick up to put some bread on the table. On one of my visits to Peter's workshop, he introduced me to one of his Cub customers. This event was to end up strengthening my relationship with him, even though our interface was not always plain sailing. It was often punctuated by the odd rift and difference of views.

Peter had always had a lifetime ambition to make Piper Super Cubs under license. He had developed an amazing workshop that was a myriad of jigs and frames and had manufactured all the jigs necessary to build complete wings. He had a local aluminium company make dies to manufacture spars and the extrusion needed for the wing ribs. With all these jigs, and his incredible stock of pre-cut 4130 steel components, he assembled wings that he had made from scratch. All he was short of was the ability to make the fuselages, which he was developing with a crazy German that he had working for him. This guy was the most amazing character, a real one-of-a-kind. He spent his day cursing and verbalising his dislike for SA, and the sheer perfection of the German race, but he still lived in South Africa! It must prove something. Nonetheless he seemed to get the work done to a good standard. Over my years of association with Peter, the crazy German was to finish the array of jigs and tools to be able to produce complete fuselages from scratch.

My involvement started when a particular customer was in the office. He had undertaken to purchase a Cub from Peter over a period and he would present his payments as the manufacture progressed. At the time they were into discussing fabric and, as was often the case, Peter had an amazing speed at which he assessed the situation and made the cards fall to his best advantage. Often his ability at situation playing had benefits to others as well.

True to form, he pulled me into the discussion. "In fact Roy and I were just discussing that he would do the fabric work for you," he said, looking at me. Knowing full well that I was looking for work, he was once again playing his cards skilfully. He was soon quoting figures that were available commercially, and saying that we had been discussing a figure somewhat lower for all the fabric work. Again his mastery at assessing a situation amazed me. Of course I was happy doing the work at the price discussed, being paid directly by the client. After all I would be working from home or in free premises if Peter insisted, and so had much lower overheads than the commercial sector. Cleverly, Peter was building in another safety feature for himself by having me contract directly with his customer.

This particular Cub was to be partly new and partly old, and in fact Peter had previously bought the damaged fuselage from me. Armed with the potential order, I rushed home and sat on the phone getting prices. I soon presented a quotation to the customer and walked away with an advance payment! Like the proverbial dog with two tails, I drove home with a huge grin on my face. Peter would not want me to work at home as the fabric work being done in his workshop, would made him look more viable. In any event, he was not charging me for the space and so it was a good deal. The next day I went to Rand to order the supplies and get moving. I chose an area of his 'shop that was quite narrow and long to suit the dismantled wings and fuselage that I would be working on. There were a number of old turbine engine boxes lying around that I stripped and used to make up a series of partitions to separate my area and to contain the over spray.

The added benefit was that I now had a super little cosy area to start work. With the wings moved in, it all began, and soon the area had it's own identifying aroma of dope and thinners. Covering aircraft components has a unique therapy for those of us that are so inclined. We start off with a bare frame and within a short space of time it assumes it's own shape. As time progresses a super shape and finish is the reward for the multitude of layers of dope that are applied. I was very content in my little world and an added benefit was the interface with all the people at Rand.

This was to cement our association, as even though I was not involved on a daily basis, I was able to keep a handle on the progress of the freight concept. Being at no more than arms length from Peter I was often pulled in to discussions, continually getting bits of extra work and I was also able to appreciate the joy of being at an airfield. Close to our hangar was a large assortment of elderly aircraft under various stages of repair, and further along was the legendary Strecker family with their maintenance facility and the colourful collection of Tiger Moths that they tended. Interspersed with the smaller craft were a number of DC 3's, commonly known as Dakotas and occasionally we would have the appearance of their large big brother, the DC 4 or Skymaster, also produced by Douglas Aircraft.

The arrivals and departures of the huge beasts were always an occasion to go to the runway and watch. As I watched them, often my mind used to romanticise and go back to my early youth when I used to spend hours at Jan Smuts Airport looking at them. Little did I realise that within a few years I would be in the cockpit of that very aircraft. With Peter's past experience on Dakotas, he was often called in to assist. You can imagine how I was right behind him in case any other help was required. I had many short flights in the good old Dak, and once even got into the pilot's seat for a short stint.

One such occasion was on a flight to transport gold bullion from Welkom to Rand. Normally a smaller aircraft was used but on this occasion there was a staggering two and a half tons of gold bars to collect! When we arrived in Welkom in the Orange Free State after a short 1hr flight, we were met with the most formidable array of weaponry, obviously to protect the valuable cargo. Fascinated, we saw the movie-type scene unfolding and the gold bars duly arriving, packed in special containers. Under the watchful eyes of the many armed guards spread around, each individual container housing a few bars, was carefully lifted onto the aircraft and evenly spread on the floor in front of the rows of seats. We boarded the aircraft with the guards, sat on our seats and prepared for take-off.

As we took off, my thoughts wandered and I realised that my feet were resting on more money than I could ever wish to have earned by my retirement!! With a jolt, my daydreaming came to an end when I was called to the cockpit. "Hop in the right hand seat Roy" was Peter's welcome, "and show us that you can handle a big aircraft, and don't bump the stick." It was my first attempt at getting into the seat in the air, and I climbed past all the obstacles and into the seat. Just at the crucial moment as I was lowering myself into the seat, I made the elementary error and my knee caught the stick and, needless to say, I was confronted with a verbal broadside. I took the reprimand and humbly fumbled with the wide, heavy, unfamiliar straps, eventually getting them together. For the first time I looked ahead over the nose, and to my complete surprise realised that I was totally devoid of the normal reference to the horizon.

This may sound rather obvious, but I had never thought about the fact that the instrument panel reference against the horizon, that one usually takes for granted, is totally deformed and different without the view of the engine cowl.

The new reference is that of the bottom of the windscreen, which is angled and neither a constant distance from your eyes, nor parallel to the horizon during straight and level flight. I immediately related to those little markers that are fitted to some short-nose gliders just in front of the windscreen to act as a reference line. I looked to my right and could not easily see the wing – that was of no benefit. Looking to the left only brought me into eye contact with the expectant captain.

His eyes said it all and I took hold of the control wheel and looked ahead. There was no nose visible and it appeared as though I was peering through a rather slanted window into the middle distance. I gently tried to keep the aircraft on an even keel, but the task seemed impossible. By referring to the artificial horizon on the instrument panel and relating back to the visual reference, a picture gradually emerged. To prevent the aircraft from porpoising up and down seemed amazingly difficult due to the huge inertia and the pilot sitting far ahead of the centre of the machine. The effect was that one seemed to be moving up and down without the aircraft pitching accordingly. The inertia was so huge that there was a time lag before the effects of any control inputs seemed to happen. As a result you had to cancel the control input almost as soon as you had moved the controls, almost before the effect had taken place.

I only flew for half an hour, but it was a new experience for me and earned a lot of respect for the heroes who fought with similar large machines under less friendly conditions. Once back in the passenger compartment, settling down for the approach to Rand, my imagination was alive. I could not help thinking of how they seem to fly overhead with such tremendous ease and how the two pilots must battle with the controls under conditions of bad weather and high winds. I imagined myself in that seat, as I looked out to the huge Pratt and Whitney radial grumbling away, and with a gentle turn onto finals the grumble began to subside and soon, with a little chirp the wheels touched and I waited for the tail to drop.

I unbuckled my strap and stood up facing the cockpit and assumed a semi crouch in the aisle. This strange stance was to become the position I regularly assumed in the Gooneys. In that position one could see both pilots and get a good vista of the panel and the world outside. We taxied off the runway with the accompaniment of the sounds of the creaking and squealing brakes that typifies the Goonies. Being a tailwheel aircraft with little directional control on the ground, the pilots use differential braking to keep the aircraft on its intended line, accounting for the characteristic sounds as each brake takes effect. We taxied up to the old terminal buildings; themselves sculptured to a likeness of the aircraft itself.

My daydreaming was brought back to the present as we were greeted by another display of weaponry. We were completely surrounded by the security force, brandishing an impressive display of small arms. With the same efficiency that we saw at Welkom, all the containers were unloaded, and the normality of the airport resumed. As we taxied back to the hangar, it was as if I had just woken from a strange dream.

This was just one of many superb flights in the old DC 3's that allowed me to perfect the crouched position between the two pilot seats. I got to the point that I would remain there even during landings and takeoffs, wedging myself into a secure position. In all the time I spent in the cockpit, nobody ever queried it and sent me back to buckle up, so I continued. The reward of almost being part of the crew overshadowed the discomfort and numb limbs. Even when we were on test flights, invariably there would be a large number of mechanics and engineers on board, making my position a bit awkward. I soon found another position behind the co-pilot's seat sitting on top of the spares box. That way I could see a large proportion of the panel and controls through a hole cut in the bulkhead. By sitting there I would not be pushed out the way by all the people jostling for a view of the crew at work.

I suppose, in retrospect, this was my first introduction to a two-man crew operation and as such cemented together my individual ideas about flying large aircraft as a career. Often I would be wedged in my position while a pilot was getting a check-out or conversion. At times it was necessary to summon all ones strength to avoid being thrown about, depending on the 'pilot flying abilities' during the takeoffs and landings.

My time at Rand, covering the Cubs being produced, was providing a living while I was hoping to get a real flying job with the DC3's. I felt that all the knowledge I could gain would not be wasted. At long last the time came when I was included on a conversion course. With great gusto I got into the technical side of the course. The time I had spent around the Goonies now paid off, and I really enjoyed the technical and flying lectures and could not wait for the flying to start.

As always, Murphy was just around the corner, peeping and about to pounce. I flew on the conversion flights of the more senior chaps on the course, but when it came close to my time, a problem arose about my not having my full Instrument Rating. I was told that I would not be able to complete the flying course without the rating. I was horrified and proposed what I thought was a reasonable offer. I suggested that if I was not able to put my IF rating on his table within a month that I would pay back the costs for all the flying that I had done at an agreed rate.

Try as I may, I could not get them to accept my proposal and, of course, soon the course ended without me being able to do a thing. So near and yet so far! I retreated back into my little den and consoled myself with the fact that I was still earning a living. The atmosphere of being around the aircraft with all the activity was still wonderful. The arrivals and subsequent departures of the huge DC4 were always a great event for those of us that are aviation 'mad'. We would all go out to the runway to herald the arrival, see the touchdown, and witness the majestic, growling taxi to the hanger.

The DC4, more commonly known as the 'Skymaster" was truly the grand old lady of the air. My attachment went back many years to my childhood when I remember sitting at the top of the ramp at Jan Smuts Airport watching them. My father was in the shipping and forwarding business and I used to get a lift on Saturdays with his delivery van. I used somehow to get from the underground freight depot, up the long ramp and onto the edge of the apron, where I would sit and look at the airliners. Looking back it was amazing that I had never been challenged. I can only presume that Sipho, the driver, would come to collect me when it was time to go back to the office.

The most amazing childhood memory was that of being inside one of the Douglas DC aircraft, looking up at the large Perspex dome used for taking sextant readings. As I stood behind the pilots' seats I recall the vast array of instruments and switches and particularly all the fittings in the roof panel above the pilot's heads. How I ever got to be taken inside I can't recall, suffice to say that it did happen.

Now, almost forty years later, I was climbing into a similar machine. Gone were the pristine passenger seats, the access stairs and the general grooming that I had seen in my childhood. Instead, climbing up a ladder leaning in the doorway, I looked to the left to see an aluminium floor, no carpets, no seats, but a series of tie-down rings attached to the floor. The edges and grooves in the floor hinted at signs of her cargo of grain, maize and other foodstuff. At the rear, a built in shelf was laden with a variety of spare parts all draped in an oily veil. The aroma of food clashed with that of oil to produce what was to become a familiar cargo aircraft smell. Looking at the shelf, the need for field repairs was all too apparent. Walking forward towards the cockpit door I looked out along the wings at the oily engines and imagined being in flight.

Opening the cockpit door I was amazed to see two bunks on my right and a basin with Perspex supports for the shelf above, a locker and small desk on the left, with the pilots' seats beyond. As in my childhood, I again wished to be in one of the seats when it all happens. Rather larger than that of the Dakota, but with a similar treatment, were the two pilot seats with a large instrument panel and centre console with its huge control levers. The whole aircraft had a large, workmanlike appearance and seemed ready to go.

Alongside the DC4 was a much smaller 'craft, a Hawker Siddley 748. This turbo propeller aircraft had just been flown across from Madagascar for repairs. As always, I had tried hard, but in vain, to be part of the team that went over to prepare her and fly back. The long-awaited machine was greeted at the end of a long over-water flight with enthusiasm that was soon to disappear when they assessed the situation. The propellers had not been properly secured and had caused damage to the propeller bosses and the shafts. A long series of negotiations took place, both parties avoiding the issue, resulting in that being its last ever flight. The particular aircraft today sits pushed into the veldt having been probably cannibalised beyond recovery.

These two aircraft types were to become major players in my future destiny but, unaware, I reluctantly wandered off to continue my covering.

Chapter 27

With Peter's Cub production line and my hopes of getting into the DC 3 scene both coming to an end, I was again on the lookout for a source of income. I was still in the hangar completing my last remaining Cub work and searching every possible opportunity for some honest, income-producing work.

The Maintenance Organisation at Rand that rebuilt and maintained Tiger Moths needed a pilot to do their flipping, particularly during the week. The income was not going to make me rich but it was good fun and after all I was there anyway. Every bit helps. Eagerly, I leapt in for a check ride to get me included on the insurance policy, and off we went. As my Tiger was out of the air for a re-cover, I had not flown one for some time and it was a joy to be at the helm again. I felt so at home that it was like putting on a favourite suit. The flipping worked out quite well as I was on the field during the week and was able to do most of the single flips then. The weekends, on the other hand, were busy as that was when those who fancied a flip in the old girl would summon all their friends together, and as a result, often a whole day would be spent flying them around.

The normal duration was 20 minutes per flip and I had worked out a rough scenic route. I would vary it a bit depending on the particular interest shown before takeoff. I would normally fly in a westerly direction, passing south of Johannesburg. This would give them a good view of the complex of motorway junctions in amongst the yellow minedumps, with the backdrop of the concrete jungle. It is very dramatic as there is a line marking the sudden end of the high-rise buildings. This results from the mine workings below ground, necessitating a restricted building line for multi-storey structures.

From there I would pass over Wemmer Pan, with the oversize Gulliver standing at the entrance of the Minitown next to it, and head towards Gold Reef City. This is a re-creation of a turn of the century mining town built alongside an old disused mine. From aloft, the view of the mine headgear and the old world city, so close to Johannesburg, was always appreciated. In sharp contrast was the new, in the form of the adjoining modern fun fair. Often we would see some of the fairground rides in action. The huge ends of the looping ride reached out of the greenery up high into the sky with the loop in the centre. It was a huge focal point seen from the air, rather like two huge javelins that had struck the earth from some giant's hand. Often we would see the merrymakers in the cars, careering up to the ends of the rails.

After a short look, it would be time to return to Rand. On the way back I would, almost invariably, go over the small ridge and fly over the rural area. This would complete the flight with a view of the open fields and gentle hills contrasting to the golden minedumps and the city as a backdrop.

The approach to Rand was usually easy, as the controller knew our schedule and we would soon be in for the landing, dead on time, after the required 20 minutes. On one particular day, I did 14 flips and by the end I was quite keen to see the last passenger, particularly when the cold started to set in.

Flying the Tiger, doing my covering, and being in amongst all the activity of the DC 3's and 4's was all good fun, but it only put crumbs on the table and not the bread that I needed. With the bulk of the covering all but complete, an even leaner time loomed and so I had to keep the flow of CV's going and maintain all my flying connections.

I then made contact with a chap that I had worked with previously on a helicopter project. The company he worked for was currently busy with the documentation for a Cockpit Procedural Trainer and he was interested in a hand. So much for the scores of ads that I had applied for, in the end it is the personal contact that matters! I had an interview, we soon came to an agreement, and I started out as a contractor for a limited period only.

The CPT, as it was known, was simply a huge, very sophisticated computer simulator, mounted in an aircraft cockpit. The huge advantage was that the correct switches, indicators and instruments were adapted to computer operation. With artificial feel built into the cockpit controls, the effect was complete and the trainee pilot could then operate everything, identical to the aircraft, while looking at a view from the cockpit projected in front of them.

It was an amazing concept and a much cheaper alternative to a full simulator requiring sophisticated hydraulics. I was sent on a trip to the Cape to see them and I was fortunate enough to 'fly' one. It was so good to see in the flesh what I had been writing about.

There were two types at the base. The smaller one was all built inside a normal shipping container as a self contained, transportable, unit, while the second was much larger, and was intended as a fixed installation, in a dedicated room with a curved, wrap-around screen. Even without the motion simulation, the feeling of flying was very real. So much so, that as I looped and rolled within 'sight' of Table Mountain, I found myself looking to my side to check the horizon. Of course each time my eyes moved nearly 90 degrees from dead ahead the view disappeared, leaving me feeling a tad foolish, looking at a blank wall.

I was very happy working on the project, the people were great, and even though they could not offer me a full time job, at least I was established for a few months at a time. Soon my initial contract was extended on the understanding that I really needed full time employment and if something came up for me it would take precedence. One day, out of the blue I had a call from Peter asking where could he meet me, close to the office, for an urgent discussion. We soon agreed on a meeting at the Snake Park for lunch.

I had no idea what it was all about and I had an awkward feeling that a can of expanding foam was being introduced into my life. I had been chasing my flying dream and now with a semi-secure post was I going to be pushed around by all the air in the foam? We duly met at the Snake Park, I must say on my part with some reserve, and I was introduced to two Russian gentlemen. I remembered one as having been a pilot with the 707, but the other rather imposing character was a new face, and he went straight to the point.

"Peter says you are good. We are starting up a cargo operation in South Africa and we need you to start with us next week."

I was totally taken aback and I tried in vain to explain about the contracts and my position with the CPT.

"Please we need you as soon as possible," were the parting words.

With my mind spinning, I went back to the office realising that this may be the one chance to come my way and that I must not let a golden opportunity slip by. Fortunately I was coming to the end of a particular phase in the contract and if I left at that point, I would not be leaving them in the lurch. Once again fate was being kind to me, as it had been over my well-timed meeting with Peter over the wheel story that got me involved in the first place. A couple of weeks earlier or later would have made the decision more difficult for me, possibly leading to a different outcome. I voiced my concerns, asking if there was any permanency in the offing. The reply was an apologetic no, that they fully understood my position and if I moved on, it would have no negative reflections on me. The die was cast, I had to try out the Russians and I was itching to find out the full story. I phoned Peter and told him that I was ready and waiting.

The next meeting was quite an eye-opener for me. We were to meet the managing director in his hotel room in the Sandton Intercontinental Hotel. We went up to the concierge and asked for him.

"Gentlemen, you are expected, I will escort you up." We were whisked up in the lift to be greeted by an amazing sight as the door opened to the penthouse. He had been given the suite that was surely made for the royalty that was always expected, but never arrived. The view from the top of the hotel, looking towards Sandton and Randburg was awe-inspiring, I have never seen a room like it. It was an enormous suite with its own lounge/function room. We were beckoned to sit around a large conference table to a full traditional English high tea. Waiters kept appearing with an array of culinary masterpieces for us to destroy and eat, while we discussed my future and the setting up of the company.

"We are setting up in South Africa to supply food into other parts of Africa. The old supply route that we used to use was through the Congo and as it is no longer feasible, we have had to relocate our operation. Thousands of people are relying on organisations like us as their only source of food."

At this stage my mind was doing unending loops of confusion. We had all heard about such stories but was I prepared to have them in my lap?

He continued. "Once you have helped Peter get the company going, we need you to set up all our aircraft documentation and other paperwork and liase with the aviation authorities and maintenance personnel. Once that is all in place you might be in line for some flying."

This all sounded good, but all a bit high flying and improbable. "Next week you and Peter go and find an office, get a computer, and you can start putting it all together. Over the Easter weekend the first few aircraft will arrive."

That rather was that. It all sounded too good to be true. It was definitely something that I could not pass up. Rather daunted by their commands that were so easy to say, but that required so much in actions, we left, each with our own thoughts. While I worked out my short notice period, he chased us until there was a temporary office. It was very small but as it was on a monthly basis and being in a rented office block we could easily expand. We moved in and soon the work was rolling in and space became a concern.

We had settled in and were getting all the paperwork in line, when one day we were again summonsed to the penthouse. He took us to a window overlooking the then new Sandton Square. "Look at that block over there. When they are finished that will be ideal for us." And with that we started off on another quest. As the building was far from ready, the timing was ideal and we spent many hours supervising the finishing to his requirements.

The arrival of aeroplanes was now getting closer and we did not yet have an airfield base. Peter gave a long dissertation on how much easier and cheaper it would be to operate out of the old airforce base at Pietersburg. Considering the cost of road transport as the only disadvantage to offset the various huge costs at Jan Smuts Airport, the decision was made and we were sent off to seek out a hangar there.

Great fun and off we go to Pietersburg. The military field with all its facilities had been decommissioned and was now available for civilian use. Peter had some concept of the size required for the operation and so we went in with his high ideals and put in an offer on the largest hangar. In the car on the way home I was amazed at the extent of all the arrangements and Peter explained that together with the aircraft that were flying down, were a number of personnel that would be here on an almost permanent basis. The whole concept began to take shape.

We had measured out the hangar relative to the size of the Russian aircraft that he had given us, and only then did I realise what we were in for. The Managing Director immediately agreed on renting the hangar with the offices and a lease agreement was drawn up and a cheque made out for the initial deposit. For a bit of fun, I flew up in my Stinson with Peter and one of the girls who was to be a secretary there. We landed and proudly taxied towards our new home. Once out, we walked the short distance to the administration building, and looked for the contact person. They knew that we were arriving and I was rather amazed that nobody was there to meet us. We waited in the waiting room with the deposit cheque that would represent some months of my salary, burning a hole in my pocket. Eventually they arrived, and as we gave them the cheque, the reason for the delay was clear. Since we had agreed to rent the hangar, a number of companies had approached them for premises. They had just been in a meeting with one of the passenger airlines who were desperately trying to get the large hangar away from us. Just imagine if we had not passed the cheque over in time.

As I flew back, my mind was wandering. I felt like I was being involved in a huge film production. We had now got the sets, the actors were arriving and we were getting ready to roll, but where was the script, and when would the show start? What I understood all pointed to a huge undertaking and, as amazing as it seemed, I was part of it. Was everything going to materialise just like that? It all seemed so impossible.

We, as a family were getting on quite well with one of the Russian families. As mentioned I had met him when he flew the 707 and he had moved over with his family to live here. They had a son much the same age as my younger son and, unlike many business situations, the two families saw each other regularly. We had invited them to join us on a small game reserve south of the Kruger National Park over the Easter weekend. As the first few aircraft were due in on the Monday, he had to keep in contact with the MD in Dubai and we had to come home via Pietersburg. At the time, looking at the map it looked simple and it was on that basis that we had planned the holiday.

Well, we had a super few days together and on the Monday got ready to leave as soon as we got their estimated arrival time. In due course we got the call and got on the road. As I had planned, I left Nelspruit and headed north to meet the connecting road to Pietersburg. My heart sank as we got further along the road. The 20th century roads gave way to a narrow, winding road full of potholes, with tiny settlements every few miles. As our progress became incredibly slow, the frequency of the phone calls increased and then the mobile 'phone battery was getting flat.

"Where are you? Why is it taking you so long?" was the request from afar. The pressure was on and I was going as fast as I could. I managed to get the mobile phone on charge and things began to improve a bit. What happened to the roads that were so well represented on the map? I checked and rechecked, we were on the right road, it was just the graphic representation that needed attention.

After a long, tedious journey we drove into Pietersburg and through the entrance into Gateway Airport. As we drove towards our hangar, I saw some enormous aircraft. They were Illuyshun 76's I was told. I stopped next to them and was quite amazed at their vast construction. They had the typical opposite dihedral (anhedral) so that the wings looked like they were drooping under the weight of the four engines. The undercarriage had a multiplexity of wheels supporting the belly, and there were even four wheels on the nose bogy.

We walked around to the tail where the loading ramp had been lowered. To my amazement, I looked up to see a pair of rails extending the full length of the hold and ramp opening. On these rails were four overhead cranes. The huge hold was lined each side with a row of fold up parachute seats, and above our heads in the very rear of the fuselage, was a blister to accommodate a rear gunner. Continuing our walk around, we came to the front, and looked up above us to the arrangement of panels making up the windscreen. Below that was a bomber type Plexiglass canopy. The belly was so low that we could not walk underneath it, but because of its immense depth the cockpits were high above us. At the front we could see into the Plexiglass where presumably the bomb aimer had been. It was now presumably used only for navigation.

I stepped away in awe. Not one, but two of these monsters were alongside each other on the tarmac. Not only were they greater in overall dimensions than the 707, but because of the ridiculous girth of the belly, they were enormous. Having been involved with the loading of the 707, I could really appreciate the wonderful utilitarian design and I could not get over how easy the loading must be. I was yet to find out how the same philosophy extends into the maintenance programme as well, explaining why the Russian aircraft have become the backbone of African air transport.

That evening we had an early dinner at the hotel before leaving on the two hour drive home. Sitting in amongst all the crew, listening to all the conversation in a foreign tongue, and English, when spoken, was with such an accent, that I felt as if I was in a James Bond movie, but on the other side!! They were all very friendly and I was going to get very used to the scenario.

The time soon came for us to leave and return homewards to Johannesburg along the road that was to become so familiar. I was again carrying a huge mental vision, wondering if the picture was going to turn out to be larger than the frame. My mind was alive with ideas and prospects of the future.

Chapter 28

The temporary office to the East of Sandton City was now unbearably small. In a single office, we now had two computers, four people and a mountain of paperwork that I had been churning out, and no space. The new office was progressing well and we could not wait to move in.

Over the last few weeks we had visited the new offices many times to sort out the finishes and final touches. By this time we had a new dimension added to the office. A charter group would also be joining us. They were a small group that contracted out their flying and would be quite an asset to us. They would be using our aircraft for their freight requirements wherever possible and having someone already operating in the local environment would be of great benefit to us.

When the move eventually came, we had got ourselves so prepared that everything went like clockwork. My old faithful trailer was once again summoned for duty and after a few trips in a single day we were in our new office – it was wonderful. We rattled around like peas in a pod with so much space that we felt overwhelmed. The view from the office on the 24th floor was like flying. We had enormous picture windows in all the offices giving us a wonderful vista, and I could even see the area where our house was built, some 6 – 7 km away. The whole office had a wonderful sense of peace and well being thanks to the views of the green rolling countryside and the plethora of trees that exist in the suburb.

Once we had all settled in to our offices, I continued writing the Operations Manuals as well as all the other paperwork in conjunction with an aviation consultant in the UK, who was our official consultant, particularly regarding all the legal requirements. The aircraft were flying out from Pietersburg on a regular basis, but with my head well into the paperwork I was really not sure where the flights were going, suffice to say that they were 'in the Bush'.

From time to time I got involved with purchases for the "Bush". At one time I had to get prices for a self-contained freezer room. When I got the requirements I was astounded at the size required was almost 100 square metres of floor area and over 2 metres high! We would transport the contractors with the fridge itself and the whole structure was to be erected on site. It was amazing talking to the suppliers without mentioning where it was all taking place. I had my own visions of a clandestine operation, landing in the dead of night but in truth I had no idea where it all was. The price was accepted and the fridge was delivered with the installation team prepared to go. They returned having installed it and I was as mystified as ever.

On another occasion I was called on to go out with a chap that arrived from the Bush to go and purchase large amounts of food. I had seen him around on other occasions but had never spoken to him. On this occasion I had to take him to the large wholesale stores to purchase his supplies. He carried a briefcase and I was staggered when we were welcomed at the store and he handed it over to be put in their safe. The suitcase contained just short of 200 000 American dollars in cash. We walked around the store and he simply ordered case upon case of supplies. My mouth gaped open when we left having spent the vast amount of money on biscuits, soap, bottled water, and the bulk on pilchards in chilli sauce, for delivery to Pietersburg.

The food that was purchased was being supplied to a wholesale chain for distribution for sale in the "Bush". I did not know where we were supplying all the food, or in fact any details of who the client was. The office was also buying enormous quantities of maize, rice, and fresh vegetables. I could not wait for the day that I could see the operation and the sheer size of it all was falling into place.

As well as being in the office, as my paperwork load was lessening, I was called upon to help in a fuel installation that Peter was developing. We had four large industrial fuel tanks (the type you often see on farms) that we were all connecting together to be fed by electric fuel pumps to refuel the aircraft.

I went out and bought some 12v petrol refuelling pumps that we connected in line and eventually the whole system was put together and tested. We now had a storage system of thousands of gallons of fuel, and a sophisticated system to refuel aircraft, with pipes long enough to access the wing fuel tanks.

I was not quite sure how it was all going to get to the bush, I presumed they would be transported by road to Pietersburg but I was soon to be proved incorrect. One day while we were working at Rand, the familiar rumbling heralded the approach of a DC4. To our amazement the aircraft taxied up and parked near Peter's hangar and the crew came to speak to us. Apparently the DC4 would be taking all the tanks up in the next few days.

Back at the office, the Russian MD called me in. "Go out and buy sufficient food for 10 people for two weeks. Also get stretchers and sleeping bags and anything else they well need. Peter B here will help you". I left rather nonplussed. I got the feeling that no questions should be asked. Peter B seemed to know more about what was going on than I did, so I thought that I would just go along and see what would happen. We went down to the supermarket and soon had trolleys filled with an enormous amount of food. Up at the camping shop we got stretchers, sleeping bags, some camping stools and mosquito nets. He was also insistent that we must buy a chest freezer. We had run out of money so would I put it on my credit card and get it back from the office. In view of the urgency I agreed. We chose a good, solid-looking freezer. We obviously made arrangements to come and collect all the goods later, and left to go back to the office.

Back in the office, I was again confronted by the Russian, who said that I would be going along. Can you imagine my surprise? The anticipation of going in a DC4 was something out of this world. All my previous efforts to get included in a trip had come to nought, and now I had a trip ahead of me. I had no idea of where we were going, other than to "The Bush". My mind conjured up an image of the aircraft landing on a clearing in the middle of the jungle, and I thought back of Uncle A. being lost and crashing into the dense jungle.

We went out to Rand Airport with the load of goods and were confronted by a person who was to become my mentor and good friend. This was Captain Jack Wight, a familiar face around the family of Douglas aircraft. He was here to give Peter a conversion on the DC4 and I realised that this was to be my first flight in this aircraft. We all clambered up the stepladder into the rear hold, and walked up to the cockpit on a horizontal floor, unlike the DC3 that was a tailwheel aircraft. I watched Peter strap himself into the left-hand seat, and Capt. Wight into the right hand seat. The flight engineer swung a seat in place in between the two pilot's seats and settled himself in. I got into the navigator's seat and strapped myself in. The engines roared into life one after the other, and in due course we taxied out. Very different from the DC3, with far better visibility and control, we negotiated the rather small space between the hangars and out onto the field.

I could see the 3 crew members chatting and going through checklists, but without a headset unfortunately could not hear them. After the pre takeoff checks and engine runups, the four great radials were opened up together and we trundled down the runway. After lift-off I saw the gear selected up and shortly afterwards was aware of a strong burning rubber smell. As this is a critical phase in the take-off process I dared not interrupt and had to simply hope that they knew what was going on, but I was looking out the window with a bit of concern. Although we were off the ground, with wheels up, we did not seem to be climbing and I wondered if the burning rubber smell could have anything to do with it.

Almost as my thoughts had gelled, we started to climb and all seemed to be well, and the rubber smell had subsided. We did a few circuits and at each undercarriage retraction we had the burning rubber smell. After the last landing when we had stopped and disembarked, I enquired what the smell was all about. "Oh, it's a common DC4 characteristic, there is a strap that stops the nose wheel spinning as it retracts into the well. That is what makes the smell". What a sense of relief I had, if only I had known earlier and not had to stress as much. I had thoroughly enjoyed the flight and was beginning to adapt to the new type of flying.

Back at the hangar we were told that we were due to leave in the next few days, as soon as all the tank equipment and the supplies were finalised and loaded. I took a break from loading to phone my wife and tell her the news. She was due to go to Mooi River (4 hours by car) over the weekend to collect a Saint Bernard puppy. As we would be loading all weekend, she arranged to go down with her father for company. We continued all weekend, loading and transporting the goods from the office together with collecting spares for the DC4 to take along.

On the Sunday, Jane came past to announce that we were the proud new owners of the most beautiful Saint Bernard puppy. They had phoned in on the way back from Mooi River and I explained that, as they were almost passing Rand Airport, they should pop in and see us. It suited me as I could also tell her that the plan was to leave the following day. They were as amazed as I was at all the activity and after a rather long day we all went home, having loaded up the aircraft, fuelled up and ready to go on the following day.

We met at the terminal building, with me still unable to find out exactly where we were going early in the morning. I recall Peter B. with a collection of medical supplies in a rather serious looking box. He and Jack kept talking as if this expedition was not new to them and so I took it as a kind of reassurance. All our passports were collected, stamped in bulk, and we prepared to leave. Kisses and goodbyes to the assembly of girlfriends and wives and we set off to the plane.

Struggling with our cases, we climbed up the ladder with our minds all full of our individual thoughts. Personally, I was thinking of what lay ahead, but considering all the purchases, I envisaged some sort of camping expedition.

Chapter 29

The silence of our thoughts was broken as the engines grumbled into life and as we taxied out. I was still trying to paint some sort of picture of what was ahead. Human nature is always trying to analyse what is happening, but here I battled to understand what was happening to me. Never before had I been taken somewhere off into the unknown by another force. My mind was working hard when I was brought back to the present as all four engines roared for take off.

If I had been aware of a flat climb out after the take off on the previous flight, I had another thought coming. With the full load, and the now familiar burning rubber smell, we seemed not to climb at all. On later reflection I know that it is a normal large aircraft characteristic and it takes a lot of ground to be covered before the aircraft is in a clean, climbing mode, at the correct speed.

Once we had climbed to our cruising level, things began to settle down and we moved around and chatted. We were taking some spares up for another DC 4 that had blown a cylinder barrel, and so we had an extra crew with us. Apparently we were going to overnight at Victoria Falls before setting off the next day. One of the engineers took out a gas bottle and cooking ring, and to my amazement started to boil some water for tea. Although striking me as being distinctly odd, tea being prepared in that way was to become a welcome and familiar sight just after getting airborne each time.

We all partook in a very hearty cup of tea and biscuits and continued boring a 170knot hole in the atmosphere. I spent hours watching the crews every move. There was a great oil tank below the bunks that was used to pump oil into the engines in flight. This was explained to me as my first duty on the flight. There was a selector valve at the back of the lower bunk and a spring-loaded valve. Once the required engine had been selected, the valve had to be held down while the oil was being transferred. From time to time the flight engineer would call back to me to move the selector and hold the valve down to top up the required engine oil level.

As well as his constant vigil, the engineer also had to keep the four engines synchronised. For that purpose there is an instrument with three little propellers depicted on it. It is linked to the speed of engine number one, and the propellers rotate to show that the individual engine is either slower (rotating counter-clockwise) or faster (clockwise) than the reference engine. The engineer then gently adjusts the pitch lever to stop the rotation of the relevant propeller on the instrument. The harmonic hum that is generated from unsynchronised engines is thus minimised.

While this kept the engineer busy, the pilots took turns in flying and monitoring the instruments and indicators, their eyes continually roving inside and outside the cockpit. The non-flying pilot then did the navigating and radio work. I learned that the antiquated auto-pilot fitted had strange habits due to it's air operation that rendered it an inadvisable flight aid. Even though that was the case I always wanted to try one out one day, but it was not possible.

After a while Captain Wight got out of the left seat and came aft. Peter got into the captain's seat and the co-pilot got out. "Get in Roy and see how she feels." I could not believe my ears. With glee I got in to find that there was an enormous amount of space compared with the DC 3 and so I did not bump either the stick or my head on the array of ceiling switches as I had done in the past.

I strapped myself in and then looked around to take stock of the situation. As commanded, I took hold of the stick and continued my visual enquiry. The stick was firm like a Dak, and a similar porpoising was evident. Being so much heavier though, all my concentration was needed to maintain a decent flight level and heading. "Remember not to use your feet in the cruise". As I gradually relaxed and eased myself a bit higher in the seat, I was able to appreciate the magnificent view over the nose. One has a truly panoramic view of the landscape, and looking behind me out the window, I could see the two thumping great radials on my side doing their job

After an hour or so I was relieved of the position that had been so enjoyable. While I had been at the helm, my control of the beast's porpoising had improved so much and I was really beginning to enjoy it in a big way. Later on in the day we neared Vic Falls and we began the final clearing up for landing. All back in our original positions we settled in for the approach and landing. Never having been to Vic Falls before, and having heard so much about it, I was quite excited at the prospect.

Being used to approaching over some signs of civilisation, the long approach over nothing but the African bushveldt was so unfamiliar. Approaching from the west, it looked like the airport had been dropped in the middle of the bush. The captain executed a perfect landing and we taxied up to the fuel pumps.

Stretching and yawning, we got out of our seats, opened the cargo doors and sampled the fresh Zimbabwe air. With a feeling of elation and pride, I climbed down the ladder and looked around. In front of us, in the rather austere surroundings, was a six-seater Cessna. The little aircraft was so dwarfed by the DC 4 that it looked like some sort of suckling infant. Having given the fuel attendant instructions, Peter B and I walked up to the control tower to settle the landing fees.

Once inside the long, box-like building, we headed to the end where the tower seemed to be grafted on. We climbed up the stairs and entered the control tower where we were faced with a real birds-eye view of the whole airfield and surrounding area. The amazing amount of bush surrounding the field was very apparent. Only on the town side was there any vestige of development, and that was only the parking lot, a few buildings and the road. The other 270 degrees were all virgin bush. We paid our fees and met the others back at the aircraft.

I could not believe how long it took to fill the tanks but then I suppose that, with a total capacity of 2850 gallons, it was a new dimension for me. I watched the flight engineer open and remove the emergency exits over the wings and climb out onto the wings so that he could unscrew the dipsticks. He checked each tank content and each filler cap security. With the fuelling complete, we passed all the bags down the ladder, parked and secured the aircraft for the night and went to the arrivals hall to clear customs and immigration.

Once clear of the formalities and outside the terminal building we were faced with an array of taxis. We chose two and loaded up, heading for the Elephant Hills Hotel. Peter requested the taxis to take a longer, more scenic route as it would be an opportunity to look around.

After a rather uninspiring drive towards town, we drove alongside the massive Zambezi River towards the top of the falls. Expecting to see the actual falls I was rather disappointed to see just a seething mass of water before it took the huge tumble. Unfortunately we had to continue on to the hotel where we could unwind for what was to be our last evening in civilisation. It was all so new to me that I was on an absolute high, I was soaking it all up like a sponge. Sitting on the balcony at sunset I could see the huge clouds of water spray even though it was miles from us. I was told that it was that distant view that coined the name "the smoke that thunders." Between us and the falls was a huge expanse of green lawn, and as I looked down I could see warthogs and small buck grazing peacefully.

After a filling meal, our tiredness got the better of us and we all fell into our beds in the wonderful luxurious rooms and I dropped off wondering how the next day and night would unfold.

Chapter 30

The next day, after a very comfortable night, we left the hotel and again squeezed into the two taxis for the trip back to the airport. We took the direct route through the town itself and I enjoyed looking at all the buildings and the one-man stalls that abounded, selling mostly their local crafts. We carried along the amazingly straight road until we turned into the airport. Once through all the legal channels we carried our bags out to the aircraft on the apron. As I walked out the unknown started to build up the anticipation and excitement inside me.

She was dripping with the early morning dew and grew like a giant out of the mist as we approached. Knowing that I was a part of it all gave me a super feeling of belonging and pride. After the luggage was carried up the ladder and safely stowed aboard I became aware of a new ritual as I walked around with the pilots as they carried out their pre-flight check.

Radial engines are prone to oiling up the bottom cylinders when standing, and sometimes so much oil accumulates that the piston comes up solid with the trapped liquid. If the starter were used when this happens, the piston coming up against the incompressible liquid, driven by the starter motor, would in all likelihood bend the connecting rod or crack the barrel. To avoid this, each engine is rotated by hand a full two revolutions to ensure that each cylinder has been through compression. I was soon shown the ropes and designated for the task. I had to reach up and grab each blade and pull it through as I walked from one side of the engine to the other.

This procedure makes it possible to feel the resistance put up by the liquid before damage occurs. Pulling through six blades on each engine ensured the required two revolutions. I could soon see that this would be a good early morning loosening up exercise for me each day.

With the pre-flight complete and all of us strapped in, we started up and got moving. The take off was once again one of the low, long runs, part of her character. As before, I watched the crew's every move with a mixture of admiration and envy. I looked at them, wondering if I would ever be in their league. It was not as easy to see them as it is on the Dak because there is a step up to the cockpit level and the engineer sitting between the two pilots also obscures the view from the navigator's desk.

Once we were airborne, I got up to look through the side windows at the world outside. The ground below was virgin scrub and dry grass covered the ground that was not occupied by the typical African thorn bushes and trees. As we flew along, I would alternate between observing the crew and keeping a lookout for wildlife. I did, in fact, manage to see a heard of buffalo, but not much else.

On the previous day, before arriving at Vic Falls, I had been severely pulled up by Peter B for not having reviewed the route. Try as I did I could not persuade him that the destination had not been discussed with me, and that the location of the whole project had been kept away from me. In a later project I was also to see how the aircrew were far more aware and eager to discuss their flight details than the management was. At long last I managed to convince him that I did not even know which country we were destined for and his attitude softened.

By the second day our relationship had healed to the extent that he was now eagerly showing me the route. We headed along the notorious Caprivi Strip before setting our course for Angola. The Caprivi Strip, a narrow piece of land between Zambia and Botswana, saw military activity for many years and was a common name in many news items in the past.

Once we set our course for Angola, Peter B began explaining that there were areas that one kept well away from, known as the 'hot areas'. On our route, two towns in particular had large military airfields equipped with jet fighters and guided missiles. I was so involved and intrigued with the whole exercise that in retrospect the real meaning was somewhat diluted. Even though he diligently took me through all the difficult areas, in later years Peter was to be caught by his own rules much to the detriment of the crew and passengers on board. He was in fact forced down over the very town that he was busy pointing out to me.

The countryside changed to a series of dry riverbeds crossing our path almost at right angles. The series of these dry beds carried on for quite some distance. The vegetation became sparser and as much as I kept up my vigil for animals, I never saw any sign of wild life north of Vic Falls. In fact, the vastness of Africa was awesome. We would fly for extended periods without having sight of a road, any dwellings or any sign of civilisation. I could not be anything but be amazed that this was the continent with all the fighting about land possession. Surely these huge unoccupied areas meant that there was enough for all!

As we progressed up Angola, the land became much wetter and there were numerous flowing rivers. The signs of local life was much more apparent. Small, typical African villages were now quite plentiful, with little in the way of organised towns by comparison. Eventually, the trusty GPS and our maps warned us that the destination was imminent and we started cleaning up for our approach.

Looking out, it was again strange to be approaching the airfield with such undeveloped bush beneath us, but that was what the map showed. In the navigator's seat I could not see too much on the approach and, so when we taxied up, was quite amazed to see that the whole place was dirt with no hard standing anywhere.

The airfield was occupied by the largest collection of DC 4 and 6 aircraft that I had ever seen. They were all parked on the one side of the runway and a pair of Antonovs and a Hercules occupied the other side.

We stopped at the southern end of the airfield and prepared to disembark. A local in an old pickup, who seemed to be expecting us, arrived and greeted us. He turned out to be part of the organisation that marketed the foodstuff that we would be transporting. I was gradually putting things together and the end result was a bit amazing. It was like an old World War 2 movie and I had the feeling that everything had just been left there for years. The whole airfield and the aircraft all had a well-worn look about them.

We offloaded all our provisions, camp beds, deep freeze and loaded up the pickup, which was soon full and promptly disappeared. By the time it returned empty, we had all our personal belongings alongside us and had locked up the aircraft for the night. We climbed on the back with our luggage and left the airfield, accompanied by a guard armed with an AK47 assault rifle, much to my horror. By this stage my eyes were so wide-open that I thought they might fall out.

Not only had I been part of an amazing trip, I now seemed to be driving into this film set and I still did not quite know what it was all about. The road that we drove down had once been a tarred road, and it was bordered on both sides by an amazing collection of abandoned junk and derelict, battle-scarred buildings. Old parts of once proud farm machinery lay in various states of disrepair, and there were the odd telegraph poles sometimes with a hint of the wires that they used to support. Needless to say, the majority of the cable had long since been 'recycled'.

After a very short drive we stopped in front of a double story building with a balcony overlooking the road. Driving up, we saw that the one side of the building had been the subject of some serious arms fire of some sort. The plaster had been blown off leaving a random selection of craters in the wall.

We offloaded our baggage and carried it all into a ground floor room where the driver on the first trip had stacked our provisions. We were led upstairs where the higher ranks turned left and we turned right. We were shown to a mezzanine where all us lower ranks were to set up our camp beds, dormitory style. Having set them up, we went to the higher rank apartment next door to join the others for a welcome beer. There were two bedrooms and a lounge all furnished with some rather derelict furniture. This main room/lounge was to be our meeting, eating and command area. There was what once had been a kitchen and a bathroom with taps that had long since ceased to function. The bath was a revolting sight filled with muddy water. This water was the source of water for all cleaning and washing, but one look ensured that it was clearly branded 'NOT FOR HUMAN CONSUMPTION'. On a daily basis a United Nations tanker would come and stop outside so that the bath could be topped up with buckets of murky water. I was once watching this process, looking down from the balcony, when the worker dropped his bucket and promptly climbed into the tank to retrieve it and continued unperturbed.

The surroundings, the water system together with our guard, was enough to make you doubt your sanity. I never discovered whether the guard was to protect us from them, them from us, or was simply on another agenda completely. Suffice to say that we were guarded at all times, 24 hours a day, except when we were within the airfield boundary. The washing method was equally odd. We would stand in the shower and pour the muddy water over ourselves with a jug. I had to soap my wet body and then rinse it off with the dirty water, shivering at the mere thought. With the only alternative being not washing at all, that was how it was done, and we all survived!

Looking out from the first floor balcony, we seemed to be in a ghost town that had been taken over by squatters. Dirt and grime was everywhere. People moved incessantly from place to place, but there was no sign of any industry or business of any sort. Being good South Africans, the 'braai' was never far away and it was set up on the balcony, and a discussion followed. We were given a severe warning. The whole area had been severely covered with anti-personnel land mines and the unoccupied areas were all to be treated as unsafe. We were told never to walk off the edge of the road or airfield. Quite a sobering thought.

The plan was that on the following day the engineers would repair the second DC4 while the rest of us would get the tanks and fuelling system set up. With that in mind and after a good piece of steak and boerewors, things seemed to feel a bit better and we retired to our camp beds. As tired as I was, I could not sleep, as I was kept awake by the snoring of the rather large chap next to me. Later on, his camp bed started to show signs of overstress. The bed could no longer contain itself and eventually it gave up and the large body was audibly deposited on the floor with his feet, still supported at the foot of the bed, pointing upwards. Much cursing and swearing accompanied the bed's auto-destruction. By the early hours of the morning, he had given up and was sleeping in his sleeping bag on the floor. That enabled me to get in a few hours sleep.

The next day I awoke with a good stiff back, wondering where I was and what I was doing. After breakfast and a pot wash, the trusty bakkie arrived, we all got in and went to the airfield.

Unlike Rand, where we had cranes and other things to make life easy, here there was nothing but an interminable supply of sand. The engineers got busy replacing the barrel on the silver DC 4 in amongst all the dust, as if it was an everyday experience. We offloaded the tanks and all the other attachments. With an enormous effort, we rolled the large tanks down planks and stepladders, using our securing straps to restrain them on the way out. We moved them alongside a veritable array of 44-gallon drums of fuel and oil.

We started to move drums under the aircraft to refuel her, and to my surprise, a centrifugal, petrol driven, portable pump arrived. Looking more like those used to empty municipal drains, it seemed to be what was used. It actually worked well although I had my suspicions as how safe it was. Almost as soon as we had tediously fuelled her up, the bakkie arrived, followed by a large truck filled with provisions. One of the flight crew started to supervise the loading of the provisions aboard the aircraft and soon a large a chain of handlers were passing boxes and bags into the aircraft. The handlers standing on the truck could throw them to those in the aircraft and the end of the chain would then pack neatly in the aircraft as instructed by the co-pilot.

With the mandatory 8 tons of food aboard, and with the pre-flight complete, we watched them take-off. The sight of the grand old aircraft running down the dirt runway with a huge cloud of dust rising behind it as it climbed sedately out was one that was to become a daily ritual. We watched until she was out of sight and then returned to the task of getting the re-fuelling rig together. The engineer continued fitting the barrel and preparing the 'Silver Bird' for flight the next day.

By the afternoon the tanks and all the pipes were connected to the electric pumps and we were ready for a test run. We did not have a long wait before our DC4 announced her return and we all turned to watch the landing. Captain Jack Wight was at the helm and I could see that he knew exactly where to go as he taxied up into position next to the tanks and shut down the engines. We were then in a position to try out the new system but we were soon to be in for a surprise. The good news was that we could easily reach all the tank fillers on top of the wings, the bad news however was soon to come. With glee and some fuel in the two huge tanks on the ground we started the generator, primed the lines and on command fuel spurted out of the hand spout.

One of the chaps climbed onto the wing and we handed him the hose. To our disgust a mere dribble was delivered as the handle was squeezed and it soon stopped. It was back to the drawing board and soon it was apparent that the electric fuel pumps running off the generator could not pump enough to overcome the height required to reach the wing fillers. Dejected at the failure we got our lift back to the flat to mull over the day's events with no real hope of a solution.

Chapter 31

Amid much trepidation and expectation, we went out to the field the next day. The evenings and early mornings are cool, so we stood outside our flat shivering, waiting for the bakkie to arrive. In due course it did and I clambered on the back, out in the open. This was my first experience of the chilly early morning drive up to the field. When we arrived, my ears were completely frozen and my body shivering.

The cold was soon dispelled by excitement as we climbed the ladder to put our bags on board. We again disembarked to do the pre-flight inspection. With that behind us, fuel tanks drained for water and undercarriage locks removed, we again got aboard the mighty machine. To my absolute horror, Captain Wight instructed me to get into the right hand seat. What was happening, surely I was not to be the co-pilot on this flight, with a full load, and on a mission.

In the right hand seat

Looking around, the other pilots were nowhere to be seen. In all my haste I had not seen the Silver Bird take off as it was parked some way from ATF and must have left unnoticed in amongst the rest of the DC 4's and 6's. It seemed like this was for real, I put on my glasses, got myself ready for whatever was to be and waited. In the early morning, my glasses were cold on my cheeks and in a short space of time they fogged over. Being glass and not plastic, this was to become a bit of a problem each morning. Only recently having to wear glasses I was still getting used to them and had bought glass as opposed to plastic.

By the time we had got ready for start-up I had realised that the only thing to do was to get them warm in my inside pocket, which I did. Captain Wight briefed me on the starting procedure, how to watch and count out loud as each engine turned over 12 blades. 6 blades having been called out meant that the engine had now been through 2 full revolutions and so each cylinder would be primed. As I counted out the last blade, the mag switches went on. Cough, splutter and with a little bit more coaxing, the engine burst into life. The ritual was then repeated until all four engines had settled into a steady throb.

I was now about to get to know one of the most wonderful personalities aviation had ever bred. He had the most amazing patience and expert airmanship, bred from all the years in aviation. With the starting of those engines, a great friendship was born. The inimitable Captain Jack Wight was to become a leading figure in my life. As well as maintaining a Captain and First Officer relationship, which was vital to flight safety, he became a real friend and mentor. His flying career demanded the ultimate respect and admiration. He flew Spitfires in 1941 during the war and at the time I flew with him, had some 35 000 flying hours.

However, I am digressing. Just before starting, he had given me a run-down on crew procedures and the duties of the co-pilot. Initially, in conjunction with the Flight Engineer, he would be responsible for reading out and checking the start and pre take-off checklist. Thereafter, the non-flying pilot would hold the stick while calling out the speeds of the ASI (air speed indicator) until the pilot who was flying would take over the stick. The co-pilot would then continue calling out the speed and when she got light on her wheels, call positive rate of climb and select gear up. Although I had been exposed to the crew scenario a number of times in the 707, it was new to me as an actual member of the crew.

With the engines rumbling away steadily, I read the pre taxi list and we started to taxi. The view looking out of the RH window at the great wing with two engines on it was quite formidable. The Captain was now relying on my judgement to get past other aircraft and other obstructions on my side. Being rather cautious and apprehensive, when asked if it was clear, I replied, "It seems OK". This was a purely instinctive reply out of a lack of confidence, and I was to hear a phrase that was to become all too familiar "It is either OK or it is not, decide".

At the threshold, I read out the pre take-off check. This included releasing the control lock, a large wide band that extends from the overhead panel down to the floor. The strap, once released from the lever on the floor, returns to the overhead panel drawn in by a large spring. This is quite a good set-up as the Captain is only too aware of the great strap in front of his eyes. With the controls now unlocked, my job was to hold the stick up to 40 mph, check for full and free control movement, and to counteract for any wind across the runway.

With a large knot in my belly, a mixture of fear, apprehension and joy, we set sail. Although I had been in a few DC 4 take-offs by that time, I could not have been prepared for the thrill and feeling as we travelled own the dirt strip. I gave the stick over and continued calling off the speeds. At the designated speed we started to rotate (lift off) and my eyes turned to the vertical speed indicator. "Positive rate of climb" was my call, the reply "gear-up" was the return and my hand grasped the huge lever and selected gear up.

The elation as we flew almost level while the speed built up, was fantastic. I called out the speed as it gradually increased and the engineer removed a few notches of flap and we began to climb. The view, flying low over the African bush, was a complete adrenaline rush.

Once I had overcome my joy, the calm voice of the captain called for climb power settings from the engineer and got me to do the radio work and keep the flight log. I began to relax. No sooner had I begun to do so, I was told to take the stick.

Large aircraft seem to resist the efforts of the pilot to maintain straight and level flight and show their supremacy by having a large delay due to the sheer size of the machine. As the pilot tries to check a rather rapid climb or descent, the inputs seem to have no effect, until all of a sudden the giant says, "Too much". The input that seemingly had no reaction has now been multiplied by a great factor, thrown back at the novice pilot, and the whole mass of machinery begins to overreact to the pilot's efforts.

The resulting porpoising around the sky is somewhat degrading to morale, as it seems that the pilot has not yet learned to fly despite the licence in his top pocket. After a time, they get used to having an input to the controls, and then just waiting for a reaction before overcorrecting it. The effect on the airspeed is incredible, as one loses so much speed with the porpoising that you are soon aware of the fact that unless you master it, you can't even maintain height at a cruise power setting.

Just as I was feeling totally incompetent, I got a tap on my shoulder and was passed a cup of tea! Was this just another test? I took the tea with one hand and placed it on the glare shield as I had seen it done so often by others, and looked at the altimeters. It was climbing as a long lost angel. A gentle push on the wheel and nothing happens. More push and soon the angel has fallen off her perch and is now falling to mother earth again.

Eventually, and with a number of dry remarks, I got things under control. It seemed like just a few minutes later when the captain asked for descent power and I started to descend. Guided by the GPS and various comments from the captain, I was soon told I was on final. As hard as I wanted to believe them, I could not see any sign of an airfield. As we got closer, I saw a clearing in the dirt ahead of us. Surely this was not the airfield. There were no aircraft around and it looked like a strip of bare earth in the middle of the African bush. He took over for the landing and I went through the pre landing checks, setting the gear down and monitoring the speed.

As we got closer, you could make out that the strip was built up on the top of a crest, so that the thresholds ended up on steep banks. Things happened rather rapidly. The engineer was getting flaps down in stages and at the point just when one commits for a landing, I heard "cut one and four". To my surprise the engineer cut the two outboard engines. The captain put down the most perfect landing in quite a nose high attitude on touchdown. As we rolled at a fast walking pace, the reason for cutting the two engines became apparent. The other end of the short runway also ended as abruptly as the first, in a huge drop into the valley below.

We backtracked and I looked out the window to the right to see the wreck of an aircraft. On the other side of the runway was another wreck. This time, its Douglas ancestry was evident in the mangled DC6 wreckage.

There was an apron area on the right of the runway and we taxied into it and parked. I felt rather like the camel trophy man and heaved a great sigh of relief. There was little time to relax or think about what had happened as my next duty arrived. Amidst a great cacophony of sounds, a rather sorry ancient truck arrived and I was required to monitor the parking and off-loading.

Guiding the so-called driver into position was rather a nightmare, as such things as brakes scarcely exist. Making use of a great bolder under the rear wheel I managed to inch the truck close enough to the double open doors to start off-loading. A human chain was soon set up inside the aircraft so that all the containers could be passed along and packed into the truck. It was obvious that this was not a new task for them. The only problem was that it became a source of pushing each other to the limit until a box was dropped to break open on the floor.

After a relatively short space of time we were ready to go again. The engineer had done a minor inspection while we were off-loading and the captain had been preparing the route back. I got into the RH seat and was briefed by the captain. This was going to be my take-off. My psyche had not yet recovered from the first flight, and now I was to perform the take-off. Time had not even permitted me to think about what was happening. We got started and taxied out with the captain on the tiller. The tiller or ground steering wheel carries out the ground handling on most large aircraft. It is a wheel (or section of a wheel) and operates like a steering wheel, with no connection to the rudder.

Now, as we started the ground roll, I was not to give the stick over to the captain. He called out the speeds to me and at the call "rotate," I gently eased back on the stick. The great brute came away cleanly and with less effort than I expected. I checked forward to maintain a gentle climb while the gear was retracted. With the gear up and speed up to 120 knots I got the prompt to resume climbing. The climb out gave me the most wonderful feeling. One can never re-explore all the firsts in your life. This first take-off of mine in a large aircraft was something I shall never forget.

The sight of the end of the runway disappearing behind and the feeling as we flew along the valley with the ground falling away rapidly was ethereal, having an untrue feeling. Without the large nose and propeller ahead of me, the new aspect of the nose dropping sharply away and the huge vista vision was difficult to comprehend. One kept feeling that something had fallen off. Strangely enough, the porpoising effect is not as predominant on the early climb-out. Whether it is a result of airspeed, ground effect or possibly a combination, it was soon back.

Once in the cruise, the aircraft was again showing who was boss. Without my being too aware of it, the engineer had left and returned with the 'traditional' cup of tea, the water having been cooked on the gas ring! In the cruise I was given a de-brief and it looked like my captain/instructor was pleased with me. In point of fact he did not have any option, there were no other pilots around! We went over the approach speeds and procedures and soon we had the field in sight.

Compared to the field we had just left, this seemed enormous. The runway was long and it stretched out ahead of us unlike the other short field that kept its identity hidden until you were on top of it. I continued the approach and when on final approach I expected to be relieved of the stick, but to my surprise I was told to continue.

"Remember she is just like a big old Tiger Moth. Fly just like you are used to". These comforting words I was to hear many times and they are perhaps what cemented our friendship. "Keep the centre line between your legs" came the most familiar phrase and obediently I continued. After a long hold-off she settled so gently that I was absolutely amazed. The nose high attitude softened everything and the landing was something to make you really proud.

Feeling that I was on cloud nine, we taxied up to the apron area that we had left a few hours earlier. The perch in the cockpit was so high (being about 40 feet up) that it felt like I was doing a very slow flypast. The whole scale of the airport was double that of the one that we had just left. The approaches were clear and even though it was far below our local standards it was quite reasonable. The only major problem was the lack of hard surface and the enormous resulting clouds of dust.

The rest of the first day was spent trying to assemble the tanks that we had brought up. The philosophy of the design was that it would be easier to fill large central tanks from the numerous drums that had come from SA, and use the 12-volt pumps to fill the aircraft. After much connecting, the system was now ready for a try. Much to our disgust, the flow from the 12-volt pump was less than the tried and tested old system. This made use of a centrifugal water-type pump driven by a petrol engine. The flow from it far outweighed that of the new system. All of that, despite the fact that we had been assured that the whole system was tried out at Rand.

After the disappointment of the second half of the day, I resorted to my earlier thoughts, and I sat in the back of the bakkie in the proverbial seventh heaven. Back at the flat, the rest of the chaps had already prepared themselves for the evening. With beers in hand, they looked over the balcony watching us as we all got off the vehicle.

We had a brief meeting that evening detailing how the crew roster would work. We were to each spend three weeks up in the bush, and then get relief of 7 – 10 days. I was obviously now a firm part of the one crew as there were only four pilots left to fly the two aircraft. I fell into bed in a deep slumber, with a host of wonderful memories of the day to feast my dreams upon.

The next day was an early start. As the sun was giving the horizon a pink hue, we were eating our pre-packaged breakfast and preparing to go. Even before we were finished eating, the bakkie arrived. Hurriedly the last tools of our trade were put into the nav bags, we jumped aboard and drove past the little old church on our way to the airport.

I thought of my wife as I looked into the garden of the church. An old, obviously Portuguese church had what was left of a once proud front garden. The paths were still there, with their stone edging, although now rather overgrown. What had caught my eye were the huge Frangipani trees, with the early morning dawn showing through the foliage. I know how fond Jane is of these trees and I wished I could convey to her the vastness and beauty of the trees. I could not imagine how old they must have been to sport limbs the size of my legs, absolutely covered in the small, flawless pink and white flowers.

Accompanied by a youngster in his late teens sporting an AK47, we passed the church, and could see the old broken power line or telegraph poles devoid of any wire. We were at all times accompanied by a guard and there were two or three at the flat while we were there. They became a part of life and after a bit one was almost not aware of them. The initial feeling though, when bumping along with a child next to you with a loaded sub-machine gun was a bit frightening.

The road up to the airfield was very short and in fact, the flat was so close that we could see the aircraft on finals as they approached to land. Shortly we arrived at the field and drove up to ATF, our DC4. She stood proud in the early morning sun as she waited for us.

We opened the cargo door at the rear, positioned the ladder and climbed aboard. After a brief cockpit inspection, it was down the ladder again to turn each engine over by six propeller blades. I learned a neat trick. The outer engines are so high that it is almost impossible to reach the next blade after having turned over the first blade. The trick is to have a cloth and with one end in each hand, it is just enough to be able to throw the centre over the blade like a sling and bring it down to within reach.

With all four engines now turned through the 2 revolutions, it was time to enter the aircraft. As I walked around I double-checked that the three undercarriage pins and chocks were out and removed the tail post. Up the ladder, pull it up and close the doors. The next duty was to remove the overwing emergency panels and climb out onto the wing to check the fuel levels. This necessitated a bit of fancy footwork to climb over each engine in turn to get to the outer tanks, the last one almost on the wing tip.

Just in case we had not enough to do, the inboard dip stick on the one side of ATF was broken, so I had to go onto the other side to borrow the RHS dip stick, use it to check the left side and return it to its position. By this time the captain was asking where you I was, so rather panting from the gym type exertion, I got all my bits and pieces, dropped into my seat and got ready to go.

The starting routine with all the counting blades, smoke and spluttering was always a joy to behold. Out to the runway and away. This was the daily, early morning routine. The mornings as the sun was rising were always cool, so I used to wear my favourite windbreaker. I then used to look out over the rise at the earth below. Although the landscape looked very welcoming for wildlife, I never saw any game in Angola.

We used to cross a very picturesque river that we used to call the Rio Grande. The river was by no means huge, but was set in a wonderful environment of green foliage. As we approached, the ground rose slowly until suddenly it fell away. Looking back, we could see the steep rock cliffs extending almost vertically to the soft yellow sand that made up the flood plane of the river. The river itself was a fast-moving blue snake that boiled in a fury of white foam regularly along its path.

The sheer size and uniqueness made this river a regular landmark. Often we would veer off track by a few miles just to see a new section of this proud river, a welcome change from the typical South African dry riverbeds. Our daily route northwards with our full load took just over an hour, and the southbound empty return took just on an hour. It was soon after we had our look at the Rio Grande that we had to start to plan our descent. We elected to use a slow rate of descent and so started about 15 minutes before our expected time of arrival (ETA). From the time that we reduced power, all eyes were eagerly peering forward to pick up landmarks.

We approached over a small river and rather conveniently there was a little island just before final approach. This was our indicator because the field was almost impossible to see until you were on top of it. We had our height above the island noted down, and from that point on, we knew our exact approach path. One must remember that there was no question of an alternative or even going back to the point of departure. The control tower was simply a bloke with a portable radio on a strap around his neck. There was not even a hope of any radar control or even anyone who could give you any encouragement if you got lost or had to abort a mission.

Settling down to final approach with wheels down and the glide set, we used to watch the steep bank that made up the threshold approach. On our right was the broken DC6, our constant reminder not to undershoot.

The landing at this short strip was always a bit anxious due to its length and the loose surface that prevented us using brakes to any great extent. Once we were parked and shut down, there was only time for a quick stretch before the local was on board asking for the manifest.

I then had to supervise the offloading, having first watched with terror each time the huge old trucks used to back up against the fuselage with the inevitable large stone being used as a brake. In all the time we flew there, we only had a few occasions when they actually made contact but never with any serious results.

I almost invariably did the take-off and landing on the return journey which I always looked forward to. As we passed the threshold with the great step, it felt as if we were shooting up as the ground fell away, into the river valley below. The flight back always seemed to be much shorter as we would arrive either just before lunch, or dinner depending on whether we were on our first or second rotation.

If we got there in time to take a break for lunch, the engineer and I would take turns as to who would be able to go back to the flat with Uncle Jack, as he was affectionately called, and have a spot of lunch. The other person would remain with the aircraft and load up the next load of food.

In the evening, after a repeat of the morning's flight, we would settle down to re-fuel. This was all done from the 44-gallon drums and the pump that I mentioned earlier. By the time we were finished re-fuelling and checking for the next day, it would invariably be dark.

I remember one occasion when Peter was with us, when we were talking some way from the aircraft while the refuelling was going on, when a local lit a lighter to see the gauge so that he could see how much fuel had been pumped. The frightening thing was that the pump oozed fuel a bit and so the area was all a bit fuel-soaked and highly flammable. Peter saw it first and jumped, what seemed to be 10 yards in a single leap, shouting at the top of his voice. How we all did not go up in a puff of smoke I will never know.

This was our routine. The days were always full of excitement. Other than the demands and expectations of each flight, one had a most super interface with all the other aircraft and aircrew. We were not supposed to mix with them, but at the airfield it was beyond this scope to keep an eye on all of us. I suppose it could be likened to a playground for the oldest of children as it brought out all ones childlike attempts to confuse our AK47 toting guards.

Chapter 32

We continued going back to the flat for lunch whenever time permitted, and as time went by we got a little more adventurous. As we got to know the system we started walking back to the flat instead of waiting for the bakkie. On the first attempt the guards at the gate held their AK47 rifles at the ready to prevent us from passing through. We explained in a mixture of talk and sign language that we wanted to go to the flat for lunch and it seemed to have the right effect. We were followed by one gun-toting youth as we sauntered down the road to the flat where our normal guard took over. This soon became the norm and we thoroughly enjoyed our constitutional walks whenever we could.

One of the crew had organised to bring solar heated shower bags up with us, he must have known something that the others did not! They were simply thick, black plastic bags, with taps at the bottom and stings to support them while showering. We filled them in the morning with the rather dubious washing water from the old, stained, foul-smelling bath, and put them out on the balcony in the sun during the day. We were then able to have a welcome warm (or rather lukewarm) shower when we came back home in the evening.

That was our non-drinking water supply. We dared not even open our mouth while showering, let alone drink or even cook with it. We only drank, cooked, or made beverages with the bottled water that was an integral part of most shipments from SA. All our washing and showering was done with the brown water taken from the bath.

By this stage there were only aircrew for two aircraft left and so we were able to move upstairs and use the downstairs room for our food and aircraft spares storage. The next room had a toilet and drainage from the floor, and so we used that for showering. We could spread out a bit and our living area became more comfortable, and our evenings became very sociable, with our standard barbeque out on the balcony overlooking the road and the buildings opposite us. Our side of the road was made up of apartment type buildings and so we had a view of what was going on over the road from the balcony. We looked down on a collection of scruffy houses, which always got me thinking of the past. They had all been supplied with water, electricity and water-borne sewerage in the civilised past but scarcely fragments remained.

We would watch as the locals carried the water about in containers balanced on their heads in typical African tradition. There was no grass or any other foliage and there was a constant flow of human traffic, seemingly all day and night. There was no apparent direction as there would have been if they were on the way to work, but just a constant movement in all directions. The number of women and children that would normally be expected were not visible, and the population was mostly men and boys in the upper teens and twenties. Seldom was there any sighting of anyone older than their mid thirties, a strange phenomenon. Whether it was as a result of the requirements or affects of the war, or in fact from illness or landmines was never to be known, that was just how it was. I once was taken to the office in the heart of the town and saw the freezer room that I had purchased. I was really able to appreciate what a well-established town it had been before being reduced to its present shambolic state.

As time went by back at the airfield the activity increased and the other DC4 was dispatched to operate from and be based at the other airfield that they had been flying to with the supplies. We therefore no longer saw them at night, but used to make a point of seeing them for lunch. As we were almost invariably both airborne at daybreak we used to communicate in the air. As soon as we heard each other on the radio we would 'go numbers', in other words change our frequency to 123.45.

We could then chat freely without cluttering the airwaves. I remember Peter telling me that he was convinced that we were under radar surveillance. I was amazed, as the popular belief was that there were no radar stations in the area.

"Help yourself," he said, "switch on your transponder and see for yourself." Sure enough I switched on the transponder and there was the flashing light!

A transponder is a device that responds to a radar signal and transmits a code if correctly set. When it senses the radar beam it indicates the condition by a flashing light. Therefore if the light flashes it means that radar is in operation and therefore somebody was monitoring us.

It was to be some time before we flew to C1 where the other crew were staying, but even then we never got to see where they actually lived. They boasted that they had a house with proper furniture, their own cook and that they had even been given a car because no one could afford the petrol and it was just standing around unused. They just used the avgas from the aircraft, making sure that the locals never saw them as knowing that they could use it in a petrol car would be the saviour of many vehicles but with drastic consequences to our fuel supply. They seemed to have a supply of diesel fuel, but petrol was an impossibly scarce and expensive commodity when it was around. To us it all sounded too good to be true, we were never able to put them to the test.

One day when we were returning on our last leg, I could not believe my eyes when I saw a Boeing 707 on the apron. Apparently this was not a totally unusual occurrence, but for me, seeing a 707 on a dirt strip was a first. Unfortunately I was never able to see it take off, the sight must have been awesome. A few days later we were told that we would not be permitted to return that night and that we would be put up at C2. We had not realised that presence of the 707 was in fact an indication for us that something was up. Even though we always carried an overnight bag in case something went wrong, we packed bigger bags and set off the next day. We were unaware of the full implications and that it would be some time before we saw the flat again and then only for a few brief spells before we lost our access completely.

707 and our Antonovs at A1

We did our usual two round trips, filled up with fuel and loaded the cargo for the next flight. We flew to C2, landed, secured the aircraft and left the unloading of the cargo for the next day. We climbed into the maroon Landcruiser that was waiting to fetch us. Having landed daily but never venturing beyond the airfield I was intrigued to see the surrounding area. From the air we had seen that it was a much smaller village with far less organised building. We drove some way through largely informal settlements and soon the sun had set and we could not see too much, but were certainly bumped around in the most amazing fashion. We drove for almost an hour before we arrived at a dilapidated warehouse in a slightly larger town.

Alongside, almost attached to it and equally shabby was a house where we were to stay. The house appeared to be owned and occupied by the wholesaler and his brother, who welcomed us inside and showed us our rooms. The problem was that there were only two rooms, one with a double bed and one with a single bed. The unfortunate and obvious decision was that the captain, from both seniority and age, would get the single bed, leaving the two of us to sort out the double. That meant that I would have to share a double bed with the same huge engineer that had snored and kept breaking his stretcher all night on our first night in Angola. Anyway they say that these things are sent to try us and so, I had to get on with it, much to my disgust. The only saving grace was that we slept in our own sleeping bags.

We were shown around the warehouse and I was quite chuffed to see a huge pile of pilchard boxes that I had initially bought in Johannesburg. I had also been on the Antonov flight carrying them up to A1 and had flown them myself from A1 to C2 in the DC4. It was quite a stimulating feeling that I had been involved with the supply chain from the inception to the final delivery.

Our bedrooms adjoined the shop front where the boxes were sold over the counter to the individual vendors. They in turn took their box, set up a stall in the street and sold off single tins. The next few days were a bit short of flying, and I realised that it was as a result of the huge birthday celebrations of the country's politicians. The 707 had flown in all the goods and overseas dignitaries, and so its presence was a poor omen for us. Even the flying, the backbone of the food chain there, had slowed down to an erratic pace.

As a result we had a chance to have a look around. We were in a small town, with dirt roads, absolutely buzzing with people. Every two metres another vendor was selling his goods on the street, mostly the goods brought up from SA either by our company or one of the other operators. The street price of an apple was between 4-50 and 5-50 US Dollars and that of a tin of good old Castle lager was a staggering 8-00 US Dollars. It was amazing that the community could support the prices that were virtually ten times the cost back home.

Sleep that night was not easy, firstly having to share the bed with this huge man whose snoring would break Guinness Records, and secondly because there was a huge, high powered disco over the road. The locals would play loud music at full volume while they drank and made merry until the small hours of the morning. Fortunately the situation changed after a few days and I moved in to a room right next to the sales counter. The disadvantage was that I was now right on the road and the disco was even louder, but at least I was on my own.

The only place for us to relax was in the lounge that seemed to double up as the meeting venue as well. It became the centre of activity in the house and we were privy to the most amazing comings and goings. The number of people that used to pass through while we were sitting and relaxing, or even at the table eating was quite phenomenal.

Street scene in front of the wholesale store

From the tones of various conversations, in tongues foreign to us, it appeared that most of the time business was discussed there at the top of their voices. I was even drawn in when one of their local female associates appeared to take a fancy to me. She was a tall, slim Angolan lady wearing long hair extensions. She wanted me to source a supply in SA and supply her for resale. I explained that I would only be back in SA in another two weeks. I explained that we were up on a 3 week on and 1 week off basis, and that I would investigate it and contact her when I was back. This met with her approval and, much to the crew's amusement, she showed it with a great big hug. I was to see her many more times, each time with the same greeting and was to be a source of great mirth for the rest of the crew.

During the period at Caicesse, the workload was very tenuous, and we did not know from day to day whether the next days flight would be cancelled or not. Obviously it was at the forefront of our minds, as our future depended on what was happening, but all we could do was speculate and go with the flow. When we did fly across to A1, things were different. We were not permitted away from the field, and felt totally lost without access to our provisions and spares.

On one occasion when the flying for the day was cancelled, just to see a new perspective I went down to the river to see where they collected water. They stopped the vehicle at a ford where the river flowed across the road surface and I was met with a most amazing sight. There was a conglomeration of people at the ford. One person was washing his vehicle in the water. He had taken off the bonnet so he could clean the engine. Next to him were people washing themselves and their clothes in the water, and next to him was our guy filling up our 25-litre water container.

It made it all to clear how aware they all were that the land mines posed a great threat and that it was not an option to walk off the road to gain access to the cleaner water. This was quite an education and reinforced the reason for not drinking the water, and in fact I almost did not want to wash in it anymore but there was no other choice.

Not having access to our supplies at A1, and not having a regular contact with the flights from SA we were being fed the local store keeper, but the food was not very palatable, and we longed for a bit of our own cooking. Most of the time we just ate without asking too many questions, as there was no other option. At one stage they brought out a chicken and our hopes of a good meal rose. Now that the freezer room was working well, surely it was one that we had

Collecting water at the river

transported and so would be good. Some considerable time later the beast reappeared as if it had run through a veldt fire, getting totally scorched. The flesh had even shrunk away from the bones, leaving long, charred ends to the drumsticks.

That evening pushed us over the edge and we had to make contact with Johannesburg and the only contact was with satellite phones. They were all under lock and key at the military headquarters near the airfield. To use the phone the call had to be monitored by one of the guards, during daylight hours, and we did not particularly want to be overheard on this occasion as we intended to find out what was happening with our arrangements.

The only unguarded phone was in the hands of the crew flying the DC4 for the diamond mine. As we obviously knew them we were off to their house, even though we knew that we were not permitted to mix with other crews. We persuaded our driver to take us there at night and it all seemed to be going well so far. After the usual bumpy ride we duly arrived at the house and were welcomed in. I will never forget the sight that met my eyes. They were sitting on wonderful looking chairs, looking at current television. The house looked like a five-star hotel, it was magnificent. They had electricity, a microwave, oven and a proper stove.

They must have seen us looking at their empty dinner plates and offered us some leftovers from their lunch. It was wonderful to eat good food again. While we sat and ate, we watched the famous boxing match when one of the world-class boxers had his ear bitten off by his opponent.

Suddenly the door burst open and a collection of young guards arrived waving their AK 47s around in a most unsafe manner. Shouting and screaming that we were not allowed to socialise with other crew, they took hold of us and roughly and unceremoniously marched us out. They escorted us, in our vehicle, back to the warehouse and eventually left us with just a warning. We considered ourselves very lucky considering what strange and horrifying stories we had heard. Despite the interruption Uncle Jack had managed to get through on the satellite phone and told us the story of our immediate future. We would soon resume our full flying missions but would no longer be able to stay at A1.

Gradually the flying picked up, but we were never allowed to go back to the flat again. We had a problem as we had accumulated an enormous amount of spares, fuel, and oil, all at the mercy of scavengers and we had also left vast quantities of food there. At least the spares were back at the flat with the remnants of our belongings. He said that at a later stage arrangements would be made to get all our goods back to us.

Just before our return to SA when the three weeks were up, the shop owner told us that he had secured a house closer to the airfield for us. We duly climbed into his vehicle and went to see the house on the way to the airfield. What greeted us was not quite what we had in mind. An old, grubby, derelict house was presented to us. It was a little way off the main road that we had been using and was well away from the informal settlements, but close to other derelict buildings.

The thought of being on our own and not living in his house was so strong that we jumped at the invitation. He agreed that by the time we returned he would have fitted doors to all the open doorways, fixed all the shutters, cleaned and painted it. One must realise that there is no glass freely available and so one lives either with open 'windows' or closed shutters. That is probably why the mosquito/malaria problem is so severe.

We flew back to A1 where we meet the Antonov to fly back home. and on the way my mind wandered. As we flew along I was excited at the prospect of the house and the hopes of having a 'new' base to work from. As we chatted and our thoughts became more realistic, our positive thoughts were centred on getting all our possessions back together and a firm base to live in and to work from. The potential difference would make daily life much more workable and productive. A mental image was now forming in each of our heads and I wondered how similar the images were.

Chapter 33

The prospect of being able to live a life of our own, even in the somewhat derelict house, was enough to keep us inspired enough to plan our new home from home. True to form, when we returned after our break that always seems so short, we had doors and shutters. They were in the process of being painted and so we had to put up with a bit of paint smell, but it was a small price to pay for what it would offer us. The whole place looked so different with all the holes closed and fresh paint, although their choice of colour was a trifle strange to say the least.

He had chosen dark green, blue and brown and combinations of these basic colours led us through the house. A strange and somewhat dreary choice but perhaps in fairness it was all that was available, We longed for the light colours that we were used to, particularly in the minimal lighting that we had at night. We wished he had contacted us as we could easily have brought paint back with us. At least it was neat, but rather oppressive in the poor light.

We moved in with rather mixed feelings. Our basic drive was positive enough to overcome the greatest hurdles. The first few nights were spent in sleeping bags on the floor, and gradually, with each flight to A 1 we brought back enough to make us really comfortable. We brought back divan type beds, the deep freeze, and the petrol generator and we settled down quite comfortably.

Rather remarkably, we discovered that most of the electrical wiring in the house was still intact and soon we had the generator coupled up directly to the house wiring and we had lights that we could switch on. Each evening we would do a bit more cleaning or fixing and soon we had a real home. As time went by we brought back four fuel drums from the airfield, mounted them on a large tower at the back of the house and plumbed them into the remains of the house plumbing. This meant that we had taps in the kitchen and bathroom, and cool showers. I attacked the flushing system and sometimes, if the drums were full enough, we even had a flushing loo.

The house now became a real home. There was a palm tree in front of our house and on the odd occasions that we got home early enough, we would sit on the porch in the evenings and watch the other aircraft coming in on finals. Watching them, and seeing the setting sun through the leaves added a rather romantic ring to the setting. With the sun down we would move into the lounge and with the heat such as it was, sit with the shutters open to get a bit of draught through the house. At that stage, unless we were liberally protected by creams, we would be at the mercy of the mosquitoes and their malaria threat. In fact at one stage 50 per cent of our crew had contracted malaria at some stage.

This was a huge issue based on whether prophylactics should be used or not. One view was that the medication suppressed the symptoms resulting in them being masked and making diagnosis more difficult. Personally I found that the medication caused such degradation of my eyesight that I went off them and relied on barrier creams in preference. When I rose each morning I would cover myself in cream, repeat it when the sun was going down and again before bed. That certainly did the trick for me and, touch wood, I have not had malaria.

In a nutshell we were as happy as we could be. Unlike anywhere else in the area around about, we had light and water, comfort, evening sunset views, and even better, we were spared the dreadful drive to Caicess twice daily. The drive from the house to the airfield was along a road that had once been tar. Now all that was left was just a central hump of tar in between the traffic on the dirt in either direction. The surfaces had been so eroded by use that the tar centre hump was well above the road level on each side. As a result overtaking was only possible if the hump of tar was crossed, and as it was so much higher it was a hazardous exercise with the vehicle slewing sideways.

The twenty-minute journey always produced something interesting while we bumped along with out teenage, armed guard in the car with us. We passed through an attractive area where we crossed the river, and we would see all the workers walking to work with their diamond pans. The diggings were visible from the road but we were never able to get permission to visit them. Further down the road we passed a series of shelters made from 44-gallon fuel drums that had been flattened out into panels. It showed what resources could be summonsed when the need is there.

On one particular occasion I saw a small child, carrying a huge stone running alongside a truck and to my horror I saw him throw it under the wheel as it went too fast. As the truck thumped over it with both axles it would slow down a bit and the kid would collect the rock, run ahead and repeat the operation. We were used to the rock system of hand braking at the airfield, but to see it on the roll was something else. I guess as they say; 'necessity is the mother of invention.'

The approach road went past a Land Rover graveyard and then the military base where our satellite phone was held. Onto the field we went down a huge bank and past the controller with his portable around his neck, standing next to his wheeless caravan shelter. Even though it was quite small, there was an enormous hive of activity and at most times there would be six or seven aircraft, mostly DC 4's or 6's on the field, three of them resident and remaining on the field every night. Then on the right we passed what once was an active fuel depot, and quickly accelerated past a huge unexploded bomb protruding from the ground on the left. We then arrived at our aircraft parked on the northern end of the dirt apron.

Passing the bomb each day I often wondered about it and in the end my curiosity got the better of me. We came to accept it as part of the surroundings. The fact that it had not yet exploded seemed to indicate a measure of stability and so I went to look closely at it. Wearily I walked up and was surprised at its size. The girth where it penetrated the ground was so large that I would not be able to put my arms around it, indicating that almost half was buried below the surface. As I stood next to it the stabilising fins were at chest height so that the whole bomb must be taller than I was. The others thought that I was nuts to go up to it, but I am happy that I had a good look at it. I am sorry that I never had anyone take a picture of me standing next to it, but after all pictures were taboo.

The freedom to move around was much more relaxed than at A1 and we gradually got to know the other crews better. Our life now settled down to a routine. We were usually in the cockpit starting the engines as the sun rose and would put in two rotations each day. We would fuel back at A1 from the drums before our last trip home. We would seldom get back to the house before the sun set. The days were wonderful and happy; we loved old ATF, really enjoyed each flight, worked hard, and slept well.

On one occasion two new pilots and a flight engineer came up to get some experience and to relieve us when the time came for us to go back. The new engineer was directing the truck into position to load the cargo. I was looking on from a distance when I heard a dull thud and I immediately realised that the truck had hit the aircraft. The other new chap ran from the front of the aircraft, under it towards the cargo door. Concentrating on the source of the noise, he ran straight into the corner of an oily undercarriage door. The DC4 is high enough to stand under and so the edge of the undercarriage door is just at head height. He opened up a huge gash, and as with most head wounds, it bled profusely.

I grabbed the cleanest cloth around and held it on the wound to stop the bleeding. One of the others had the presence of mind to grab the vehicle that always followed the truck before it left. No explanation was needed and we climbed into the vehicle and I continued to hold the cloth on the wound as we bumped along. The suggestion that he visit the local doctor was vehemently dismissed and he insisted that he would rather put himself in my hands. By the time we got to our house the bleeding was no longer as severe as it had been, and my mind had been racing, trying to keep ahead of the developments.

Back home, I set myself up on the porch where there was plenty of light, with disinfectant and my nail manicure kit, my only possible source of equipment. It had been given out at a promotion years earlier, and had never been used for much other than the odd nail cutting but it was now in for the real test. I cleaned up the wound as best I could with the antiseptic to find the most enormous four-inch gash, exposing his white skull. I am sure that my stomach would have turned if I had not been so involved, knowing that he was relying on me. He again refused any local help and said that he would rather be flown back to SA for treatment. I agreed with his sentiments but explained that my concern was with the bleeding, as there was no flight until the next morning.

I disinfected my nail scissors and tweezers and started pulling the hair out of the wound and cutting back the hair. The hair had been forced into the open wound by the aluminium edge and I had to gently extract them. My idea was to clean away the hair and leave a few tufts on either side. I could tie them together in an attempt to keep the wound closed. After some time it all began to look a lot more manageable and clean and the bleeding stopped. The others all came home and, much to their surprise found everything under control. We ate supper rather mechanically and after all the tension we just fell into a deep sleep.

The next day Butch was wearing a big grin and on examination his head was looking good and had not bled at all overnight. In due course the car arrived and we all got in. As he got in he banged his head and the bleeding started all over again. We took him to A1 with us in the DC 4 and shipped him out to Pietersburg on the Antonov. As he would only get there towards nightfall, one of our guys had phoned Pietersburg from the satellite phone at the military headquarters and warned them to arrange an evening consultation and stitching.

I was astonished the following day when we met the Antonov, there he was, stepping off the aircraft. The doctor had sewed him up and there was no holding him back, he was all ready to go. The doctor was very impressed at what had been done, and said that the patient owed me a vote of thanks. I must admit that I was quite chuffed at having succeeded at my first (and I hope my last), bit of medical care.

On another occasion we had a free day and so we decided to look at ATF's brakes. She had never had any brakes to talk of and so we thought that there was no time like the present to give it a go. We set ourselves up and started. To remove a wheel we carried a balk of timber with a chamfer on one end. Each main undercarriage leg has two wheels and so to lift one wheel off the ground the timber was placed up against the other wheel and the aircraft taxied up onto the timber. It all sounds so easy, but is it in fact so? I was nominated to do the taxi as I was the only pilot about. Rather ill at ease at being on my own in the three-crew cockpit, I started two engines on the required side and carefully rode up, lifting the wheel off the ground. I had anticipated that the difficulty would be in stopping on top of the wood and avoiding galloping off the end of the wood. This was successful and with one wheel off the ground I joined the engineer and started stripping the brakes.

Obviously following the Flight Engineer's directions I assisted removing the wheel to gain access to the brakes. An initial check revealed nothing and so the brake discs came under fire. As we released the pack of brake discs, the whole lot fell apart and onto the dusty earth on the apron. The individual brake discs had cracked and broken into up to as much as five pieces each. We were faced with a dilemma. What to do with the bits, there was no possibility of getting any replacements in less than a week. We started on the only option; the brakes worked before, make them work again. Picking all the pieces off the ground we started cleaning them and trying to piece them together like a jigsaw puzzle. Holding thumbs we started assembling the discs.

We had just started to make progress when disaster struck in the guise of an Antonov 76. The AN 76 is a twin engined, high wing jet, a typical Russian cargo aircraft. Unlike western aircraft the engines are mounted on top of the fuselage, on the centre section of the wing, to minimise dirt and dust intake. The resulting high exhausts just blew us away as he turned his tail towards us. Helpless I watched the 20-litre container, with all our tools inside, get blown onto its side and roll off into the distance, spewing its contents out on the way. As I saw it come to rest up against a bank, I began to follow its path, collecting bits. By that stage the rest of the crew arrived and they also helped collecting all of our tools and pieces, but one small union was missing, and we racked our brains for a solution.

I offered to go to the wrecked DC6 that lay on the opposite side of the runway. Years earlier the aircraft was coming in to land and had approached the short strip a little too low. Probably not realising the extent of the bank on the threshold, he had pulled his main gear off against it. He then careered down the runway like a wheelbarrow, on his remaining one nose wheel. It must have been quite some sight trundling along on the single wheel until it drifted to the side and off into the rough where it stopped.

I figured that was the most likely place to find some spares and so with a handful of tools I looked for a local to escort me, hoping that he would take adequate cognisance of the land mines. I carefully followed his every step in the blind hope that he knew a safe route. I climbed all over the aircraft looking at all the remaining pipe work, but there was incredibly not anything useful left. The carcass had been picked clean and even the cylinder barrels and magnetos had been removed.

On the other side, closer to our aircraft, was a Lockheed Electra wreck. Although it was not a DC series there might have been a union that we could have used. We crossed the runway to get to it, and as I approached I saw that it was completely burned out. We were so far that we carried on to have a look. The inside of the craft had been totally gutted by fire and the floor of the cargo hold was covered in burned out AK 47 Assault rifles. I would have loved to bring one back as a souvenir, but obviously it was not possible. Other than an interesting jaunt there was also nothing to be had at that wreck, and we walked back to ATF.

At the end of the stint I got back to find huge grins all around. It had taken them almost as long as my walk, but they had all scratched around until they found the missing part. I think I had more fun though! We each lent a hand and soon the jigsaw was together, and there were no spare parts left over! As expected there was no improvement, but at least we were all back together and fortunately, no worse off. We carried on with our daily routine and soon it was time to return to SA.

On my return, I was questioned about C2 and the possibility of getting the AN8 in there. I described the strip in detail and explained that an AN32 and an AN76 were regular visitors. Soon the company AN8 was flown in as a test and a regular daily flight from Pietersburg was put in place. Yuri flew the aircraft in and became such a regular visitor that we could expect him at exactly 1030 each day. This was quite a bonus for us as it meant that we could get a lift with him from Pietersburg without going via A1. It was a wonderful contact with the outside world and each day we made sure that we would get back from our first sortie before he arrived. We were always eager to meet him as he often had bits of mail or tuck boxes for us.

As time went by even going up with Yuri was a bit of a drag as to catch his flight at 0630 I had to leave home at 0430 to get to Pietersburg in time. Jane used to keep phoning me on my mobile every half-hour to keep me awake as I drove along. I looked for a solution to avoid the long drive and soon found it with one of the other suppliers. They regularly flew up from Lanseria and whenever I could I caught a lift with them to save the tedious drive.

On one particular occasion I was in their AN76, and decided to sleep on top of the cargo as per usual. I was the only passenger on that flight and so fell fast asleep, just to awaken some hours later with a horrific smell. I had not realised that the cargo was frozen fish, as it had not had a smell while it was frozen. I settled in my sleeping bag on top of the load and was soon fast asleep. The serenity quickly changed however when my body heat defrosted the top surface and I ended up smelling like a trawler at the height of the fishing season.

Subsequently I flew up from Lanseria on a number of occasions but became a bit weary of what the cargo was.

Chapter 34

The daily routine continued for quite some time. We really enjoyed the house and our way of life in the Bush. We had got quite house-proud and most evenings some time was spent getting it a bit better. I recall Uncle Jack and I on our hands and knees in the lounge/dining area scraping the floor on a daily basis. We were eventually rewarded when we revealed quite an attractive multi-coloured floor that had been hidden for years. I had made a side table cum shelf from boxes next to my bed and each one of us had made a comfortable lifestyle for himself .It was a completely new life for me with the constant moving between my two homes. The flying was superb and all of us crew got on really well.

We used to commute back to South Africa after each three-week period of duty, and return after a week at home. I found that both Jane and I had adapted easily to the new way of life. I had anticipated that she would have found it difficult being without me for such long periods, but she coped well. From my side, there were no distractions or any interesting diversions and so the fact that we were so busy was a blessing. By the time we got home after the day's flying, had made supper and eaten we were tired and fell into bed. Time flew and the three weeks did not feel as long as it was. Soon we were enjoying our families at home.

On one of my flights to C2 on the Antonov, I took my courage in my hands and decided to fly the whole way in the bomb aimer's position in the nose of the aircraft. From the outside, standing next to the fuselage, the bubble was at shoulder height and so I thought it would make for an interesting flight. I was certainly correct. As we took off with me looking straight down at the tarmac whizzing by I knew that I was in for a new experience. All the way I was able to look down at the earth passing below and the view made me feel like a huge eagle. On finals I began to appreciate what I had let myself in to. As we got closer to the threshold I felt like I was being thrust face down onto the runway and I'm sure that I was pushing myself up to counteract it. It was quite an experience, one that I will not rush back to repeat.

My ill-timed advice to the company about getting the AN 8 into the short strip was soon to have its effect. I had unwittingly showed the management the way to dispense with the DC 4's in favour of the AN 8. As a result the time came when I was sadly to make my last trip back to C2 and 'our' house. The AN 8 had taken over our job and was flying in daily. I suppose it was only to be expected that it was a more cost-effective solution, and that probably I should have kept my trap shut. In any event they would have soon found out that the one from the coast came in quite often.

In any event ATF was out of action as she had engine problems, both on the same side. I was not there when it all happened; suffice to say that there had been no drama but that both engines had to be changed. Two replacement engines had been brought up by the regular flights and we were sent up to fit them and bring her back.

As we came in for the last landing on the now familiar runway I casually looked to the left at the parked aircraft. To my horror I saw that ATF was facing the wrong way, she had been turned around 90 degrees. I jumped out as soon as I could and went over to see how she had possibly moved. It appeared that prop wash from the other aircraft each day had, bit by bit, caused the chocks to dislodge and as soon as one was out she had moved. The small stones from all the mining activity, covering the whole apron area had probably made it easier for the chocks to move.

We opened up the door and I went into the cockpit to have a look around. The windscreen on my side had three cracks from top to bottom. How could we fly back like that? A natural reaction was to feel the cracks with my fingernails. On the inside the crack was not discernible, but when I had the side window open so that I could feel the outside, the penny dropped. The glass was the old type of 'Triplex' glass made of a back and front piece sandwiching a plastic sheet. This prevents a panel from disintegrating once it has cracked, as the plastic holds it all together, but what about at 300 km/hr. With the crack only on the outside, and no possibility of a replacement we would just have to see how it fared. Remember they did not even have glass for the windows in the houses. Not a happy thought.

When we got to our house we were in for a bit of a shock. The AN 8 crew had been using our house and was it a mess. The freezer that had kept us going for so long was absolutely caked in frozen blood from the meat and the rest of the kitchen was disgusting. The house itself was dirty from head to foot. It was rather a slap in the face that our house that we had put so much care into had been so neglected in such a short space of time. As my wife will bear out, I am no cleanliness freak, but it showed us what sloppiness could do. We had to console ourselves with the fact that this was probably our last visit, and just turn a blind eye to it all. Nonetheless, as always after a full day, we had a good night's rest.

Up at the field the following morning Jack and I were checking out the aircraft while the others were completing the engine change. Once our preparations were complete I spent some time helping with the engines, as I always find the mechanics interesting. In time the engines were test run and pronounced fit. We started fuelling from the 200 litre drums in preparation for the trip home. Test flights were an unknown quantity there and so we just had to check it all out meticulously. In fact on one occasion we had aborted a take off when the fire warning went off and had been reprimanded by the head of the military. As far as he was concerned an aircraft that did not complete its take off was unfit for flight and no amount of reasoning would convince him otherwise.

While we filled the tanks, a brand new Pilatus passenger aircraft landed and taxied in next to us. As we watched we heard the sound that we knew well and always avoided. That was the high-pitched series of pings made as a propeller sucks up the small stones and hurls them around at great velocity. The Pilatus was picking up an enormous quantity of the smooth pebbles and it was quite frightening. As we tried to take shelter we could hear them hitting our fuselage. When it had all died down we continued fuelling and preparing for the next day's return to South Africa. As per normal, the General kept all our passports during our stay and so we had to notify him of our intentions to depart the next day so that they would be returned in time.

We arrived bright and early to get our departure clearances and passports to be met with a bit of a shock. The general insisted that we take some passengers to C1 on our way. As much as we explained that it was not possible, that we only had limited fuel, he would not take no for an answer. The only way out was via C1 with the passengers, which would extend our journey by an hour. Happy to get our passports, but knowing that we would just have enough fuel, we had to agree.

Back at the aircraft we waited impatiently for the pax to arrive, and as soon as they did we were off. We flew to the left of the river, turned right onto base, then finals, and landed at the rough, uphill runway at C1 and taxied up to drop them off. Without the passengers we called up for clearance, just to be told that we had to wait for some other passengers to take back to C2. By that stage our tempers were being challenged. They arrived and we still did not have clearance. We all sat next to the aircraft waiting and I looked up at the engines. As the oil dripped down it gave me an idea. I followed each drop with an exaggerated move of my head and soon the rest of the crew caught on and mirrored my movements. Soon one of the prospective passengers asked me if the aircraft was safe. With as much reservation in my voice as I could muster. I replied giving them a very obviously false, weak reassurance

They soon began to wonder about their safety, particularly when I had told them how envious we were of the safety of the Russian aircraft. It was not long before they wandered off to the easily identifiable controller with the one and only radio around his neck. They returned to announce that they had made arrangements to fly out with the Russian aircraft – my plan had worked and we had won. It was not long before we were given permission to leave, and we could depart. By that stage we had lost quite a few hours and so would be running well behind time.

Relieved we trundled down the runway, took off and turned onto our course for home. As we droned on we monitored the 'new' engines, particularly their oil consumption. We all started to relax after the bad start to the day and the flight began to take on the usual form. We leisurely had tea as we ate up the miles to S. A. keeping a constant watch on the world outside and the machinery inside. In time we ate lunch and from there on, as we got closer to home things looked better and more like home.

We continued making our hole in the sky and soon I was talking to Johannesburg approach. Before I transmitted I had been listening out as normal, and they were having a really busy day. Uncle Jack, as always came up with a bright idea. Instead of getting entwined with all the approaching traffic and risking the inevitable delay we could cancel our IFR (Instrument Flight Rules) flight plan. Doing that would then transfer us to a visual approach and we would avoid the high traffic density congestion. I requested cancellation, and as soon as it was granted, the rumbling lessened as the power was reduced and we descended to below the controlled airspace. Just as we were approaching Hartebeesport Dam (a compulsory reporting point) we had lost enough height to be visual and the flight engineer gently increased power.

Just as I started to relax I was violently jogged to my senses as the one engine coughed. Our tight fuel situation leapt up and hit me between the eyes. All I could think about was a four-engined forced landing and I glanced at the fuel gauges. Even though we knew that they were a bit dodgey they all showed fuel in the tanks. Just before my heart stopped in sympathy with the engine, Neves leaned forward and moved the fuel selectors around. While I was looking seriously at our height, the healthy roar of the engine welcomed me, as it came back to join us. One tank had run dry despite the gauge showing otherwise.

With that frightening moment behind us the approach to Rand Airport was textbook smooth. I was flying as we turned onto finals on runway 11. Jack had just called finals when the controller advised us that he could see that we had an engine fire. Jack declined any assistance and told me to continue our final approach. It was dark and I landed amidst a flurry of flashing and rotating beacons and the frenzy of the controller who had sent out all his fire trucks and ambulances. Jack in his quiet inimitable manner reassured me and told me to ignore it all, as we had no reason to suspect fire and we taxied up normally. We stopped surrounded by all the emergency vehicles and calmly went through our normal procedures.

We got out and inspected the aircraft. It appeared that the scare was due to the exhaust rings (manifolds) not being properly maintained by our previous engineer. The same chap that had been such a problem before had struck again. I was the first to be accosted by the fire chief who demanded that we file an incident report. No amount of persuasion on my part would convince him otherwise. The fact that the controller requested them without us requiring them was not to be accepted. Soon Uncle Jack was onto it, they disappeared and no more was ever mentioned. Rather relieved that the long day had eventually ended well, our various wives took us home for a peaceful night's rest.

The next flight up north was to be my last into Angola. We were to transport eight tons of beer up to C1. Peter was the captain and I was relieved to have Neves as the engineer again. We were taking the other DC4, the Silver Bird up just for an overnight stop to drop the beer off. Neves had put the whole deal together and he was hoping that it might have the promise of a bit of future potential to save the DC4 plight. Peter had spent very little time in the Bush, but having heard the stories and with his little experience, he realised a few limitations. He was insistent that we would be totally self-reliant, sleep in the aircraft, and avoid going into the town.

I knew that he had never flown into C1 and was not familiar with the area so I spent some time describing it to him. I knew the airfield and, even having drawn a sketch, it took some convincing to get him to accept that our destination was an airfield that was marked as unused on the map. On my sketch I had marked the cross-runways and I explained to him that the longer one was unusable. What we had to do was use the shorter, uphill one and at the junction turn the 20 odd degrees on to the other runway to give us the last bit of length needed to stop.

Only when Neves agreed with me did Peter begin to believe me. In retrospect I probably would also find it hard to accept if I were in his shoes. I explained how difficult the approach was due to the large grader parked just before the incoming threshold. I also warned him about the gradient at the threshold and the poor runway surface. I illustrated the approach alongside the river onto the downwind leg and referred to the AN32 carcass lying at the intersection. The reaction to all this was not quite as interested as I expected, but I had done what I could.

With all of this as a plan we met at Lanseria for an early departure. To our surprise Uncle Jack popped out of the DC4 next to us. He was also on a flight to C1, also refuelling at Victoria Falls. While we were doing our last preparations for takeoff we watched him start up and taxi out and as we were preparing to start up we saw his ladder on the apron next to us. We loaded it up, knowing that we would see him when we both refuelled. We had a pleasant flight up, chasing Jack all the way. When we arrived at Vic Falls we just saw him taking off, I could not believe how fast he had been.

We took off with a full load of fuel and set course for C1. After a pleasant flight we approached C2, our old home. We had been told to not fly directly overhead as in the interim the town had been taken over. Flying past with that in mind I had a strange feeling. Never before had I ever been involved in an area that had been in a conflict zone and taken over by force. I wondered what had become of the house and all the belongings, I could imagine. We continued and as we approached C1 I pointed out the area to Peter, referring to the discussion the previous day and I was now reinforcing all that I had told him.

As we got closer to our destination I suggested that we start our descent. Peter started to get uneasy. He was unfamiliar with the undeveloped area and questioned my knowledge for the first time. I realised how futile it would be having a dispute even though Neves also knew his way around and would back me up. I racked my brains to find a way to convince Peter that I was right. I realised that by showing him that the sketch I had drawn the night before was correct I would gain credibility.

I asked him if he had the sketch map and he produced it. I began showing him that the landmarks around us were correct and he started to be receptive. "The airfield is over there." I pointed. He immediately disputed the likelihood of any field in such an undeveloped area. I again referred to the sketch, explained that the controller only had a small hand-held radio, and showed him the approach path.

Much against his better judgement he agreed to try my idea and we headed towards the downwind leg on the left of the river. I kept up my description, referring to the sketch map, describing the final approach and reminded him how rough the surface was. A newcomer was on the flight deck behind us, and afterwards he described how as we turned onto finals, he saw Peter's jaw muscles tighten up and he started sweating. I was concentrating on the approach and landing, and so was not aware of his reaction. After a positive landing, I reminded him about the slight dog's leg to the right onto the other runway, and we came to a halt on the terrible surface. I could not understand why we had come to a complete halt and did not taxi off until Peter turned to me and said.

"Roy, I will never again not believe you, you don't exaggerate."

His acceptance at the conclusion the night before now made sense, he had been not taking me too seriously, thinking that I was exaggerating. With that we proceeded to taxi and park next to Jack's DC4.

The truck duly arrived and we offloaded the beer and Peter told them of our intention to sleep in the aircraft. They soon returned with strict instructions that we were not permitted to remain on the airfield after dark and were to return with them. Peter soon realised that he was not on a winning streak; we collected our belongings and left the aircraft. I had never been away from the airfield at C1 and so was interested at how the town compared with C2.

After a long drive over roads that were only just short of impassable, we turned off the road. I found it difficult that roads so poor were in fact in daily use. There were no traces of old tar centre humps. The road was eroded into a series of huge potholes held together with little bridges of hardened mud. On both sides of the area where we parked were rows of low, long, single pitch, prefabricated buildings. We were shown to our rooms, to find that the rooms were just roughly partitioned off sections of the building, with a single bed in each, one door and no windows or other openings.

We all put our kit into the rooms, and were soon greeted by a voluble series of expletives as Peter looked at his room, and the day's events culminated verbally. There was a table and some chairs and we sat outside waiting for Peter. He joined us and asked where the toilet was. I was the only one who had enquired about it earlier, and so took him to the wondrous creation. It was just a roughly dug, aromatic, hole in the ground that one had to crouch over. This was the final straw. He exploded and I was seriously worried that he was in for a heart attack. He stormed off to his room, refused their food and said that he had had enough and was going to bed. With that he disappeared leaving us to enjoy a pretty reasonable meal by local standards.

Much to my surprise Jack and his crew were also staying there and were at a nearby table. We moved the tables together to make one big group and continued chatting until quite late. To keep our sanity, we always made sure that we had an adequate beer supply and so there was always a very social side to our flying.

Loud compulsive coughing suddenly broke the convivial atmosphere. As we turned around to see who was at the source, we saw a dazed Peter staggering out of his room, coughing hysterically. After he quietened down a bit we got to the source of the problem. He was always paranoid about malaria and in an attempt to ward it off, he had lit three mosquito coils in the small confines of his room. The resulting effect was that he had fallen asleep, just to be woken by his own coughing, all but poisoned by the fumes from the coils. He was seriously ill, and it would just take time to get out of his system. The party dispersed shortly after that, and I was asleep by the time my head hit the pillow.

Peter was still rather poorly the next day, particularly as he thought about the strange airfield. He was at least able to partially function on the flight back. This time I had full credibility and when I suggested a taxi to the uphill part of the disused runway to start our roll there was no objection at all. We started our run and he was now quite happy to follow the kink to the left to get us onto the 'serviceable' runway. Earlier Jack and I had chatted about how much faster the DC4 was that he was flying, and he was soon to prove it again. We followed him out and he just left us standing. We both flew back to Lanseria and, by the time we got there, he had already cleared customs and had left.

I only flew that particular aircraft once, and the conditions did not permit me to appreciate its performance as much as I had done chasing it. Uncle Jack and I had been asked to ferry her from Rand to Lanseria after some maintenance. When we were about to leave I would phone Jane and she would meet us to take us home from Lanseria. As is so often the case one waits for the maintenance to be completed, and this occasion was no different. Eventually it was ready and it became clear that it was going to end up as a night flight.

Once we were at the holding point the controller gave me clearance, and warned me of high, gusting winds. I acknowledged and we discussed it briefly. When we collected the aircraft there was no appreciable wind, but at least we had been cautioned. It was Uncle Jack's turn for the take-off and just as he rotated the left wing dropped out of the sky. I have never seen reflexes like it. Uncle Jack was as fast as lightening and at well over 70 years of age it really showed how on top of it all he was. I am sure that I would have been caught out if I had to do the take off.

We continued on a bumpy, dark, journey in the unfamiliar aircraft. I have never before or since encountered such turbulence. As we flew to the west, the buffeting was so bad that I was trying to hold the instrument panel with both hands to stop it shaking, while I tried to read the ribbon type directional gyro. We turned right and continued on to Lanseria and the turbulence did not let up for a moment. There were heavy gusts as we landed and we taxied up wondering what it was all about. Once out of the aircraft the wind did not seem unduly harsh and only when Jane arrived did we know it was not all in our minds. She arrived, wide-eyed, having battled to drive through treacherous conditions. Somewhat amazed and confused we secured the aircraft and left.

On the way back home the proof was there in the form of a number of road signs that had been uprooted and deposited all over the place. At home the television told of the freak windstorm that had reeked havoc just where we had been flying. The report said that between Johannesburg and Vereeniging there were a number of buildings that had been damaged and others with just the roofs blown off. All this and some of us had been crazy enough to fly through it.

Chapter 35

By this stage the DC4 operation had come to an end and the company was investigating other potential work for their aircraft in Africa, particularly the AN32's that they had acquired. I had become quite involved in the Pietersburg operation and was involved in the aircraft registration, documentation and airworthiness, and I spent many hours commuting to and fro. The company had the AN 8, two AN 12's and the three huge IL 76's that were busy all the time. As a fill in, they had purchased four AN 32 aircraft to increase their short haul capability.

These aircraft were turbo propeller machines that had been specifically designed to operate out of high altitude locations. As a result they were fitted with two huge 5 000hp engines mounted on top of the high wing. They had all been flown in from Europe and were a bit tatty on the surface, but basically very sound. At Pietersburg they underwent a complete paint strip and respray and came out looking as good as new. They were finished in white with imaginative blue stripes and looked really fresh. Our own staff in the large hangar did all the work, and, being able to look back to the time when I went up to pay the first deposit, I felt really proud to be part of it all.

Management had decided that the time had come to include some South Africans in their flying staff to fly the Russian aircraft. The aircraft that were already operational were well catered for by the Russians that they already employed, but the AN 32b fleet needed pilots, and they would train some of us for them. In addition the language difficulty also meant that the AN 32b fleet had to be placarded in English. It was a huge job and in between my trips to the hangar I was producing flight manuals, checklists and other manuals in English.

As the AN 32 was not able to be registered in South Africa we considered registering them in Swaziland. A few trips there proved the viability and soon I was preparing reams of paperwork to get them type approved in Swaziland. At last they were approved and they proudly sported their African registration, and together with the English placarding they were beginning to shrug off their heritage. I was put forward for the conversion course and, having been so involved with them, was quite excited.

The day came when the course was due to start and we all made an early break to get to Pietersburg on time. I drove the 90 minutes up the all too familiar road and turned left into the entrance to Gateway International Airport, as it was known. As I progressed down the long entrance road my mind was probably roving a bit with the thoughts of the weeks to come. Suddenly I was jogged back to the present as a policeman stood at the roadside and stopped me for speeding. They had actually set up a speed trap up on the access road; I was humiliated at my stupidity. All the other pilots passed me while he stood alongside my car writing up the ticket. Needless to say this was the subject of much hilarity when I walked into the class.

That over, the class began. Our main lecturer was a full blown Russian, whose broken English was far from presentation standards, and so he was assisted by a translator. It was far less rigorous than it sounds, particularly as he could understand and talk enough English to field questions. We spent a week on quite an intense technical, followed by another week's instruction in the aircraft if we passed the written exam. Even though I had been exposed to them earlier, the aircraft were amazingly different from the more traditional ones that we were used to. The new treatment of different crew duties was altogether very different, particularly on the engine management side. Once we had passed the final technical exam we were free to go home for the weekend, and to return on Monday for the flying.

The following week was amazing. Even though we had all been inside the aircraft and browsed around it, we were surprised as it screamed to life like a huge banshee. I had been used to the 8 and 12's, as I had seen them on an almost daily basis, but I was not prepared for this monster. With the first pupils aboard we covered our ears and watched as the sound rose to a crescendo and the aircraft taxied off to the end of the runway.

Soon my turn came and we got in to the AN32b. I was sitting in the LH seat preparing for my take off and listening to the briefing. In the aircraft there was no interpreter and we had to listen attentively to catch all the information that the instructor gave over. In essence we each would take off, go and do some upper air work and return to do a few circuits. In the air the next student would get in the LH seat and the exercise would be repeated. The take off was fairly as I expected, the rudder control was very adequate without the tiller steering that we had on the DC4, and all the flying control responses were much as I expected. The amount of power however was phenomenal and our climb out was beyond my expectations. Long gone were the long, low climb outs that I had become accustomed to. After a session of upper air work we returned for a series of circuits and then I gave up my seat to become an observer for the rest of that flight.

The evenings were very enjoyably. The students got on well as a group, we seemed seldom to eat at the hotel, and spent most of our time next door at a steakhouse. The atmosphere there was very vibrant and conducive for a group get together. When we arrived we used to choose our table according to the waitress who was serving that table. They were super and one in particular took my fancy on one occasion when we arrived to find the steakhouse birthday being celebrated. They were all kitted out superbly in various interpretations of birthday dress, particularly my favourite who was in pig tails. As Jane says I have never grown up and if a girl wants something from me, pig tails will do it, I love them. I found out, of all things, that even though she was born in SA, she had a Russian mother and a Russian Christian name. We used to stay there until late and in retrospect they probably cursed us for not leaving at a self-respecting hour.

The following day we met in the lecture room for the briefing. As on the previous day we would return to do a few circuits, all regular enough, and then came the crunch. When the instructor considered us up to it, each student would come to a full stop and return to the holding point. On the take off he would cut an engine at V1 and we had to continue to take off on one engine. I could not believe what I was hearing. V1 is the speed that defines the moment that the pilot makes the decision to continue with the take off. Every pilots dread is that an engine fails between that and the next decision speed V2 where there is ample speed to continue on a single engine. We were now being tasked to do it as an exercise. I could not believe it. We would also see the automatic feathering system in use. When power is lost the propeller changes the pitch (blade angle) so that the propeller stops rotating completely to minimize the drag

My turn came for the full stop landing and I taxied back to the threshold with my mind full of thoughts. I started the take off roll and waited, I made extra sure that my feet were listening to me properly, and waiting. I saw the instructor's hand move and I knew the time had come. I pushed like mad with my right foot as I saw, out of the corner of my eye, the left propeller slowing to a stop as it automatically feathered. It was certainly dramatic but far more under control than I expected. We climbed out at an initial climb that old ATF would have been proud of and turned downwind. I prepared myself for the engine in-flight start, but I was still amazed. As the engineer started the engine, I watched the stationary blades slowly move. Suddenly, as the pitch began to change the rotation dramatically increased, and I had to push even harder than on take off to keep her straight. Once the engine revs increased I was able to reduce the push required and soon the engine was under full power and the situation was back to normal with full power.

This rather dramatic conversion technique was certainly unknown among Western aircraft but not among the Russian counterparts and it was certainly a unique experience for me. That evening when we got back from dinner, I got a message that I was going on a flight the following day and to contact the instructor. This all sounded a bit strange and so I called him. In his broken English he explained that they were to take a cargo load from Jan Smuts International Airport to Blantyre and return to Pietersburg and they needed me to go as co-pilot. Even though he said that the flight planning had been done it was all a bit daunting, but I was certainly looking forward to the flight.

The next day I met the crew at the Operations in our hangar and went through the maps and planning, preparing for our departure. I climbed apprehensively into the right hand seat and strapped myself in. Suddenly the lack of the old familiarity of the DC 4 struck home. This was for real. I was sitting in a barely familiar cockpit, with an instrument panel decorated with Cyrillic script, as that particular machine had not yet been completed, with a crew that did not even speak my language properly. What was I doing? I wished for the old familiar cockpit with dear Uncle Jack beside me. But the die was cast, I had to make a go of this flight.

We took off, climbed out and when we were out of the Pietersburg airspace, I changed over to the Johannesburg Approach frequency and called them on the second radio. Although I could hear them clearly, even after repeated calls, I got no response and could not fathom out the problem. It was only when Pietersburg came in on the other set that it all became clear. If we did not comply immediately and contact approach our flight clearance would be terminated. I had not realised that there was an intercom/transmit selection switch on the control stick, and it was in the intercom position.

During all of our training it had been left in the intercom position and so we had been unaware of its existence. I hurriedly switched over and made contact with them. Soon things started to flow smoothly and we were coming in on finals. The Russians had assumed that I was familiar with Jan Smuts, but in reality I had never flown in before. To make things a little more difficult, they had cleared us to 03 right, this made our taxi route a bit more complex, and so I had my nose down looking at the airfield layout trying to pick out the correct route around the field. Adding to the complications was the insistence of the crew to taxi at the most incredible speeds using bursts of reverse thrust to slow down slightly. None too soon we reached our designated parking area and shut down the engines.

The cargo arrived and was soon loaded up the rear ramp, and we prepared to depart. After start clearance the screaming resumed and we taxied out. The fully loaded take-off was amazingly short and the climb equally impressive. We were soon at our cruising level and whistling along. I was shocked at how noisy the cockpit was. Having flown so often as a passenger in the AN8, I could not imagine the fact that the AN32 was so much noisier, no wonder the flight duty hours in the cockpit were restricted. Other than that it was all fairly comfortable and as time went by I even began to feel a little more at ease.

The approach to Blantyre was a little unusual as beyond the town is a sizeable mountain. After an uneventful landing we taxied up at the now obligatory maximum taxi speed, and parked as shown. Enjoying the peaceful early evening atmosphere, I walked to the tower to pay the landing fees. As I was on my way down the stairs from the tower, a person wanting a lift to Johannesburg accosted me. I was amazed, even in deepest Africa I would not expect a person to be hitch hiking at an international airport. I tried all I could to put him off but without any luck. He explained that we were, in all likelihood, the last flight and his last chance to get out. I made sure that he had a passport and put him in touch with the captain who agreed to take him. The cargo was soon offloaded and with no daylight left we started up to go back home.

Flying back at night it was calm but very cold at over 20 000feet. The air conditioner controls are on the right side panels, controlled by the co-pilot. Almost halfway home I suddenly realised that there was probably no heating in the cargo hold and I visualized a totally frozen, stiff human form being carted off at Gateway. I eventually managed to get my concern through, and the engineer just shunned it off and told me I worry too much. We soon saw the long line of lights far ahead and soon landed in the usual Russian manner with the engineer doing all the power adjustments on his own and the pilot pointing and flying down the glide slope.

Once we were stationary in our parking bay and the engines and all the systems were shut down I could not wait to see if our hitch hiker was in good form, all I could think about were the ramifications if something went wrong. I need not have worried for as soon as the door was opened he could not get out fast enough, almost to kiss the good old S.A. soil. I often wondered if the truth was quite as innocent as he made out. In any event he came with us and cleared back into SA in the usual manner so we will never really know.

The following day, back in the classroom, the others had completed their flight tests while I had been away but were amazed at my quick dash up north. The conversion course was a success for us all and all that remained was for the work to come rolling in. We all bad farewell and left for home with a good positive feeling. Despite our best wishes and hopes for our future with the AN 32, as usual the crunch was on its way.

Three of our chaps had a short-lived enjoyable career flying the AN 32b's before the whole of the show folded. One of them was repatriating aliens to surrounding countries in the AN 32 on a regular basis and even that came to an end.

Chapter 36

The company was having increasing problems with their staff on two fronts. The immigration authorities were throwing as many stones as they could in their path and the hotels had had enough of their behaviour, particularly as they had been away from home for extended periods and they were a bit restless, to put it mildly. International politics had also come to play and had stopped the food supply to the area that we had been supplying by air. The AN 32 program had started off with the three local pilots and the Russian crew but they ended up being rather more active outside SA.

The management then made the decision that they would relocate their whole operation to the Central African Republic. We were all offered the option to move with them, which the three SA pilots eventually did do. For me, having a family and the whole scene that goes with it, it was not a proposition and I declined in the hope of trying to keep something going on locally with the DC 4's. As always there was the promise of work, but not yet, was the all to common plea.

An enquiry came in from Nairobi, and again every effort was made to try and capture the possibility of work. There had been an ongoing season of floods and torrential rain in East Africa, and Somalia particularly had been severely hit. Scores of people and relief organisations had been pulled in to offer disaster relief to them using Nairobi as a base. I was notified late in the afternoon that I was on the crew and that we would be meeting the customs at Rand at 0600 the following day and departing immediately for a period of two to three weeks. You can imagine the rush to get things in order, but I guess that is a pilot's life.

We had a rather long take off the next morning in the Silver Bird. Loaded with a spare engine, a mountain of other spares as well as 2 500 gallons of fuel the DC4 took a bit of runway length to get airborne, albeit only at a few feet over the numbers, and the usual distance to clean up and get climbing. She climbed amazingly well and by the time we were requested to turn on to our track we were over the West Rand and had got to almost 8 000 feet. After a right turn we were on course and had another eight hours in the air ahead of us. One of the younger pilots, being groomed for the future, was along for the experience.

While we were cruising along just leaving the Reef behind us, he announced to Uncle Jack that he had left his passport behind. He had driven up to the aircraft to unload and without realising it, had left his passport locked safely in his car in the parking lot. With his usual calmness Uncle Jack explained that one does not just go back and land a heavy aircraft full of fuel as you do a Cessna 150, and that that is where it would have to stay.

Soon the traditional tea was served, and this time flying the silver bird, we were lucky enough to have the electric hotplate to use, as opposed to our gas hot plate in ATF. Jack as always reached for his biscuits and I was able to beat him to the draw. I pulled out some jam filled biscuits from next to my seat that I had bought. With his sweet tooth, he really enjoyed them while we rested our cups of tea on the dashboard coaming next to the rudder trim wheel.

We flew on up Africa for some hours, reporting in from time to time to the various African countries. We encountered large amounts of cumulus cloud all the way. This kept me busy choosing a flight path through the thinnest cloud while maintaining track. We spent almost half of our time in the cloud, an indication of what was ahead. We flew up Lake Malawi, my introduction to the Great Lakes of Africa and eventually the famed Kilamanjaro came closer, but as the top was covered in cloud I was denied the sight. We started a clean up in preparation for the long, gradual descent.

Because radial engines suffer from cracked heads due to super cooling during rapid descent, a long approach from the west was chosen. We would then go around the mountains and avoid a steep descent. I called repeatedly but no acknowledgement was forthcoming. The radio silence persisted even when we no longer had the mountains between us, and eventually I got a response giving us the landing permission. We were on the desired heading, according to the map and the ADF radio aid, and after not long an airfield was visible in the distance. As we both peered through the screen to identify it, we realised that though on our direct path it was the smaller Wilson Field. Beyond the National Park was our destination, Jomo Kenyata Airport, and it slowly approached us. We were given a direct approach and flew straight in on final approach. When we got closer I realised what a busy airport it was and no sooner had we touched down than taxi directions followed.

No simple instructions were given but the controller talked as if we were familiar with the airfield. As a result we turned off to the south, looking for the freight section. After we had been taxiing around for some time trying to decipher the instructions, we were told that we were on the wrong side and that we should be on the northern side of the runway.

We then had to cross the active runway and things made more sense. Once she was parked and our luggage was offloaded our transport ferried us to the customs and immigration. I looked back at the aircraft to see the setting sun behind the aircraft and there was just enough light to get a super atmospheric picture. The whole sky was a golden bronze with the clouds making streaks in the colours. Our silver aircraft in the foreground seemed to be radiating all the sunbeams away from it.

On the way, the subject under discussion was the missing passport and as usual, Jack's experience came to save the day. If all of us cleared under a General Declaration, then with a bit of luck he would not have to show his passport. This worked and we all proceeded to the centre of Nairobi. Our host kept up a continual patter, warning us that the town was oft' referred to as Nairobbery for just cause, and to be aware at all times.

Sunset behind Silver Bird at Nairobi

As we drove through the streets I was aware of the most frantic driving in the traffic. When we approached circles or roundabouts, the driving became frantic and a race ensued to beat the cars around you into the circle. The resulting grand prix around the circles was something to behold, the amazing thing was that in all the time we were there I never saw an accident. The standard of vehicles was better than I had seen in other parts of Africa but not what we were used to at home. Booked in at our hotel we dropped off to a well-deserved rest.

Bright and bushy tailed the next day we looked around while we waited for our meeting. Out of the hotel window I had a superb view between the multi-storey buildings. I was amazed at how relatively modern the city was even though the tattiness of Africa was apparent. The streets had the hum and vibe of a busy big city and I looked down on a multitude of tiny vehicles and people going about their tasks. The weather was very strange, but considering why we were there it made sense. It was not raining when we got up, but looking out, the streets were totally sodden. Puddles of water were everywhere. By mid morning it was bucketing down in a torrential fashion and we soon learned that mid-morning and mid-afternoon torrents were the order of the day.

We were met and taken to the meeting where our task was outlined. A number of aircraft had been brought in to offer relief aid. The main supporters were the Hercules and Buffalo aircraft because they had opening loading ramps at their rear. They were successfully dropping supplies to the flooded areas on a daily basis. How could we help? The DC4 was a military version and so had a small paratrooper's door set into the cargo doors. Unlike the cargo doors, the smaller door opened inwards and could be opened in flight and the supplies pushed out through it. A picture began to develop in my mind, I began to see a sort of slide to direct the cargo to the door.

More details came out colouring in the picture. There were no parachutes available to us, and so, unlike the others, we had to develop a suitable technique to counteract our lack of parachutes or loading ramp. We were to drop at an airfield called Sacco Uen, deep into Somalia. The 1 000metre strip was rough and was flooded so the aircraft with the supplies destined for them could not land there. Later on we would be taken to the operations office at Wilson Field (the one we flew alongside coming in) to sort out maps, routes and other details.

My mind was working hard as we drove back to the main airport. All I wanted to do was stand inside our aircraft, looking at the door and visualise a possible solution. Uncle Jack and I chatted on the way about how the concept had changed. From the initial discussion we had before we left to what was presented to us was a drastic transformation. From a gentle flight, landing and offloading we now faced a vision of being unable to land and dropping supplies without parachutes. We continued driving along with pauses in conversation conjuring up disastrous visions. The picture now looked more like a flooded plain, littered with broken containers and people being struck down by flying boxes. Surely this was not really happening to us?

When we got to the aircraft Jack and I stood inside and battled to open the parachute door that had obviously not been open for many moons. As we worked at opening it I again visualised a chute arrangement so that the packages could be lined up and just pushed out of the door. That would minimise the chances of boxes getting stuck in the doorway. The more I thought about it the more convinced I was that I could make it work. By the time the door was opening freely we had discussed a number of ideas. Uncle Jack, as always, put the finishing touches to the scheme. His idea was to drop from only 100 feet as he felt that that would minimise damage and scattering, and use the parachute alarm as a signal to the people pushing goods out of the door. At that stage we had no idea of what the goods were and what shape or size they were.

The parking area around us was dedicated to the relief programme. The aircraft were either the well known Hercules or Buffalos, a type I had not seen before. They were twin-engined, high wing aircraft made by de Havilland Canada. They were ideally suited to the role having a large opening rear loading ramp. The pilots told us that they were designed mainly for flying into high lying strips where they could land, unload and take off before the aircraft sank into the mud. Wish we could be so lucky.

Around the aircraft was an enormous collection of boats, and I went up to look at them. Their hulls were made of formed and welded aluminium sheet, fully equipped for any sailor to be proud of and with a visibly powerful outboard engine attached to the rear. These were also being flown in to the flooded areas with the other supplies.

With my concept firmly planted in our heads we were taken to Wilson field, where the airport office was. Maps were spread out on a table showing us our route to Somalia, but, and in flying there is always a but, there were no maps available of our destination itself. Not a problem, we were told, we will give you the GPS co-ordinates of the airfield, and the radio frequency of the relief worker on the ground. After a perusal of the maps the plan was to fly for three hours to the GPS position of an unknown destination, push out a whole load of cargo without destroying it or people below, fly back for another three hours, land and the job is done. My mind boggled. To lighten our load the chap produced a sketch of the airfield to help us identify the place.

On the way back I asked the whereabouts of a carpenter or handyman to make up a chute for me from the dimensions I had taken. When we stopped at the carpenter I explained the concept to him and drew a dimensioned sketch of what I wanted. He assured me that it was a simple task and that it would be ready the next day. We spent the rest of that day deep in our individual thoughts. by that stage we were being somewhat acclimatised to the hazardous drives around and were getting used to the look of the hotel precincts, and as always, Jack and I were enjoying the hotel and its menu to the full.

The next day we waited at the typically English front entrance, small flight of steps, curved walls up to the entrance door waiting for our lift. It arrived, proudly showing off my chute, we climbed in and left for the aircraft. Once through the airport entrance the driver weaved his way through all the stacks of relief supplies, the boats and eventually we got to our machine that looked so foreign amongst the other dedicated aircraft. Once aboard I put my chute in place and we carried out a dress rehearsal using some boxes and bundles. It looked good. There were handlers that had been assigned to go with us and we got them to mimic the offloading procedure and it looked very promising although what would happen once the load was out was anybody's guess.

Back to the waiting game for the next few days. We had mentally flown the route many times and I had rehearsed our route out and back with the imposing Mount Kenya on our left as we climbed out. I had earmarked ground references to keep us well clear from trouble and had noted their GPS positions. All we needed was the load so that I could work out our final estimate of time for the drop. Jack and I had come to the conclusion that we would make contact with the relief worker on the ground and ask him to drive a vehicle along the length of the runway. We could then see the condition of the surface from the tracks and decide whether an attempt at landing was feasible, even though we were told it was not. While we waited, the two of us did our usual walk about and got to know bits of the town.

When we had been paid in the past it was in US dollars, and mostly in $100 bills. Due to the amount of counterfeit notes around they were most often not accepted around parts of Africa. In Vic Falls there were even large signs up notifying the public of the fact that 100-dollar bills were not accepted at all. As a result I had to find an outlet for my bills, which I found at the Intercontinental

Hotel. They had their own bank with a counterfeit note scanner in the shopping area. I went there whenever I could and asked them to split a couple of notes into smaller denominations. They would check my notes on the machine and give me $50 notes. In addition we enjoyed the walk there and back. As we walked along we could see the residential area on the hillside with the huge Kenyata stadium in the foreground. Jack and I vowed that we would walk up there, which we did do.

We had mentally mapped out a route that we could see looking up the hill from below, and we could see that there was a probable connecting road between the two roads up and down the hill. We set out on the road towards the stadium early enough to be back before the daily deluge. We turned right to cross the stadium as this was our short cut to the road, and soon we were climbing. In no time it felt as if we were climbing a mountain as we walked up the road. I was quite worried about Uncle Jack as he had seen the better side of 70. Was I pushing him into something too strenuous, what could I do if he fell over gasping and clutching his left chest?

It was too late now to change it as we were already there. I had earmarked what looked like a hotel on the side of the hill as a stopping point but it still seemed a long way away. Eventually we got there and I bought us each a light refreshment before we continued. Even though it appeared to be an upper class residential area it had still suffered the ravages of time although not as badly as the town itself. We continued along the upper road and started our descent back to the town. I need not have worried about Uncle Jack. He coped so well that I'm sure he could have done the route again. He never ceased to amaze me at his ability and determination.

We were eventually notified of the load's imminent arrival and went out to receive it. It looked more and more like I was going to be carrying the can for the success and so I carried out another dummy run to confirm my estimate of how long to expect the drop to take, now that we had the proper load. To my amazement I saw that there were numerous packages of different sizes. As that would complicate the dropping procedure I looked at consolidating the parcels. I sat up in front of the open parachute door pushing various sizes out until I established the size that I felt suited best and began consolidating the packs. Small medical supplies were wrapped with larger items, and then wrapped with the softer items until I had a couple of standard types of packs to drop.

Even with my consolidation, there were just short of 400 to drop. The whole load was taken aboard and we carried out a full dummy run against the clock, even moving the goods towards the rear to get a true simulation. While one person pushed them out in the half-minute that it would take us to do our run along the runway, the others had to continually move the goods to the rear to keep him supplied. I extrapolated the results and came to an estimate of 55 minutes to drop the load. That would give us 3 hours there, 1 hours drop and a 3 hour return, a total of 7 hours if all went well.

We got to the field early on the day and prepared to go. I went up to file a flight plan, but the difficulty explaining that we would be away for 7 hours, fully loaded at take off, and return empty without landing was difficult to put over. Eventually I succeeded and went back to the aircraft. We taxied out with an air of the unknown hanging over us. The helpers that we had been given to move the load under our control had been briefed and shown the ropes, but the fact still remained that they had never flown before. Oh for a crystal ball, what did the next few hours hold.

Luckily the weather was on our side and we took to the skies before the morning showers broke and slowly climbed out. I sat next to Jack and looked to the left, all too aware of Mount Kenya, and thinking of our return journey. We flew directly over the edge of the dam that was my chosen waypoint and I made sure that I could get there on the way back. We droned on for hours in and out of rain and clouds until we fell off our printed map. Now the true stuff starts. I had the sketch map on my lap, the GPS co-ordinates plugged into the GPS, and a relief worker behind me supposedly in contact with the destination. Jack had briefed us on dropping at 100 feet above the ground and then doing a circuit while the handlers moved the next few bundles onto the chute.

To my amazement the elements were kind to us, it was not raining at the destination, and at the appointed time I saw a field looking like the sketch, just beyond a small village. The relief worker had been in contact with the ground and no sooner had we got there than we saw a vehicle driving down the runway as far as he could. As we had been told we saw that piles of branches had closed off the ends of the runway.

We saw that hoards of locals, kept out by the bushes, had congregated at the end of the runway and it was a great safety concern to us. We carried out a precautionary pass along the runway and looked at the tracks left by the vehicle. It was clear that there was not even the slightest chance of a landing, so we prepared for the airdrop. Uncle Jack did the first circuit dropping a few boxes to see how they fell. On downwind they opened the door, got ready, and as we turned onto final approach I called out the height so that he could keep at 100 feet. He reached up for the bell switch above his head and as we crossed the threshold he pushed for a single ring, and the handlers started pushing bundles out. As each one left the aircraft we heard and felt the thump on our ears. At the end of the run he gave a double ring to indicate that they must stop until the next pass.

As Jack turned away the engineer supervised the movement of the load towards the door and got the first full drop lined up on my chute. As we turned onto final I was aware of how the mass of humanity up against the bushes was growing. As we were turned over their village at 150 feet onto finals, there was a snake of people leading to the strip, obviously to collect the spoils. As we flew towards the runway we looked along an amazing sight. There were boxes and bundles that we had thrown out. They were well placed along the centre line and away from the mass of people at the ends. As the huge bird flew along at 100 feet dropping our first full drop I wondered how impressive it must look from the ground. With the load now exiting at full speed the thumping on our ears increased its tempo until the double ring again signalled the end of that run. In total we did fifteen circuits that we shared.

It was my turn to do the last seven, and the feeling as we roared down the runway was indescribable. Not only was there the rush that low flying stimulates, but we were less than a wingspan off the ground doing over 150 miles per hour. After each circuit the number of boxes and bundles would multiply as by hidden magic and amazingly few had broken open. The positioning was perfect and so was the adrenaline rush. Every so often we would feel the trim alter drastically and we would shout to the back. We would hear it relayed:

"Take from the back, move very slowly from the front."

In an amazing 45 minutes the aircraft was empty and we turned for home. We had not realised what stress we were under and as we climbed away we felt exhausted and hot and all but totally expended. As I flew I realised that the screen was covered with locusts. They were stuck under the wiper blades and plastered all over the screen. In the heat of the moment we had not even noticed them, as we flew through the swarm. All that and we still had three hours to fly back! The relief worker with us had been talking to his counterpart on the ground the whole time and was very complimentary as to how the job went, although a surprise was to follow in the next few days.

We were all sweltering and the helpers, who had done so well, had reactions setting in. They were moaning about not feeling well and the engineer went back to get some air flowing. He opened the emergency exit over the wing and was all but pulled out along with the exit panel itself. It did however do the trick and things got cooler and people felt better. It was not long before the ever-present rain hit us, also helping us to cool down, and we flew out of sight of the ground for quite a time. Again fate was with us and by the time we got near Nairobi the rain let up to low cloud that gave us a bit of visibility.

As we got closer to Nairobi, I flew along with Mount Kenya visible on my right, waiting for my waypoint on the dam. Sure enough it drifted below us and I corrected course slightly to bring us in on the approach path. As we touched down we felt a unanimous sigh of relief as each one of us let go and relaxed. In our parking bay we were welcomed back and congratulated on our success. With the aircraft all locked up we went back to the hotel for a very welcome bath, dinner and nightcap (the order not too important!).

Post mortem time the next day, and we walked to the now-familiar office in the high-rise building. The stairs up the side of the building were in a semi circle, enclosed by full a height, Perspex, semicircular, dome. The result was that, as you looked at your feet, you would look down the side of the building. Initially we would use the lift but from their reception we would often use the stairs up one floor to the offices. Strange as it may seem we both used to cringe at the view over the side. On that particular occasion it struck me that the day before we had being doing our air drop from almost the same height but it still made us back away from the edge. It is odd that people who do many strange things in the air are affected when a link exists from them to the ground.

We got in to the meeting to be shown a report written by the relief chap who had come along with us. Instead of the accolades he offered on the day, there was a report damning the aircraft as unserviceable. His biggest criticism was that the windscreen wipers had not worked and to him this showed the whole exercise up as unairworthy. Never did he query it at the time when we could have explained it to him. The reason was simply that they are not necessary at cruise and one does not use them at speed except in the circuit. He had condemned our whole operation on that basis and we were never given the opportunity to justify ourselves. If it had been raining at the Nairobi airport we would have used them. The other feedback was that we had delivered so much that they could not collect it all off the runway that day and had to resume the following day, hardly a fault of ours I would have thought.

Uncle Jack and I used to walk to their office almost on a daily basis, just to be told that it was all going to happen, they were just waiting for another organisation to confirm. And so it went on. In the meantime, while keeping tabs on them, we started to get around a bit and see a few things of the area. They had a taxi driver who used to take us around and so by chipping in a bit extra we got around to see a bit more at the right price. We managed to get as far as to see the rift valley from one of the mountain roads. Stopping at one of the numerous roadside informal shopping areas, we overlooked the huge valley, reputedly the source of the Nile River. It gave me a bit of an eerie feeling knowing that it actually flowed into the sea on the northern coast of Africa.

We also visited the Naivasha Park and Country Club, on the shores of Lake Naivasha, a very picturesque setting. We walked all the way onto the jetty where for the first time in my life I saw fishermen collecting huge fresh water crayfish on a commercial basis. The Country Club however did not quite share the beauty of the lake, showing ravages of time and signs of the lack of the membership support afforded in the old colonial days.

On another occasion we visited the National Park, on the edge of the main airport. Having flown over it on arrival it was a must to see and we got our 'driver' to organise it. He said that we would have to pay $20-00 each, I think it was, but that he being a local got in for just a few bob. He drove us around and it was wonderful to see the typical East African landscape and game. The amazing difference was the huge grassy plains that one associates with East Africa. The amount of game that congregated together was also very different from our normal sightings. It was not uncommon to see three or even four species at a single sighting point.

The amount of water in the area was apparent when we passed alongside the high ground. Presumably unusual due to the floods, water continually seeped out of the sides of the ground on either side of us. Sadly we had to end our trip in the Park and go back to the hotel. Uncle Jack and I were so impressed, that we wished we could bring our respective wives up and even got as far as enquiring about flights at the travel agent at the hotel.

Things were not progressing with the flying side and Christmas 1997 was getting closer. Uncle Jack and I in our walks around Nairobi did quite a bit of shopping, especially the Scotsman's type, and thoroughly enjoyed it. He helped me chose a pair of rather gorgeous sapphire stones to have made into earrings for Jane. The two of us visited the shop a few times before the deal was ultimately made. They will always be a lovely memento of Kenya. Sadly we left soon afterwards to come home by airways leaving the 'Silver Bird' up there. The ordeal was not yet over as our one member was still passport-less and we all had to get back in to SA.

When the day came to go home we all dolled ourselves up to the nines, looking as professional as possible with all our stripes and badges and got our final lift out to the airport. As we sat and waited to board we surmised how we would get through the immigration at home. As always, Jack was not fussed and we had no option but to bask in his optimism. On arrival as we were walking up to the immigration counter, we were called to the crew queue as the others were completely backed up, and we simply whistled through. Lucky for those without their passport handy!

Chapter 37

We were preparing for another long flight in the DC 4, this time up to Entebbe. The company had responded to an enquiry to work together with a local businessman to move perishable goods around, very similar to the Angolan operation. Negotiations had got to the stage that they had to relocate an aircraft to start the operation. We were going in my old favourite ATF.

I was expecting a visit from some Australians that a friend and I had a joint venture with, and so could not be away for long. I was only required to fly the 'craft up and then would be free to return to SA. The importance was to get the aircraft there so that the client and relevant authorities could inspect it prior to the start of the flying. As soon as my visitors left I would return and the timing would work out well as I could then return to Uganda. Having ATF there was the only way that the deal would be finally clinched.

This time we were due to leave from Lanseria, which would make life a little easier than the Nairobi flight out of Rand. Amazingly, as close as it is to them, Lanseria is 1000 feet lower than all the other Reef airfields, and the runway is longer and less obstructed than Rand Airport.

The usual packing of supplies and spares came to an end as the departure day arrived, and the next day found us at the airport fresh and early in the morning. Once all the good byes to loved ones were through we clambered aboard. When we were seated, while we were getting maps and things all sorted out we could see our families on the tarmac below. As usual, I was still waiting for the clearance but was assured by Andrew that it would be forthcoming soon.

Being human, I always have the anxiety of the flight ahead and this was not helped by the wait for a clearance number. We saw a figure way down below, waving a piece of paper trying to attract our attention. Before a flight I always have my side window open to get a bit of a breeze through the invariably hot cockpit. I poked my head out and strained to decipher him above all the airfield noise and got the gist that he had our clearance to fly over all the neighbouring countries. The vision in my mind as I looked down at the seemingly small person below, was of this long-awaited piece of paper taking off from between our hands, and it was too far down to try to grasp it from him. Neves got up from the Engineer's seat between us and opened the side door. Stretching down as he lay at the opening he was handed the valuable document. We were now all ready to go. I called up for start-up clearance and soon we were counting propeller blades as we coaxed the giant engines to life.

With the engines settled to a steady rumble, and the clouds of start-up smoke disappearing behind us we were ready to taxi. When we had taxied into the holding position we could look down the nice long runway, and we knew we were in for a far more relaxed take-off than the previous long flights. We lined up, pushed the four throttles forward and effortlessly we climbed out and settled in to the long trip ahead.

Other than during take-off and landing, every 20-30 minutes each crewmember does a routine check and reports back over the intercom. As I looked back at my engines, I had to take a second glance. Oil seemed to be streaming out from a pipe on the front of the engine nearest me. I called to Neves, who also looked hard to try to find out what it was. It appeared to be emerging from near the wiring harness, which obviously made no sense at all. Our fear was that oil was being sprayed onto the harness tube causing the apparent oil leak from an electrical harness! It was visibly black and therefore not a fuel leak, so all we could do was to monitor the situation with an eye to turning back.

As we continued to bore a great hole in the sky, Neves kept a beady eye on the oil contents and the consumption. After some time it was apparent that no excess consumption was taking place. As logical as it seemed, it was very difficult to be at ease when I had the vision of the huge spray of oil each time I looked out my side window. The longer we flew the bigger the spray of oil seemed to get. I was wondering if I was suffering a similar illusion to that which pilots get when flying over large stretches of water. The further they get from land the rougher the engine seems to get.

Despite my fears, I had to obey the logic portrayed by the instruments as they were registering some consumption and so were not stuck. Our safety reasoning was that we could shut down number 3 engine and still have almost the same range, albeit a trifle slower. My notes show that at that time we were managing a presentable 185-190 knots so that we even had a bit of time in hand.

We were all lulled into the cruise mode with the strange sensation brought about by the peaceful droning of the engines. The flight was all going well and so Uncle Jack announced that he would be off for his usual little shut-eye. "Wake me up if there are any problems or when it is time for lunch." And with that he settled himself into the bunk behind me.

Neves settled into the left seat and we droned on. No amount of speculation could resolve the apparent oil problem, and still the consumption of all four engines was within the usual acceptable limits. As we approached the long Lake Malawi I made contact with Tanzania who asked for my over-flight clearance. I confidently relayed the number that we had been given, only to be told that it was not correct and I hurriedly asked Neves to give Uncle Jack a prod. Woken from a good nap, Uncle Jack joined us and I told him what had happened. He asked why had I even spoken to them, but now we would have to sort it out. With his normal presence of mind he told me to tell them that we would alter our route to avoid their space.

I carried out orders, plotted a new route up the lakes and gave it to them. As I started to alter course I was put in my place and told to continue on my original course. "We only tell them we are going that way." He glibly remarked, and I continued on my heading. I was rather anxious about it all, particularly when I saw a fair size airfield approaching. Calmly Jack instructed me to pull up the few hundred feet into a cloud that was slowly drifting overhead, and we continued. All I could think about were those below who could clearly hear us but not see who we were. I just continued until, relieved, I flew out of Tanzanian Airspace. Soon our stomachs were complaining and we got our appetites in line for lunch, as always prepared by our on-board Flight Engineer cum Chef!

Later that afternoon we saw Lake Victoria in the distance. As I read later, it is the largest inland stretch of water in Africa. We sat transfixed as the panoramic view unfolded. The water's edge looked like an ocean coastline and the water stretched into the distance as far as we could see. In total disbelief I looked at the vista ahead, the gentle swells all around, and the full-blown beach below. Looking from side to side all that was visible was the huge expanse of water.

As we started to fly over it I thanked Pratt and Whitney for their four great engines that were holding us aloft. They were droning on so peacefully, removing what would otherwise be concern from our minds. As I carried out my regular check of the engines, the oil really appeared to be pumping out but Neves assured me that the contents remained normal. One mystery was that even after all the flight time there were no tell tale oil streaks visible. The border between Tanzania and Uganda is in the middle of the lake and so as soon as we crossed the imaginary border I called for descent clearance. Once it was granted Neves pulled back the power and we settled into a long, gradual descent.

I was so absolutely transfixed by the huge expanse of water that I made a calculation that we would have been flying over the lake for just on a full hour, making it 360 km of water. As we got lower things got larger and clearer. There were swells on the water just like the open sea. At one stage an island slipped below us with a reasonable size runway running on it, virtually taking up its full length, and all I could see in any direction was just miles of water.

My attention was drawn back to the task at hand as we approached Entebbe. The feeling as we descended and prepared for the approach while still over water was very weird. On the map the airfield is indicated as in the lake, and as we approached I could see why. It was on the edge of the shoreline and had water on two sides of it. On long finals I looked at the signs of activity ahead of us. On our right, much to my surprise, was a long line of aircraft of all shapes and sizes parked on the apron. I had not expected so much activity.

We landed and were told to taxi off to the eastern side. As we taxied away from all the activity, down a rather derelict taxiway, I queried the instruction. "Yes we were correct, just proceed further," came back the reply. We obliged and soon we fell into a creation worthy of Disney World. We were on an old, deserted airfield with relics of buildings and machinery all around us. Unlike Angola, there seemed to be little, if any, life around.

I looked to the left at a derelict building, pock marked with shell holes, and recognised it as the actual terminal building from the Entebbe Raid. I could not believe what I was seeing. Clips from the film came rushing through my mind and I felt like I was in the middle of the raid itself. There was a lull, I waited for the shots but they never came.

A baton man appeared and directed us to park facing the derelict old terminal building. We shut down and I looked out, transfixed. On my right, leading away from the building, were a number of equally derelict old hangars, and the whole atmosphere was totally theatrical. We got up, stretched our legs, and walked back to the cargo door. By the time we opened it a ladder was in place and our welcoming party was looking up at us. I was brought back to reality as I remembered the 'oil leak' and could not wait to go and investigate it.

I walked around to the right hand side and looked up at the top of the engine and cowl. There was no evidence of any leak and everything looked normal. We got a ladder and climbed up and, to our amusement found that a piece of electrical tape had come loose and, flapping in the wind, had looked like an oil leak. As it flapped about looking like a huge leak it unwound further it so that the leak seemed to be getting worse. It had us all fooled.

We packed all our goods into the waiting vehicle and were taken to clear customs and immigration. As we drove past the hangars, elderly vehicles and helicopters peeped out of the half open doors. The whole scene looked like Hollywood at its best. At the end of each row we passed the usual armed guard, until we drove out onto a road to the modern part of the airport. We cleared customs and immigration in the modern terminal building, and once again my ID cards worked wonders.

As the car took us out of the airport grounds onto the main road we passed the old part of the airport, where we saw 'ATF standing in the middle of the time warp, and immediately opposite the road I saw two derelict aircraft in the bush. I recognised a Boeing 707 and a Caravelle. Amazingly these were the two that had been shot up and destroyed in the raid. Seemingly they had just been towed away and dumped.

After a drive through a complete variety of living accommodation, we arrived at an almost conventional house where an elderly lady welcomed us. She explained that she was the mother of the dealer who required our services, and that he was called away for a few days. This was a bit surprising, as after all we had flown all day to get to the meeting! She went on to say that we would have dinner with her and then be taken to the Entebbe Beach Hotel, where we would be staying.

As she led us to the front door, away from the paved parking area we walked over a walkway above a large pit. I looked over the side rail and was startled to see a fair sized crocodile resting up against the stone retaining wall. The house was otherwise rather normal with the exception of a blowpipe that was used to project darts at the dartboard. Being rather amazed with the entire goings on at the airport and the crocodile as a welcome mat, I walked through the glass doors to join Uncle Jack in the garden. I looked and saw a flock of geese milling around and in the centre of the lawn a couple of wild buck chewing at the grass. I enjoyed the view for a time and then turned to go inside. Uncle Jack, who had seen too much of Africa to be amazed, had gone in ahead of me and was standing with the blowpipe in his hand. I watched as he blew darts into the dartboard as if it was an everyday occurrence. With a bit of encouragement other people had had a try during the course of the evening. We sat relaxing in the lounge and were offered a very welcome beer before dinner.

We were served meat that was entirely different to anything that I had eaten before. I had been used to the Angolan style where everything was overcooked to a point just short of cremation, but together with all my previous culinary experiences in Africa, this was a first. During the meal I could not help wondering what the meat was, although I did really not want to think about it. The sweetish taste of the meat, other than Chinese sweet and sour, was something new. It did not seem to be in the preparation and spicing but rather in the meat itself. After the meal discussions gravitated towards the fact that the meat was goats meat. Suffice to say that it was edible (albeit rather strange), it filled the gap, and none of us were sick as a result. In due course we were taken to our hotel and, after a very long day, had a well-deserved, brilliant nights rest.

The next morning we opened our eyes to a beautiful day, and when we left our rooms to walk down to breakfast we were met with the most awesome sight. The Entebbe Beach Hotel, as its name implies, was built right on the water's edge. So much so that the lush green lawn went right down to the light bronze beach sand where the water gently lapping at its edge. There was not a sign of the waves that we had seen the previous day as we flew in, although we were told that the water does get very rough at times. To our surprise, probably only 50 metres from the shore, we saw fishermen in their boats casting nets and pulling them in, heavy with fish. The impression of being at the seaside was complete.

A railing, placed at the edge of the grass defined the hotel property, and as I turned around and looked towards the hotel buildings with the high ground and the road on the boundary behind it, the typical scruffiness of so much of Africa was lost. The buildings were terraced as the ground rose away from the beach, and they looked superb.

We walked into the restaurant and were treated to a surprisingly good breakfast as we looked out over the wondrous lake. The plan was that we were to be collected mid-morning to go to the aircraft and thereafter back to the house for lunch. That left us just enough time for a little exploratory walk. As was so often the case Uncle Jack and I were always available for a look-see type walk whenever possible but the others were seldom as keen.

We walked parallel to the beach, out of the entrance and turned left into the road. We walked, alongside the hotel boundary, up the steeply inclining tarred road towards the boundary road opposite the beachfront, and above the terraced buildings. Once we had turned left onto it we had a view that was quite something to behold. We were high enough to look over the hotel buildings and out over the lake. Immediately below us were our rooms in a separate little block with the lush lawn leading to the main building and beach. My thoughts were that it was surely one of the most beautiful places that the Creator has given mankind.

We turned away from the magnificence and continued along the dirt road and soon became aware of a huge difference creeping in as we looked to the right. The road we walked on started to show its age. Great gullies of soil erosion made a mini Grand Canyon and it became narrow and just short of impassable. The verge on our right, away from the lake, had the most amazing luscious foliage with huge leaves, which on further inspection yielded a surprise.

As I parted the greenery I found the reason for the growth. The edge of the road was a veritable rubbish dump. Every manner of food waste and general garbage had been dumped there. The green leaves were the products of waste that had seeded itself, mainly tomato plants. The contrast as we then turned and looked over the expanse of water, with all its beauty, was incongruous. Shortly thereafter we walked back in time to be collected from the hotel.

We drove down the typical African unkept roads, past numerous scruffy, makeshift dwellings. The difference here was that the dwellings were separated further from each other. They were not on top of each other like so often seen and as I looked at the unending array of dwellings my mind wandered. What became of the proud African peoples that are written up in the annals of history. Where are the traditional huts that were so much part of their culture? Here the neat grass huts and mud buildings were replaced by a collection of metalwork no longer required and thrown out by western commerce.

I became aware that the centre of Entebbe was in fact no more than the few buildings in the vicinity of the hotel. I suggested to Uncle Jack that it might well be the focus of our next walk. We again drove past the amazing sight of the two destroyed aircraft in their lonely graveyard as we proceeded towards the main airport gate, manned in the usual style. Again my crew cards did the trick and we went straight to the old section of the airport.

As we headed towards the old terminal building I thought what a super hotel one could make out of it. I visualised the lounge area where all the action had taken place being an exhibit in itself, decorated with memorabilia all around. The rest of the building was huge enough to be turned into a number of luxury suites while keeping the historic external look to blend in with the scenery. A finishing touch would be to drag the two damaged airliners to their historic positions during the raid.

My film set feeling was again on a high as I saw an Illuyshun 76 in front of the historic building. As I watched, I saw vehicles approach laden with men in camouflage gear and armed with a lethal selection of weapons. As our car stopped I hurried into the DC 4 and into the cockpit where I had a commanding view of the exercise. Uncle Jack joined me and we watched as the troops climbed aboard the aircraft and it taxied out. Needless to say, my trusty camera just happened to also get a glimpse of the proceedings. Shortly we had cleaned up the cockpit and my next task was to dip the fuel tanks. I opened the wing hatches and walked on the wings to the tank fillers. Neves was on the ladder checking the engines and so we chatted about our amazing surroundings, each with our own ideas as we watched the play unfolding.

We left ATF all trussed up, as we did not know when the next flight would be, and drove back to the house for lunch. As I crossed the walkway I saw the crocodile basking in the sun. I enquired about him and she said that unfortunately he had eaten the other crocodile that they had, leaving them with only the one. Amazed as I was, that just seemed to be how life was out there. I walked into the garden and strolled quietly around looking for the buck. I found them under a hedge, shielding themselves from the sun. The hens and geese seemed not too perturbed about anything and just moseyed around the lawn.

After a lunch, not unlike the strange meal some 17 hours earlier, we were all invited to pit our wits against each other with the blowpipe (using the dartboard of course). When my turn came I was looking at a fully-fledged, potentially lethal, blowpipe. As I toed the line on the floor, facing the board, I thought about the poor animals that were traditionally at the receiving end. The strength that we had to use to pull the darts out of the board was an indication of how lethal the 'pipe really was.

In the early afternoon we returned to the hotel and agreed to meet later for sundowners on the deck, next to the restaurant. I went for a stroll on my own down to the water's edge. I walked through the gate in the picket fence and onto the beach. I was soon walking barefoot on the beach, feeling the soft, warm sand between my toes. I sat down and lazily watched the fishermen casting their nets, enjoying the tranquillity of the scene. Unlike our beaches there was no huge, masculine, crashing of the waves. The gentle lapping of the feminine waves soon added to the atmosphere and I lay down and soon fell asleep with their caress.

My sweet dreams were suddenly shattered by shouts from my colleagues. They hastened to chastise me for firstly being alone on the beach, and secondly for not realising that the Nile crocodile inhabited the lake, and that they are to be found on the beach periodically looking for food. I collected myself together and joined them on the deck. As the sun began its descent we were looking over the lake, listening to the cry of a fish eagle and watching kingfishers diving at the fish behind the fishing boats as they travelled homewards. As the sun settled lower we watched the lake flies gathered around the lights next to us. They are tiny flies, like small mosquitoes, that gather in such large swarms that they can blot out the sun. I was led to believe that if drivers encounter a swarm they cannot see and have to stop and wait for them to pass. With a short life span of a few days they die nightly in huge numbers. So much so that in the morning huge piles are swept out of the buildings and I believe that the locals cook them and eat them.

As most often is the case, I slept like a baby and woke the next day to get my return ticket organised. There was another co-pilot available locally and as they were hoping to fly soon the others stayed on, and with a lump in my throat I had to leave Uganda behind me. A wonderful country, a place I could easily have seen more of.

As was so often the case, Jack did fly a sortie but it was not as envisaged and it all fell apart and the crew also flew home commercially. Poor old ATF was left there for some time, only to be returned and ultimately scrapped. I remember seeing her being cut up and I all but cried out loud. My heart certainly cried at the sight of my 'home' for so long being destroyed. I had to severely restrain myself from buying the severed cabin to make into a pub.

Chapter 38

After two unsuccessful attempts at getting on a 707 crew, a new development arose. Peter had been made aware of a 707 that was standing at Denel, the former Atlas Aircraft Company. It had been operating in Kinshasa, had been withdrawn, needing some attention and was possibly up for sale.

The aircraft was the subject of a court case around a labour dispute and had been impounded. He appeared to have some entrée to an operator and the long and short of it was that we could possibly gain access if we got it flying.

We went out to Jan Smuts International Airport, where the Denel personnel would show us the aircraft. From afar things looked promising, but when we got closer it was apparent that the aircraft had been sadly neglected. We climbed in through a hatch behind the nose undercarriage doors, through what was to become a familiar but awkward access, the lower 41.

A Boeing 707 has this very useful feature if no stairs are available. The hatch opens behind the nosewheel and you climb up and onto a ledge. You then squeeze through an area full of electrical components, and again upwards to enter through a hatch in the cockpit floor. Once we were through and had managed to stand erect again, we opened the door into the cabin to be met with a distressing sight.

All we could see was an enormous pile of junk against a backdrop of bare fuselage sides. The structure, normally covered with panels, was decorated by insulation hanging loose among a maze of wiring and piping. On closer inspection the floor was covered with a collection of spares, both old and new. I felt somewhat despondent but Peter brightened me up with the prospect of using the spares to help finance the repairs.

Climbing over them we made our way to the emergency exits over the wings. We opened them and climbed out onto the wing, behind the Denel engineer who explained their concern about corrosion on the wings. He showed us where it was on the wing root, and on the top skin around the rivets. We then climbed aboard and through to the other wing that was not as bad. After leaving Kinshasa she had spent time at the coast with the one wing on the seaward side, explaining the worse state of the one wing. We then locked the aircraft and took our thoughts back with us.

On the way back to Rand, I was a bit disillusioned, but the ever optimistic and inimitable Peter raised my hopes. As always, he was able to see through the doom and gloom to a golden opportunity. He was an amazing person eager to tackle the most daunting of tasks, and he had us as a team eager to support him. I attended a number of meetings around the 707 before we eventually took charge of it.

The day arrived when we were to tow the aircraft to its new temporary home. Peter had arranged to park on the end of a disused taxiway for an undefined period of time. The tug towed us to the spot and we began offloading the spares in earnest. After a brief inspection and listing we packed them into the holds below the deck and we cleaned up a bit and assessed the workload ahead of us. As well as assisting Peter with all the documentation, I was to dress out all the surface corrosion on the wings, prepare and paint them as well as any other painting and sign writing required. We would hire a generator and I would bring my compressor along to handle the spraying and to power the air-driven tools. It was soon clear that this was to become our base for the next few months.

I started working on the wings in the blazing sun and soon realised that it was very tiring, so I armed myself with a large beach umbrella and stand. With it set up on the wing I had some shade to work under and I got stuck in to the task at hand. Day after day, using a drill and abrasive wheel powered by the generator, I dressed out all the corrosion on the rivet heads where the old paint had cracked and flaked away. I had to constantly ensure that the maximum metal removal was not exceeded, and soon there was a definite improvement.

At the end of each day, because we were working outdoors, the raw metal had to be chemically cleaned and painted with an aluminium primer called Alodine. When a large area had been worked on it was then primed and painted. After many days of this ritual, I eventually painted the wing with primer and then grey using the correct specification of Boeing paint. The transformation was wonderful and I got the real satisfaction of a job well done despite the awkward conditions. While I was doing it, the others were engaged in a large belly repair. Corrosion had set in under the air conditioning system and instead of accepting that it was beyond repair, Peter in his usual form had an idea.

The restrictions called for a maximum of two repairs to the underbelly skin, and there were already two. He came up with the idea of replacing the large area including the old repairs and the new corrosion with a single large repair. This necessitated a patch of almost three metres in length, and about one metre wide. While the local experts muttered and looked in their books, Peter sent drawings of his proposed repair directly to Boeing and asked for approval. Much to the surprise of all, except Peter, they replied with an approved repair scheme based on his drawings.

The repair started in earnest and soon the air was alive with an orchestration of air driven power tools driven by my compressor, as well as my electric drill and spray gun. The generator ran all daylight hours supplying the electricity and a whole workshop was in place out in the open. All sorts of aircrew used to walk past us on their way to and from work and used to look at us shaking their heads. At long last we had two beautiful wings and a re-skinned underbelly approved by Boeing and the head shaking by the passing crews decreased.

While the engineers climbed into the aircraft systems. I continued with my painting, this time on the tail and fuselage. Fortunately I only had to repair the paintwork, paint out the old names and do the logo and sign writing. The tail was the biggest job as it was the height of a two-storey building. We hired a mobile crane with a working platform that I could use to access the tail. Commonly known as a 'cherry picker' it was a strange machine that I could even drive around controlling it from the platform two storeys up. I had never used one before and so I quite enjoyed it, and it certainly made the task a pleasure.

Once I had painted out the old logo, I made a template of the huge sail that Peter had as his logo, and then proceeded to transfer it to the tail. I had an ongoing battle with the wind. As soon as I had attached part of my template, and moved along to attach it further along, the whole thing was loosened by the slightest breeze and fell to the ground. I eventually overcome the battle by getting a couple of chaps to stand on the tailplane and hold the template against the tail with long sticks. A bit crude, but soon it was all attached and I finished masking and began spraying. Later on I was able to remove all the tape and paper to reveal my masterpiece, a 3 metre high sailing ship sail, on the fin and rudder. I repeated the huge red sail, with its black outline and shadow, on the opposite side but the elements were not quite as kind to me. By the time I was halfway through the spraying the clouds began to build up. I had already painted enough to be upset by rain and so I had no option but to continue hoping against the odds. It did hold off for quite a bit and the paint was touch dry by the time it rained, but when I checked it the next morning the effect of the water was evident. The surface had been pock marked by the surface tension effect of the water. Luckily enough it was not bad enough to be noticeable, but it upset me nonetheless to know that the blemishes were there.

I then helped out by making templates of the wing root repairs. I took the existing reinforcing plates and then made a new template to include another row of bolts all around, as per the instructions from Boeing. I had a new set of plates made and once they had been fitted with the special bolts, I painted the repair to complete the wing painting. We refitted the fairings between the fuselage and wings, and stood back to view a job well done under trying conditions.

My next task was to repair the fuselage paintwork and replace the old logo. I scraped, sanded, primed and painted all the rough areas and then set about planning the logo. The only place where I could paint a 7 metre long mock up was on the wall in the workshop at Rand. I could then plan out where it would all fit in around the crew and cargo door openings. After hours of masking and painting the striped, three colour letters stood proudly on the front fuselage sides and the painting was over at last.

While I had been busy, all the mechanical repairs had been completed. All the rivetting had been professionally done and the new belly patch looked superb. They had used my high-pressure washer to clean the undercarriage wells and engines and had checked out all the systems. The interior panels were all in place and soon the engine cowlings were fitted to give an incredible transformation to the aircraft. She was now ready for retraction and the other system tests.

Painting the 707

We towed her to Denel Aviation, who had agreed to carry out the tests, much to the astonishment of all the passing sceptics. Their biased view of our rebuild was being challenged and the wind had now been taken out of their sails. In the hangar the aircraft was under cover for the first time in many moons and it all looked a bit strange to us, having got used to seeing her outside for so long. With bated breath we waited for the first power up in years.

To our utter relief and amazement we witnessed a bank of lights come on as the power was applied. The array of instruments got new life as their little indicators began to move about hurredly. The hydraulic pump whined as it hungrily sucked up fresh fluid from its tank and pushed it back into the system. Workers with forklifts positioned huge jacks under the wings and nose, and she began to rise. Soon she was off the ground and we watched the undercarriage fold up, and she looked like she was on a low flypast through the hangar. On the second retraction there was a huge rushing sound and as a jet of dangerous hydraulic fluid shot out from below the right wing, there was a mad dash out of the path of the fluid. One of the pipes in the leading edge flap system had failed but the undercarriage had passed the test. With the jacks removed and again on terra firma, she waited to be taken back to the parking area.

The tow vehicle towed her back and we immediately started on the leak repair and checking for and repairing any other signs of weeping. With the engine cowlings open they were prepared for their first run for years. Soon she was towed up to the freight section and connected to the ground power unit. The fuel bowser arrived and connected its pipes into the fittings on the apron surface. Thick pipes were connected onto the refuelling unit in the wheel bay and the Jet A1 started to flow. I am sure that as it flowed I shared the thoughts of all those who worked in the fuel tanks sealing them by hand with the PRC compound. Would it leak? And all we had were a few moist patches under the wings, I wondered if we would open them up again.

Carrying our heads high we got into the cockpit and Peter energised the systems from the left-hand seat. What an amazing sight as the array of lights and dials came alive for the second time in as many days, and even more so when we heard the whine as the first engine began to turn. We heard the blast as the fuel ignited and it was not long before the other three engines had followed suite. Our eyes wandered back to the engineer and his panel to see that all four vibration meters were on their lower stop. The best news we could have wished for. All the pressures were normal and soon the temperatures settled into a similar routine.

Peter opened all the power levers and we started to move. I felt like a little child with his first big toy. I was so impressed. Without any fuss or problems we taxied to the runup area and stopped. All four engines were soon shouting their reincarnation loudly to the world as we watched the instruments. The vibration meters wavered gently on the bottom stops, better than we could have wished for, and all the temperatures and pressures were normal. With the engines at a gentle idle Pete released the brakes and we started to move back to our parking area. An excited crew disembarked to check the engines for leaks.

Fortunately there were none, which meant that she was ready for a test flight. None too soon, because the pressure was on for the first commercial flight. We were required to take 40 cows and 5 bulls to Rwanda and the aircraft had not flown yet. We waited while Peter did everything to hurry up the paperwork and it was only on the afternoon of the flight that he succeeded. I met the cattle trucks at the entrance to the cargo section and led them to the machine. The loading was easy as they were split up into 13 containers that were loaded by the scissor lift, and soon the crew were preparing to depart.

I was not destined to be on the first flight but I watched with my heart in my throat as she taxied to the threshold. After an effortless run, I was relieved to see the huge bird aloft with its full load on its first flight to Rwanda. With a mixture of pride and sadness at not being on the crew, I drove home with only my thoughts to keep me company.

In due course I got the information that they were on their way back and I went to 'Smuts to see them in. With a wonderful feeling of warmth and well being I saw the telltale, smoky bird come in for a gentle touch down. As she taxied up I could see the grins through the windscreen, a sight to behold. With the stairs in place we went up to meet them, the smiles telling all. Not only had they had a superb flight, but it was a test flight as well and they were returning with only a few minor snags and a promise of a good future ahead.

Chapter 39

I had always had a craving to visit the Antarctic. My visions of the huge white cliffs breaking away, falling with huge splashes into the sea had called me for many years. I could see the seals scurrying away as the blocks of frozen water fell, while others dived off the shelf into the water. Further inland I could see the people who lived under the snow in underground shelters, melting the snow to supply their water. On the surface others were buzzing around on snowmobiles. Little was I to suspect that this vision, after some 40 years in my mind, was to almost become a reality.

The British had put out a request for an aircraft to take supplies and a change of staff down to their Antarctic Base for the new season. The charter group that was affiliated to us had put in a quote that had been accepted and were looking to us to help them make it happen. The concept was easy. They had an Illuyshun 76 that they had been using locally and was earmarked for the job. As its range was insufficient to get there and back we would simply fit long range tanks.

For someone not on the aircraft it was easy, just get us to do the job. Peter then threw the heavy, hot ball into my hands, and as there was no one else around for me to throw it to, I was stuck with it. He explained that it was very simple. All I had to do was fit the bladder tank that came with 707 into the hold of the 76 and connect it into the fuel supply system. Our little petrol driven pump would then pump the fuel into the system as we flew along.

And so to me, his right hand man, who was always called in at the crunch. I went out with Peter to look at the 76, and we stood in the cargo hold looking up into the roof at the rails for the gantry cranes and above them the bulge housing the centre section of the main spar where the wings were attached. Just below that was a spaghetti junction of pipes carrying fuel, air, hydraulics and whatever else flowed. There were a few great couplings on the fuel pipes that seemed an easy target for a refuelling attachment. I was assured that it was an easy job for me, and after three days I would be back from the Antarctic in time for my Veteran Car Rally on the weekend.

The next day I set out for Jan Smuts International Airport with my car trailer full of equipment. I had fished out the rubber fuel tank, and was assured that of course it was leak free. At the freight side I met the IL 76 crew who looked at me, my helper, and the trailer with disbelief. At the aircraft we lifted the roll of rubber onto the cargo floor and laid out the tank for the first time. On inspection it looked good and there was no sign of tears or patches. In the roof I loosened the blank that the crew indicated led into the cross over feed, and was somewhat drenched in fuel. That was to be expected said the Russian crew, who nonetheless had not made any reference to it prior to my drenching. The flanges, with the quick connections that Peter had made up, screwed in to the fittings without any problems and I started connecting up the hoses.

Peter arrived and he helped laying out the tank. We started securing the rungs on the tank to the tie down lugs on the floor with the 9g aircraft straps. As we worked he described how the tank was reinforced so that it would retain its shape provided that it was full. When the fuel was pumped into the aircraft system, the bladder tank should be emptied as soon as possible. He then left me with the 'simple' task of completing the securing and filling the tank.

Somewhat weary of his assurances, I requested the fuel bowser and when he arrived we started pumping 10 000 litres into the tank. As I watched I saw the huge black shape begin to rise and take on a form of its own, and even though it retained its shape, I became somewhat concerned. Firstly, as the shape emerged and I realised how much weight there was I had serious doubts as to the safe restraint of the huge mass. Secondly, the liquid inside moved with a life of its own, as if a hippopotamus was in internal residence. If I prodded it a wave motion would start up. The weight shift that it would cause, as the pilot lifted off, would be incredible, and the centre of mass would go towards the rear. I began to have serious doubts about Peter's assurances.

With all this rushing through my mind, I halted the filling so that I could try to pull a few other ideas out of the hat. An obvious idea was to get a few more tie-down straps and strap them over the bladder. In that way I hoped that with them tight, if the tank was filled they would be very secure and tight against the upper surface. A quick visit to the cargo department to collect some more straps and then back to the aircraft to fit another set. Again the fuel bowser arrived to continue the filling. Even when filled completely, pressing hard against the straps, I did not have enough confidence in the system.

Phone calls to Peter, safely at the office, merely got the reaction that a few more straps would do the trick. By the end of the second day I had got no further. No amount of extra strapping would stabilise the situation and prevent the horrific wave motion. By the end of that day we still not progressed any further. No amount of extra strapping would have any worthwhile stabilising effect on the situation. As soon as one of us sat on the bladder the waves came alive. I agreed to meet at the office the next morning to discuss the position.

At the office I explained the position and suggested that creating some form of exterior boundaries might help. The other problem we had encountered was that the fittings that he had made were not entirely compatible with the Russian fittings. We had fitted them in the roof onto the fuel transfer lines as intended. We then transferred some fuel and as soon as the pipe carried the weight of the fuel, the fittings pulled out and those nearby were all soaked in fuel. This smelly drenching in fact led us to an even better solution. The fuel was not needed until the return trip and so it could be transferred safely on the ground (or rather ice) at Blue One. The extra concern of transferring fuel in flight and flying with a half-filled bladder was no longer a problem.

I was soon on my way back to the airport, now towing the trailer loaded with boards, a life raft that he had secured, and a centrifugal petrol-driven pump. We were now running short of time and would soon have to take off for Cape Town. By lunchtime I had strapped up as much as I could and the bladder was restrained with plywood sides also strapped in place.

Again we carried out tests but no amount of effort and positive thought would help and the problem persisted. Our deadline for leaving Cape Town was looming and so we had to prepare to depart. We transferred the remaining fuel into the aircraft and prepared to go. It was imperative to take off that afternoon for Cape Town and had only one day to work there before embarking on the long journey and we still had no tank.

We took off in the afternoon into a beautiful, clear sky. In spite of my involvement with them at Pietersburg Aviation, it was my first flight in an IL 76, and in fact my first flight in a big, dedicated cargo aircraft. I sat back enjoying the flight and the fact that at least nothing required my attention on the flight, when the Captain summoned me. I clambered up to the cockpit and, as I opened the door was greeted by a sea of stern faces. The captain pointed to an amber light on the panel and explained that it indicated a fuel restriction in one filter, probably caused by fuel contamination. All I could presume was that even though we had flushed out the bladder there must have been a certain amount of sediment remaining that was causing the problem.

By the time we were well into the flight two more lights had come on, indicating that another two filters were blocked so 3 of the 4 filters were blocked. The crew were not very happy and explained to me that the filters would have to be cleaned in an ultrasound bath before the next flight. I felt that a bath would be available at a large airport, and so I agreed. We landed at Cape Town and were met by a taxi that took us straight to the hotel. I explained our time problem and that we would be out after checking in and dinner to continue working. At the hotel I was shown to the most superb room with a wonderful view of Cape Town and the bay. Reluctantly I put down my bags and left the room for a long night's haul. We all met at the dining room as arranged, and took the time to relax over dinner. It seemed that no time at all had passed before it was time to meet the taxi and go back to the airport.

On arrival at the airport, we went to the freight section where the Illuyshun was parked. As always when at an airport at night, one is greeted by the eerie glow put up by all the lights and the sounds of the activity seems to fade into a background hum. The overall effect, as one looks at work being carried out in small, brightly-lit patches, becomes very dramatic and stage-like. But enough of the emotional stuff, and we got down to work.

The tank was empty and so I set about strapping up the whole affair from scratch, using all the straps and the wooden supports that I could. I was able to try to plan where to place strategic straps as opposed to gaily adding more in a rather random manner as we had been doing. By the early hours of the morning I had a veritable spider web of straps going in all directions. I had concentrated on supporting the wooden sides as well as using a cargo net over the whole bladder. I felt that if it did not work then there was no possibility of using the tank without a proper retainer. The more I thought about it I was sure that the bladder was only intended to be used when under restraint in the small cargo hold under the 707's cabin.

By that stage the sky began to glow to announce the arrival of the new day and so we left my huge spider's nest and went back for a wash and breakfast before having to return again. We had to have the strapping finished as we were due to fill up and have an inspection by the client later on in the morning. I left knowing that I had done all that was humanly possible. I was fresh out of ideas and if it did not work I would have to throw up my hands. With Peter not there I had to try to carry the responsibility myself, as unhappy as I was with the safety situation.

We had a revitalising breakfast and I crept up to my room on my tired legs. I calculated that I had two hours to put to good use. As I walked into the room I looked at the inviting bed. It was a strange feeling to look at a perfectly made bed, when it was time to be waking up, and being dog tired having had no sleep the previous night, and little the nights before. I went into the bathroom to freshen up. The loo was the cantilever type fixed to the wall, having no pedestal connection to the floor. Well with a sigh I sat down and relaxed and heard a strange creaking sound. I was trying to identify the sound, when, without any other warning, I was deposited with a crash onto the floor among a few bits of broken china bowl.

The whole bowl had parted company with the wall and it all lay smashed on the floor, with me in the middle. This was the final straw, I could not believe what was happening to me. As I pulled myself together I tried to get my brain working and find a solution. I walked past my inviting bed again and went down to the reception. I explained the events and said that I would return in 30 minutes for a new room so that at least I could get a little rest.

I walked along the street to calm myself down, as if I was on instruments. The events all tumbled through my brain and I began to wonder if it was actually all happening to me. My faith in the hotel was restored as I walked into my new room. I fell into a deep slumber and all too soon my alarm woke me and it was time to go back to the aircraft and meet the client.

I was introduced to the local liaison personnel and the lady who had flown out from the United Kingdom to orchestrate the flight. I outlined the range issue, the fuel situation, and explained how we were trying to cope with it. As we talked the fuel bowser arrived and started to fill the tank. They watched with me as it grew to its full size. I showed them how the bladder was restrained and as I tested it I explained my reservations. A bright idea hit me and I called for a pushback truck to carry out a final test.

When it arrived I carefully explained to the driver that I wanted him to give the aircraft a sharp, rearward jerk to test the tank arrangement without over stressing the nose landing gear. My eager audience, including the captain, arranged themselves around the tank and I gave the order to move.

The tank came alive, a huge wave motion inside the tank appeared to double the height as it got to the end of the tank. In unison all the observers jumped up and grappled for a handhold above them, so effective was the demonstration. I was horrified at how much the tank had deformed despite all my efforts. It reinforced my reluctance to try to take off with such a load on board. All I could visualise was this huge wave moving to the back, as the nose pitched up on take off, carrying our Centre of Gravity with it to beyond safe limits.

At this point I must digress slightly for the lesser technical types. The distance between the centre of gravity (the point where all the weight acts) and the centre of pressure (the point where all the lift forces act) must be within a certain limit so that the flight controls can exert sufficient force to balance it out. If not, the aircraft would be uncontrollable. The backward movement of the fuel in the tank would result in an enormous shift of weight to the back of the aircraft.

My hopes of containing the 'Loch Ness Monster' in the tank were now at an end. Despite every effort, I had to admit defeat, despite all Peter's calls for more straps. The problem was that there was no alternative. The distance was well beyond the most optimistic range of the aircraft and there were no airfields on the way. The onlookers were so distressed by the demonstration that they completely dismissed the idea of using the tank. My thoughts were rambling on. Would I phone Peter? Could there possibly be another alternative? The time constraints required an immediate departure due to the season, food supplies and the fact that a patient had to be evacuated.

Just when the whole exercise was about to be doomed to failure, one of the Antarctic Team spoke up. "We have about 160 drums of jet fuel at the base that could be used." The pearl of wisdom saved the day and I was left to undo all my work while they rushed off to develop their strategy. I managed to get the fuel bowser to accept the fuel back. This was amazing, as it is not normally permitted to return fuel into the bowser to avoid contamination, particularly by bacteria that live in jet fuel.

With the tank and straps neatly rolled up I thought about my next job and I went off looking for an ultrasonic cleaner for the fuel filters. I was sure that I would find one but after some time I realised that I was wrong, none of the maintenance organisations had one. The Russian crew had made it quite clear. No clean filters, no go. Well out of their sight I resorted to the only remaining option, the old-fashioned brush and Jet A1 fuel in a basin. I sat and scrupulously cleaned the four filters in the basin that I had scrounged. When I had finished the last one, with my heart in my mouth I presented the four filters to the Captain. In my mind an engine run would immediately pronounce them good or bad. They clambered up onto the beast and fitted the filters, and soon the engines started. I held my thumbs as the engine hum turned into a crescendo. The engines were shut down and the crew arrived to pronounce them all serviceable. What a relief.

I went to find the Antarctic team, found them in their office and enquired about the current status. They had spoken to Peter, offered him the fuel and everything was again on track. We would uplift the fuel with the petrol driven pump while the offloading took place at Antarctica. This seemed a much safer solution. Being responsible for the fuelling I was still concerned that the fuel was in fact there and was clean and useable. The thought that it was not all there, or contaminated did not even bear consideration. We packed up and went back to the hotel.

I crashed that night and woke early the next day ready to go. It was Saturday and I thought of the Veteran run that I was missing. Jane would still be going and I had invited Uncle Jack and his wife Annie to meet us. I had been looking forward to it for months and was really sorry to be missing the run. If only the drums had been revealed at the onset then we would have been back in time as was originally planned. At the airfield we were met by the Antarctic team who handed us our huge orange thermal suits as promised.

Shortly the passengers and the cargo joined us. They arrived with skis and sleighs as well as all the provisions that they were taking down. I enquired about the sleighs and was told that as well as the relief team, there was a group that would be attempting a crossing of Antarctic on foot, pulling sleighs. We started loading all the goods noting that it would all have to be unloaded under appalling conditions. As the day wore on the departure became more imminent, and soon we all sat on the parachute seats and strapped ourselves in while the engines began to scream.

We taxied out and were soon airborne with a huge sense of anticipation and dread of the unexpected. As we climbed out we all relaxed a bit and I looked out at a beautiful view of Cape Point, the south most tip of Africa, as we headed south. That was the last clear view and my hopes of a visual flight were dashed as we were gradually enveloped in cloud. The 6-hour flight was in and above cloud from the time I saw Cape Point until we were well into the ice world with only one exception.

As we approached Antarctica, while we were still at 37 000feet, we broke through the cloud for a few minutes. It was just time enough for me to take a few shots of the enormous ice floes, broken from the solid ice pack, and to see the icebergs with their one side glowing orange in the setting sun. Soon we were in the cloud again and after another half-hour, or so, we started to descend. The order to buckle up came and we stowed all the loose objects. The passengers who had been sleeping on the floor returned to their seats. The seats are fixed to the fuselage sides facing the cargo area in the centre, which was where they had slept. Behind us the whole width was covered with the cargo and behind that was the huge cargo door.

We all sat facing each other as we waited to break cloud. With the windows above and behind us we could not see outside other than through the window opposite us. We sat in silence as the engine power reduced and the aircraft descended into the icy gloom with its fuselage hissing as it slipped through the air. The stillness was suddenly broken by the harsh sound of all engines at full thrust as the pilot took power. We had expected the hissing to end with a gentle ice landing and our expectations turned to wonder as the cabin floor tilted to the heavens as he aborted the landing and went around.

After the initial surprise we accepted the situation but were still amazed at the way he flew her like a light sport plane. I sat hoping that he was not taking heavy avoiding action to clear icebergs or mountains, but my fear was soon laid to rest. As quickly as the gyrations started they stopped with a rather determined landing on the ice and we were exposed to a new sensation. The whole aircraft shook and juddered as if we were driving an old wreck down a seriously corrugated dirt road. This together with the harsh reverse thrust and a weaving from side to side, was altogether unpleasant, and made little contribution to confidence. Soon it all came to an end as the giant came to a halt and we were all relieved to loosen our seatbelts and stand up.

With the aircraft stationary we flexed our legs and tried to contain our excitement as we all stretched to look out of the windows at the new white world around us. The door was opened and we were greeted by a fairytale world. The landscape (or icescape) was flat for miles, with a few mountains penetrating the otherwise flat vista. There seemed to be little lead up to the mountains and so one had a strange concept of distance. I had already put on my ice suit and prepared to leave the aircraft. The cold, even standing near the open door was intense.

I looked down from the open door and immediately had a visual confirmation of where we were. 'Blue One' was aptly named, as the ice below had a distinctly blue hue. As I climbed down the ladder I was in awe at the colour. The blue ice was scattered with wisps of snow, so that wherever I looked no more than half the ice was covered so that it looked like a huge embroidered mantle had been thrown over the blue sheet of ice by some giant hand.

Wisps of snow blew around, coming to rest up against any stationary object. I looked back to see the runway, not quite knowing what to expect, and to my surprise saw nothing more than a row of plastic bags acting as runway markers, presumably filled with snow. Looking at it all, the reason for the missed approach and subsequent rough landing was evident. The surface of the ice took on the appearance of water, with the surface disturbed by small waves. It was as if the waves on the water had been frozen in mid cycle leaving the surface quite uneven and I'm sure that it was as much a shock to the captain as me when the wheels made contact.

The ice, we were told, was 1 000 metres thick where we stood and was thousands of years old. The thickness and weight of the ice literally forced all the oxygen out of the ice and it was that that gave it its blue colour. As we looked further the large uneven and craggy mountains just looked as if they had been placed on top of the flat surface. Looking back at our landing path the mountains looked too close for comfort, presumably the reason why the pilot chose a go around on his arrival. The optical illusion that it was creating was very disturbing.

I then went about my duties. I met the camp chief who showed me to a pile of snow and said that the fuel drums were in there, much to my consternation. No longer had the thought crossed my mind than I saw a couple of chaps set to with spades to move the pile and reveal the drums. This came as a bit of a shock. The thought of digging fuel drums out of a snowdrift and then refuelling the aircraft was a bit beyond my normal scope.

Fuel in the ice next to the Illuyshin 76

He explained the local rules, stressing that no waste of any sort was to be left on the snow and ice. Everything that we brought with us must go back, with the obvious exception of the supplies intended for consumption there. This included fuel. On no condition was any of the snow or ice to be contaminated by fuel, and if it were we had to remove it as well. All the empty fuel drums must return with us.

He produced an enormous absorbent blanket that I was to use under the drums, pump and connections. By that stage the Russians had taken the pump and fittings out of the hold and were waiting for instructions. We brought the pump onto the mat and began connecting it all up. The one problem that we had not foreseen was that the auxiliary power unit would have to run during the refuelling process to keep the transfer valves open and to prevent freezing of critical components.

I tried in vain to start the pump motor but it would not run. The unit was brand new and had only been used in our tests, but that did not help me get it started. I checked that there was a spark and that the fuel was getting through but to no avail. I was getting into a bit of a panic thinking about how crucial the motor was. Uplifting the fuel was the only way for us to get out and back to Cape Town. I thought about the thousands of litres of fuel that we had pumped in Angola, without a single falter. The prospect of hand refuelling on top of the wing was not even worthy of consideration as we had no means of lifting the drums and the risk of contamination was too high.

Obviously, seeing my predicament the camp chief came over to enquire about the cause of my distress. I asked him if there was a chance that there was a pump around. He said that he would enquire, as there was a Twin Otter that came in from time to time.

He invited me to climb on the back of his snowmobile and we set off for the camp. The ride was quite an education. Instead of the smooth feeling that you would expect, thinking of skiing, it is terribly rough. It feels like what you would expect if you rode a big motorbike at full speed on flat tyres. Every little undulation in the ice is transformed to a jolt through your whole body.

We arrived at the camp and I was amazed at the lack of amenities. It was only a service facility for the comings and goings at the airstrip and not a full size camp. Apparently the Twin Otter was quite active in running supplies around the area, sometimes refuelling there. My host produced a pump as if drawn from a hat. We loaded it on a sleigh, which we towed back behind the snowmobile. Back at the aircraft we offloaded it onto the fuel mat and held thumbs. I coupled up the hoses again and, with my heart in my throat, set the engine controls, and pulled the starting cord. In answer to all my hopes and prayers, the engine coughed into life and soon a steady stream of jet A1 was flowing into the '76.

My initial optimism soon took a bit of a tumble when I looked at some figures. Even though we were pumping continually at the maximum potential, it seemed to take forever to empty each drum. It would take in excess of 10 hours to pump the 150 drums into the aircraft. As we changed drums there was some spillage and soon my shoes and gloved hands were soaked through. My wet gloves and shoes no longer insulated me and the cold was getting right through them. Every 15 to 20 minutes I had to retreat into the aircraft so that I could take them off and massage my feet with my hands in an attempt at getting the blood to flow again and thus avoiding the dreaded frostbite. The wet material acted as a conductor. I would probably have been better off if they were soaked with water as the temperature would probably not got much below 0 degrees Celsius. As it was the fuel froze well below zero and so the temperature of my extremities plummeted.

This routine carried on all night and I monitored our progress on a continual basis. As I worked I watched with keen interest as the sun just slightly lowered its place in the sky as the night progressed. It was quite an honour and pleasure to watch the sky change into its midnight hue and colour, something you always read about but few people get to see. At midnight I took a picture. The clean air offered super visibility as the sky turned to a reddish hue. Even at midnight there was no need for artificial light, and it was September, not even mid summer.

By the time early morning was approaching it became obvious that I was running into a time problem. We intended to take off before midday and even though I was bettering my 10 drums per hour, I was literally losing one drum of fuel every hour to the auxiliary power unit that was burning 200 litres per hour just keeping the transfer open.

I consulted the crew who agreed that an uplift of 138 drums would be acceptable, as it would mean that we could take off an hour earlier and get back to Cape Town before sunset. I guess they felt that a daylight arrival would have less chance of time delays incurring extra flight time. With that as the revised plan I returned to my assistants and the refuelling. As I watched the sun get a bit stronger as 'day' broke, a weariness in my body began to emerge. The cold and tiredness of my muscles and bones was beginning to win and the sky lightening up made me aware that we had been working right through the 'night', broken only by regularly going into the aircraft to unfreeze my extremities.

As I was doing my stuff, I saw somebody getting ready to go on a snowmobile to do a check of the runway with one of our guys on the back. I called to him to take my video camera along with him, as I could not go myself. With longing I watched the two heavily clad figures disappear in a snow haze. I longed to give up the pumping and go for a ride myself, but I had my duties and I had been for a snow drive to the camp the previous day. I watched as they went tearing up the strip along the row of snow-filled black bags. Again I was amazed at the mountains that seemed to be on top of us.

Two of the Russians had decided to walk to the mountain despite the residents trying to dissuade them. I had been unaware of their journey until I noticed people staring into the distance. I enquired and was told that they had left some hours earlier and were now just visible on their return. As I peered I could see the two distant figures between the mountain and us. It gave the distance some perspective and only then could you understand how far away they were. The sight and sound of the snowmobile tearing up the runway also probably hurried them up. The two chaps returned from their runway inspection with a good amount of footage on my camera, and a huge grin on the passenger's face. The foot weary Russians arrived back sometime later with a few rocks to prove that they achieved their goal.

As we approached our last drum they started loading up all the empty drums and tidying up. Once the fuelling was complete I started to disconnect it all and load the remaining equipment on board. With great thanks and relief I returned the loaned pump and fuel mat and we all got ready to depart. As much as I had dreamed about a visit to the Antarctic I had now had enough and was ready to get aboard. Sadly I had not witnessed my visions of large chunks of ice breaking free while the seals frolicked around, but at least I was one of the few privileged to have been so far south.

The flying crew had spent the night sleeping and so, unlike us, were fresh and ready to go. I waited to see if the aircraft had settled into the ice and whether the snow blown up against the wheels would be a hindrance, but my fears were unfounded. Once the engines were running only a little extra power was required to get us moving towards the runway. After an uneventful takeoff we climbed out leaving the white wonderland behind us and we settled in to the flight home. As on the trip down, as soon as we had some height, the cloud prevented any further views of the landscape below. The bad news was that not only had the Russian crew taken the opportunity to rest, but they had also eaten almost all the food for the return trip. Those of us that had been working were as mad as snakes. All we had been looking forward to was a snack on the way back and I could not believe that they had opened the dedicated return trip food box without asking. It had been reduced to an assortment of scraps. With little choice, but an appetite worthy of eating the proverbial horse, I picked at a few bits before dozing off to a well-earned rest.

Some time later I woke, somewhat refreshed, and took an interest in the trip ahead. I had not even registered that the patient that we were evacuating was aboard; it showed just how tired I must have been. He sat rather quietly next to the doctor sent to accompany us. There were only a few passengers this time and, as before, most of them lay on the floor sleeping. By the time that we were two hours away from Cape Town, the captain was regretting his decision to only uplift 138 drums. He was having second thoughts about his fuel load and called for me to confirm that 138 drums had indeed been loaded. I confirmed it and mentioned that the confirmation was that all the empties were behind us in the hold. From then on we both took a lot more interest in our progress and fuel consumption, although he did not power back to get a slightly better range, as I would have expected.

With glee I looked out the window some time later to see Cape Horn slip gently beneath us. At least we were over land. By that stage the captain was taking serious strain as some of the low fuel warnings were showing and by the time we had the airport visual all four low fuel warnings were glowing unhappily. Relief came as we were given clearance for a straight approach. We had no excess fuel for a circuit, and all I wished for was an unobstructed landing. The feeling of relief, as those multiple wheels touched the tarmac, was a wonderful, secure feeling. We were safe, we were home, and all that remained was to taxi in and park.

The relief at it all being successfully over was tangible and we needed to paint the town red in celebration. We went to a restaurant on the Waterfront for a slap up meal. I can't remember why, but the meal was on me, to be reimbursed later. We enjoyed a super meal punctuated periodically by the Russians calling for vodka. We soon finished the restaurant's own supply, and the waitresses were getting what they could from surrounding venues. Suffice to say that the ten of us (8 Russian crew and 2 South Africans who were not vodka drinkers) went through 8 bottles that night. What a relief to have it all behind us!!!

The vodka ran out and so did our red paint and so we crept off to bed for the most wonderful night's rest. The next day the crew amazingly had survived the onslaught on their livers and we were wending our way back to the Reef with memories and undeveloped film to take home. That was not all, we had the intense satisfaction of a job well done, probably being the first large jet to land there, and I had two small pieces of rock to give my sons.

In the final analysis the books were not as happy as we, the workers were. We had done the job well but the management, on negotiating the uplift of the fuel had not discussed price before we left and it seemed that all the profit was eaten up in the price of the drums as they were required to pay the delivery to the Antarctic as well!!!! Needless to say there went my promise of 800 US Dollars that I had been allocated for the job.

Chapter 40

By this stage most of the labour intensive work on the 707 had been completed and I was again spending most of my time back at Rand Airport. Even though it was quite a way from Jan Smuts International Airport, where the 707 was kept, it was a very convenient and cost effective base. The 707 operation was using the offices in the front section of Peter's premises where the Cubs were being built. We had a library set up an area where all the 707 paperwork and manuals were kept as well as a central office area that would be used for planning and administrative work as soon as we got flying. In addition the Cub workshop was there to support any of our manufacturing needs.

After the first flight with the cattle everybody was very involved in all the paperwork and final touches to the 707 in preparation for other flights. It would be some time before the 707 would be in full operation and actively flying so I was looking for something to keep me going and put some bread on the table in the interim, while I could still keep in touch with the 707. While we had all been busy with the repair project, one of our fellow operators at Rand had shown a keen interest in us. He was operating two Hawker Siddley 748 turboprop aircraft and had another one to be completed. He had shown so much interest in our operation that he even hinted at getting involved with us on some sort of a cargo basis. As luck would have it, he was looking for someone to manage his maintenance operation at Rand and finish off the remaining aircraft.

I was very keen on getting involved, particularly because of the fact that when the time came I could continue to fly the 707 without a conflict of interests if he was involved with us.

This was a blessing and I was taken on as a contractor on an hourly basis, to supervise and co-ordinate all the maintenance activities of his Approved Maintenance Organisation as well as his flight operations. Like a kid with a new toy I moved in to my office in their hangar. I was going to be in the heart of all the action as well as a short walk to Peter's set-up and the conditions and understanding of my hourly contract allowed me to continue my association with him. I walked into the hangar, and there were the two HS 748's proudly bearing the South African flag on their tails. Hiding in the back of the hangar was the other 748 awaiting completion. She would still need a good few months' work before even thinking about a test flight.

This was all very new and a real challenge to me, particularly the idea of dealing with a passenger service with up to 40 passengers on a flight. I knew that the challenge was well within my capability and so I set to it with gusto and enthusiasm. I had soon isolated some recurring problems and implemented some solutions, and while the other aircraft were out flying I used all the time to get number 3 in the air. The last aircraft had a large cargo door and so was even closer to my heart. It was so convenient and stimulating to have a project to make use of the slack time that otherwise would be lost.

Nearing the end of getting it in the air we were required to do a flight test for DCA. A local contractor had replaced the original aircraft windows and they requested a pressurisation flight test before they would accept the new windows. On the appointed day the aircraft taxied out for the pressurisation test with a load of DCA inspectors on board. I remember wondering why they wanted to be on board, sitting next to the very windows that they hesitated to accept. Anyway the flight went well and the pilots were able to demonstrate the maximum pressure differential without a problem. Shortly thereafter I had the third aircraft on stream and by that stage we were flying steadily and I had my hands full, but enjoying all the stimulation and challenges.

I was getting into new areas like flight data recorders. Commonly referred to as the 'black boxes', they are in fact painted orange or yellow for easy visibility. A major problem was that our boxes were not the same type as others in use in this country, and as a result they were being hand carried to the UK for transcribing. This meant that the aircraft was not useable while its data recorder was away being processed. The requirement was that they are transcribed on a three-monthly basis and it had a large effect on our aircraft availability. I considered this tedious process a huge waste of resources and so I started to look for a solution. Faced with protests from all sides, I persevered in spite of being told categorically that no organisation in the country could interpret them. My nature was that I had to try myself to get them transcribed; I would not take a blanket 'NO' as an answer.

I contacted the chap at Jan Smuts that we got the PRC tank sealer compound through, and asked his advice and if he knew who dealt with such matters. I was given a contact who transcribed the Airways recorders and was soon on the telephone to him. As opposed to the views of the critics, he was very helpful and was prepared to give it a try. One of the aircraft was not due to fly for the next few days and so I seized the opportunity and was soon walking into his laboratory with the long, bright orange box in my hand. After some time juggling with fittings, and a lot of lateral thinking the data had been transferred to his reading bench and I returned to Rand with the data recorder and the aircraft was again serviceable. All that was then required was to identify all the traces on the printouts, rather like an ECG printout that the doctor gives you, except with three times as many traces.

A couple of days later I walked in to the office with a grin on my face, a printout from the data recorder, and a bill for a meagre R2 000-00, compared with a trip to the UK and three days hotel bills. A letter to the manufacturers soon confirmed our identification of all the traces, and I had won against all the odds of the sceptics.

Almost weekly I had similar challenges and was continually trying to find easy solutions to rather complex problems. The job was very satisfying and I felt that life was a real challenge. During my time there with all three flying we even took over a daily scheduled passenger flight to Swaziland. This was a real challenge. The word 'NO' could not be used no matter how difficult the problem, the schedule had to go on. During this period the other two aircraft had a number of charters booked as well and it was not uncommon to have all three away at a time, and I had a very tight ship to run.

Often on the weekends, I had to meet charter flights and so I would use the Stinson to go and meet them. On one very special occasion all three were departing from Lanseria together and I flew across with my son, Courtney in the Stinson to despatch them. I had pre-arranged for the pilots to park them together so that I could take a picture. I had a super feeling of pride as I flew in with Patrick at my side and taxied past them to park. We took some photographs and chatted with the crews on board as we waited for the passengers to come out of the terminal building.

In due course they started arriving and we moved on top of a bank to watch. They all filed past us, split up into three groups and began boarding. We sat on the bank watching the passengers being welcomed by the cabin crew and waited for them to depart. I was very proud as I watched all three start up and taxi out in order. We watched all three take off, the first one taking off above the last one as they taxied along.

On another occasion I was meeting an incoming flight at Lanseria. I was hoping to get a good in-flight picture and so I liased with the pilot before we took off and tried to catch up with it before we got to Rand. I rather battled to catch him and, not being used to formation flying, he would not have thought to slow down a bit. I did manage to get a couple of pictures but they were not as good as I had hoped for.

The three HS 748's at Lanseria

On yet another occasion I went with one of our pilots, an instructor, to collect an aircraft from Jan Smuts. He had been doing our training for us and had seen how busy I was, never able to do any flying on the 748's myself and so he insisted that I went with him. I flew the aircraft all the way from the take off to the landing at Rand Airport. She was a beauty to fly, being amazingly responsive and light on the controls. We were directed in to runway 29 at Rand.

The approach on this runway is very close to the approach at Smuts and I was being very careful not to encroach on their airspace. I was honoured and amazed at his trust in letting me do the landing on my first flight in a 748. As soon as I turned onto my final approach I realised that I had a bit of a time problem. The runway loomed right in front of me and I was battling to get the approach correct. Suffice to say that I had been forced to deviate from a cardinal rule, "a good landing seldom comes from a poor approach". As expected, my touchdown was acceptable but not pretty, a pity as it was the one and only time that I was able to fly it before the 707 came on stream.

He and I went to the café for a bite and true to form a number of our friends were there to witness a none-too-perfect landing. They all laid into the poor chap saying that it was below his normal standards. Sheepishly I had to admit to being the 'driver' at the time, which was welcomed by a certain amount of mirth. It just proves the point that a good landing is seldom seen by others, but a shabby one is seen by all!!

My time with the 748's was a very special time. The three aircraft were solely my responsibility with the exception of the aircrew. I was proud, particularly whenever I saw all three together. While I was with them I was also keeping a keen eye on the 707 operation and also had my little Cessna 150 in the hangar. I had bought it to initially train my two sons and to eventually form a syndicate for other pilots who had children wanting to learn to fly. My dear Uncle Jack was training them and so for a period of some months in my immediate vicinity I had the 748's, the 707 head office and my son's flying school, it was super.

Chapter 41

After the 707 had come back from the flight with the cattle the farmers vowed that there were many more in the offing but despite many meetings and effort on our part it fell flat and no other cattle flights came up. In the meantime Peter's other hope was with the North African flights. As mentioned earlier, he had to subcontract the first flight and he battled to secure the second one but lost it in the end. On the third attempt he succeeded and with big grins we planned to depart from Waterkloof Airforce Base as arranged by the client.

Peter and crew flew her the short hop to the base and started loading while I was still working with the 748's at Rand. I met them later to prepare for the departure. The atmosphere in the early evening was stimulating. Vehicles were moving all over the airfield and the whole apron was under spotlights giving a real ethereal look. A little further along the apron was a Galaxy. This and the Antonov 124 were competing for the largest cargo aircraft ever built and it was quite a sight to see it dwarfing our 707. As well as the freight there were 12 of our client's employees who were to accompany the flight and so extra seats were fitted in the front of the hold, just behind the cockpit. We cleared customs and immigration in the terminal building and then all prepared to board.

This was my first non-training flight in the 707 and so, as the third pilot, I had to look after all the passengers and their needs. Trying to look like I had been doing it forever, I loaded and secured their bags and showed them aboard. I explained the seating arrangement and that once we were at our cruising altitude they could loosen their straps and use the sleeping bags that we had provided. There was a clear area behind their seats that they could use to lay out the sleeping bags. During the flight I would alert them if the need to get back into their seats arose. I showed them the hot water, tea and coffee arrangements and the cupboard where plates of snacks were waiting for them.

All the vehicles moved away and as we prepared to start I settled back in my seat behind the captain. I wondered what our passengers were thinking at that particular moment. They all came from a technical aircraft environment, and so were not too phased by our operation (or at least so it looked) but I was very aware that they were probably watching our every move, and in some instances perhaps knew more than we did. I was sure that a few probably suspected how new we were. We were parked so that we could start and taxi without a pushback, and I waited in anticipation.

Soon the boring drone of the ground power unit was replaced by the whine of the jet engines and everything in the cockpit came alive. I felt part of the whole machine as the whine increased, the brakes were released and we started to taxi. I will never forget waiting for the great moment marking the start of this new great venture. Unlike the cattle flight, this contract had the promise of longevity and success, if we could just get it right. All our combined will and effort seemed to gel at that very moment. The unique aroma that jet freighters seem to get over the years completed the atmosphere.

In large aircraft, the crew sits virtually on top of the nose undercarriage leg. It results in a strange feeling because the whole nose moves sideways when the aircraft turns. I was particularly aware of it as we turned with the bogie almost at full lock, and lined the aircraft up for the take off roll. Then came the dropping sensation as the front suspension leg compressed as the brakes came were applied. With a clear runway ahead the engine noise rose to a crescendo, the brakes were released, the cockpit lifted as the nose gear extended and we were rolling. Freight operations tend to operate at maximum aircraft potential and are therefore generally fairly close to the safe side of the load limits.

The takeoffs are invariably interesting and this was no different. I looked forward as we rolled down the brightly lit runway. In front of me two pilots concentrated on the darkness ahead and as I looked sideways I could see the runway lights flashing past, getting faster and faster. In the distance the hangar lights moved past much more sedately until they were no longer visible. The nosewheel soon lifted off the runway and the wings began to get a grip on the atmosphere. The runway lights changed colour from the whitish yellow to red showing us that the end of the runway was approaching, and as the pilots arms gave the final pull, we were no longer on the ground and the engines screamed as they clawed for more air.

I knew we were airborne but it seemed to be by mere inches. The clunk of the undercarriage confirmed that the wheels were settled in their bays, and we continued as the speed gradually increased. Within a short time the flaps had been raised a few notches and we started climbing steadily as we headed northwards. My previous flight in a 707 had been a light training flight, and I could feel the relief through the crew as the climb stabilised. In jet terminology I had seen reference to the term 'sterile cockpit below 10 000 feet' and the need really sank in for the first time. The crew needed the few minutes to climb the 5 000 feet before they dared relax into casual chat.

I got up, opened the cockpit door and went to see all the passengers. They were all happy and I suggested that they could either have some snacks, remain seated, or retire for the night if they so wished. We laid out the sleeping bags and soon the majority were in a group on the floor and off to the land of nod. I made some tea and coffee and returned to the cockpit with some for the crew, sat down looking forward to the practical side of the flight and particularly my duty as third pilot. On long flights it is mandatory to carry a third pilot to spread the duty cycle and that was my opening. A pilot may not fly more than eight hours in any 24 without a relief pilot

I was sitting in the 'jump' seat, behind the captain and alongside the flight engineer at his impressive panel. Monitoring the flight from that position was very useful, as I was constantly able to see the relationship and the actions of the crewmembers. The flight engineers panel is mounted on the right side of the fuselage and so he faced sideways when attending to the panel. He just has to glance over his left shoulder to interface with the pilots. The seat is also mounted on a swivel so that he can rotate it and face forwards with the thrust levers in front of him for take off and landing.

Drinking our warm beverages I watched the crew's every move. I was not used to such a long night flight and the prospects had my senses at a peak. In due course I was called up to relieve the co-pilot and with joy and pride I got into the seat and strapped myself in. The extreme level of quietness was a new experience. The gentle hiss combined with the eeriness of the night flight gave me an entirely new feeling that contrasted sharply against the steady drone of the DC4.

The checkpoints came rushing up at an amazing rate and we were swallowing up the miles. Cruising at the specified cruise of MACH 0.82 (i.e. 82 per cent of the speed of sound), we were moving along at over 990km per hour. The cockpit was as comfortable as the DC4 with an equal amount of space and the controls were equally well positioned. The control inputs, particularly at that speed demanded careful thought and planning to avoid the usual porpoising all over the sky. Just to aggravate the shortcomings of the rookie pilot, a buzzer sounds if you deviate from the altitude set on the altimeter by 100 feet. Believe you me, at that speed it is an absolute mission and soon the buzzer sounds soliciting a barrage of comments about your flying ability. I almost felt that not having a working automatic pilot was intended for rookies like me.

The feeling of speed decreased as we gained height and by the time that we were at cruising altitude it was replaced by a vista of minute settlements of light far below. Referring to the map I realised that they were large towns, but at that height they looked like small groups of glowing ashes that had been dropped from above. They gently slipped beneath us as we progressed northwards and the GPS indicated our steady progress as the night grew older.

We flew steadily on until the sky started to grow lighter announcing the coming of the next day. We had noticed a distinct difference in the embers below us. The lights were no longer as closely grouped as they had been, but far fewer in number and spread out over larger areas. As we had taken off at night we had not yet seen the horizon, but in time its arrival was announced by an orange glow in the sky. Flying north I had the privileged view out of my side window. Flying at over 35 000 feet the curvature of the earth was clearly visible. The glow behind the curved horizon looked as if the dawn was emerging from a huge egg, lightening as it developed in age.

The view was beyond my descriptive ability, save to say that it was magnificent. The clarity and purity of the rarefied atmosphere enhanced the colours to new proportions. As the day developed I could look below to see a sight new to me. We were flying over a yellow, arid, flat earth and before the lights disappeared we could see that they came from larger informal gatherings. The formal towns and cities were not there any more. As time progressed the yellow sand turned into the pure desert that I had only seen in pictures. On my right a very craggy mountain range started to appear. It seemed to be made up of tortuous shapes planted in the yellow sand. They reminded me of the mountains that I had seen in the Antarctic. In both cases they seemed to be incongruous on the flat landscape.

I was relieved of my long night vigil and took a walk to the cargo deck to stretch my legs. Our passengers were still taking life easy and so I left them snoring and returned to the jump seat. Being on the left side I no longer had the full force of early morning sun streaming in at me, and I looked at the desert below. After some time I noticed a long, straight line on the left and below us. I gazed at it for some time trying to figure out what it was. It was far too long for any kind of road, and it ended in the middle of nowhere. Only then did the penny drop. I realised that it was in fact the shadow of our contrails (moisture condensation trails).

With less than an hour of our flight left it was time to contact the Approach Control. We had been in a dead area where we could not communicate by radio and could not reach them earlier for clearance to descend. With communication established we were given the clearance, the thrust was reduced and we started the descent. Peter explained that things would get hectic due to our steep angle. We would be approaching fast and the situation would develop rapidly. He was quite correct and I watched the descent turn into the approach pattern and we were soon on the ground on this airfield in the middle of the desert, only hundreds of miles from Europe.

Once the aircraft had come to a halt we opened the door and a blast of furnace air hit us in the face. The dry heat was indescribable. I looked across the runway to a normal looking control tower and passenger area, and on the ground below a series of vehicles and forklift trucks arrived. One of them drew a staircase behind it, which I guided into position from the open doorway. An immigration chap came aboard and checked our papers while other people went into the cargo compartment, checking the boxes.

With the huge cargo door open and stretching to the sky, we started to offload. Unlike the DC 4, the 707 has a roller and palette system so that the palette with its load securely strapped to it is offloaded as a unit. That was very well in theory but with them 3 metres wide and only an old forklift to lower them to the ground the fun started. The first few boxes were gently lifted off the palette by the forklift. As I watched them wobble as they neared the tarmac my mind raced to find a more suitable solution before we had a valuable, broken box to explain away.

As is so often the case, the simplest solution was the best. I arranged one of us to stand on either side of the cargo opening with the cargo straps attached to either side of the load. That way we were able to keep a positive restraint on the sides of the load and prevent it wobbling. Obviously we would not be able to hold the load if it did overbalance, but the idea was to support it and prevent the potential disaster before it happened. The sight of a forklift with a load far wider than the truck's greatest dimension, held meters in the air was not a sight for the feint hearted. The strap idea worked a treat and soon the cargo was all on the ground, being loaded and carted away on the vehicles.

As if the 9-hour flight through the night was not enough the offloading in the heat just drained us and we did not need a second invitation to get us into the waiting bus. We drove out of the airport to the hotel and I was amazed at the palm trees around. The town itself was in the middle of an oasis. Getting into the built up area I became aware that most of the sand-coloured buildings seemed to be incomplete. A forest of steel rods stretched into the sky from each of the buildings. Later on I learned that the reason was simple. Full levies were only payable on complete buildings; as a result few of them were ever completed and just left with the re-inforcing rods poking out to confirm the lack of completion.

The surroundings changed from residential blocks to a shopping area and the density of palm trees decreased. The streets were still populated by the standard transport item, agricultural rotivators and trailers. They are normally used for tilling and ploughing smallholdings and are operated and guided with the two levers, one each side. They also had trailers as an extra and with them attached it was possible to sit on the trailer and 'steer' the contraption with the two long handles. This for some reason appeared to be the single, most prolific means of transport in the area.

We drove into an area enclosing a typical sand-coloured building, the military hotel and carried our bags into the foyer. The promise of our beds took over and without taking too much notice of our surroundings we collapsed into our rooms.

Somewhat refreshed, we met in the dining room a couple of hours later to find out what was happening next. Dinner was served in a strange manner. There appeared to be no way of finding out what was being served, and it just arrived on a trolley. I did not know what it was but it was edible in any event. No sooner had I finished than the trolley reappeared laden with another course, which was served up in front of us. By that stage I had almost met my Waterloo but to keep face I slowly ate some of it. Soon, to my amazement another load arrived and despite my protests I was served with a plate. Having a hatred of waste but still unable to eat any more I had to send back another dirty plate.

That night we simply died as we hit the pillows to arise the next day faced with loading all the empty containers for the trip home. After breakfast we left in the bus for the airport, passing all the rotivator transport, through the open fronted shop area, the residential incomplete buildings and up to the aircraft. The loading went smoothly as the empty containers were so light and soon we were taken to the hangars for a bite of lunch. I opted for a large appetising hamburger that I was offered while the rest of the crew registered a measure of mistrust at its origins. Anyway it soon disappeared to keep me fuelled until the next meal.

We were towed across to refuel and I went off with Peter to settle the landing fees and parking. Amazing as it is in Africa. All the fees are quoted in US Dollars but they never have any small denomination notes. Fortunately knowing that, I always collect small notes for these occasions and soon we were off with the bill paid and the flight plan filed. We were parched and realised the amount of water we needed to consume, but after so much you just can't drink any more. I found some orange juice in the transit shop and bought a few bottles. It was very strong and so liberally diluted with water it made a new taste to keep us from dehydrating. Back at the aircraft the refuelling was complete and soon we were ready to depart.

The relatively light aircraft flew and climbed like an angel, the returning passengers were all content sitting in the seats in the cargo compartment, and the flight deck was all smiles. We had just successfully completed our first long flight, and all the systems operated as expected. We took turns flying and as night came down we saw the horizon stolen by the setting sun as it set. Again we were aware of the glowing lights below as we used them to keep our distance vision.

When a person's eyes do not focus on a distant object the muscles relax and the eye does not focus. The chance then exists that they do not see something important outside. To stop it happening the skill is look at distant objects to keep your eyes active in the darkness that envelops you. The night continued with us changing positions and monitoring the flight progress and as it drew on to the early hours my system became a little uncomfortable. I had no option but to ignore it until something happened and so we carried on.

By the time we had started our descent for Waterkloof Airforce Base I was uncomfortable to say the least and could not wait to be on the ground. We landed and entered the terminal building where we cleared immigration and customs. The previous day's hamburger called me out of the queue and guided me to other service areas. Once we had all cleared I bad them farewell and headed back to the Intensive Air offices to put in a full day's work while the rest of the crew went home to study the inside of their eyelids.

The next few flights were virtually identical except that the organisation was becoming more difficult and so Peter had gone back to his favourite Pietersburg. The huge hangar had long been leased but Peter was able to obtain a much smaller one that he could use to store the cargo before departure. This worked out quite well as it meant that the cargo could be delivered at the client's convenience and inspected by the customs before loading.

This established a standard for the next few flights. I would leave the office at Rand, rush home to change and have a quick dinner. After that I went to the client's offices in Midrand to collect a Kombi and the 15 passengers. I would endeavour to leave at around 21h00 to arrive in Pietersburg at 23h30. That would leave enough time to do the last preparations before the midnight departure.

The night flights followed the same wonderful, peaceful format with only a few unusual or outstanding memories. The flight most times was punctuated by passing through the Intertropical Convergence Zone. It is the area where the Northern and Southern Hemisphere weather patterns meet. Each time, as we neared the equator we would be aware of the increased turbulence level. Most of the time the weather was clear and we could see the stars. On one particular occasion I was flying as we approached the area and the weather conditions were a bit poor. Without weather radar and in the dead of night, we could not see the conditions. Aware of the dangers of thunderclouds I kept a good watch outside, and as time progressed we encountered a fair amount of lightening. I sat in the right seat peering through the windscreen looking at the clouds as the lightening bolts illuminated them. Soon the area ahead was split into three and there were three pairs of eyes monitoring the cloud formations. We would all make a mental note of each cloud as it was illuminated, and when all three heads were put together, I was able to negotiate my way through them safely.

On another flight I had a super view of St Elmo's Fire. It is the name given to the display made by an electrostatic discharge that travels around the outside of a moving aircraft. On that particular occasion, the only time that I was fortunate enough to see the phenomenon, it travelled swiftly around the perimeter of the windscreen in front of me. The bright blue flame looked incredibly dramatic as it leapt about in the darkness. If one did not know what it was I'm sure it would it would be taken as an actual fire. In the dead of night it left me in awe as we serenely flew through the atmosphere and thankful at having experienced the phenomenon.

In time we approached Pietersburg at the end of another successful flight and all that was left after we cleared customs and immigration was the tiring drive back to Johannesburg until the next flight.

Chapter 42

On about our third return flight from Algeria, we had taken off and were about 20 minutes out when a most amazing noise started on the cargo deck. I was not flying at the time and so I went back to investigate, and to my horror found that it was coming from the huge cargo door. I went forward and told Peter that the noise was due to the door seal leaking, either because it was damaged or because the door was not properly closed. I sat in the jump seat and waited. I had heard so many horrific stories about doors on pressurised aircraft that I was somewhat concerned.

As I watched I saw the engineer lower the cabin altitude and the noise worsened. I tried to explain to him that by lowering it the pressure in the cabin was increasing and making the leak and the resulting noise worse. We were all pilots and all the passengers were involved with aircraft, were healthy types, and were all used to flying. I therefore felt that we could easily increase the cabin altitude from the normal 8000 to 10000 feet to decrease the leakage flow through the door seal. I could not get him to understand my reasoning, and so I had to explain all my fears and thoughts to the captain, Peter.

I explained that that my main concern was about the secure latching of the door. Before we started up, the cargo door had been open after the stairs had been moved away, and so we were not able to carry out the usual locking check from the ground. We had been having the usual problems with the ground start unit and I had been up and down the hatch in the front wheel well to communicate with the starting unit. I was worried that either the door had not been securely latched or there may have been some damage from a forklift truck contacting the doorframe. Either way I was concerned about the possibility of the door opening in flight, with the resulting horrific consequences. In any event we had a problem, being unable to reach our intended cruise height, we had insufficient range to get home.

After some persuasion they all agreed with my fears and we diverted to an airfield that we had observed on the journey north. After a routine approach, we landed, taxied to the apron and parked the aircraft. An inspection of the open cargo door revealed no sign of damage other than a faulty seal. The local authorities came aboard and proceeded to demand a sum of three thousand dollars per person on the aircraft. With four crew and all our passengers it was obviously ludicrous, but as hard as we tried to reason, we failed to convince our French-speaking hosts.

Just before frustration took complete hold of us, one of our French passengers came to our rescue. Soon, supported by his language and a few telephone calls, he had reached an amiable, although still expensive compromise. Without sufficient funds left over I, as the unofficial bursar, had to do a whip around the crew and then the passengers to collect sufficient stray dollars to pay our way out.

Having lost a good few hours with the goings on and negotiations we then carefully monitored the cargo door closing and prepared to depart. Peter gave us a thorough briefing on how to pack wet cloths around the door opening. As the moisture is driven through the broken seal by the cabin pressure, it freezes due to the low outside air temperature and the ice formed seals the leak. I thought this was an obvious and ingenious way to create a temporary fix, and was keen to see it in operation.

I did not have to wait long because I was assigned to the task. Soon I was sitting at the leaking door with a collection of cloths and a receptacle of water applying the wet rags to the leaking seal. I was not sure whether it was because I was capable, reliable or just expendable, but there I was and soon the leak stopped. After some time it was clear that the seal would continue to hold and I returned to the cockpit to pronounce that the temporary repair was a success and that all was well.

The rest of the flight was uninterrupted, although I'm sure that we were all very aware of the hazard and we landed very relieved. The problem was soon cured with a new seal and our great 707 was again eager to fly again.

Another humorous occasion was on another of the early flights when we were approaching Waterkloof Airforce Base. At that particular time there was no radar approach to guide us in and so we were approaching on radio aids and GPS. As we broke cloud we were probably at just above 1000 feet and the lights of Pretoria blinded us all as the whole world suddenly lit up. I was in the right seat with Peter flying and he opted to go around to do another approach to let his eyes get accustomed to the sudden illumination below the cloud. We continued and landed in the normal way. The humorous side came some time later when I met a chap and we were talking 707's. "You will never guess what happened early the other day", he said "I had to leave very early one day and as I drove along I saw this 707 with a huge red sail on the tail pop out of the clouds and go to Waterkloof. He took power on short finals and went around for another landing, it was very impressive." I had to sheepishly admit that it had in fact been us and told him the story.

On another unique occasion we had got the cargo offloaded, the aircraft secured up for the night and we waited for the transport to the hotel. We boarded the bus and as we drove along a Canadian fellow on contract was telling us about one of the local beliefs or myths. Their folklore led them to believe that a major climatic disaster was decreed to come about every decade. It was the end of 1999, the end of the millennium and up to that stage there had been no floods, famine, storms or anything of note over the ten year period. They were all anticipating doom before the year end that marked the end of the decade. We all listened to the story with interest and scepticism at the hold that the belief was having on them.

After the usual check in we flopped onto our beds for a short shuteye before dinner and our one nights sleep over the three-day period. I dropped off to a deep sleep but to my amazement I woke only a short time later. I got up wondering what had woken me and was aware of an excessive amount of wind noise. With my eyes still a bit sleepy I went out of my room and into the passage. The windows in the passage were set above my normal line of sight, but as I looked out I could see the high palm trees gyrating madly in the wind

I walked down the passage and met Peter who said that he had also woken unaccountably early. I said that I thought that the wind was a bit strong but he dismissed it completely. We walked to the dining area and the adjoining swimming pool, which was the closest open area, and opened the sliding door. Although it was certainly blowing hard it was not more than a good gale and I was sure that it had subsided dramatically even in the short time that we had been awake.

We walked towards the reception, heading for the entrance doors, when they burst open and one of the Arabs shouted.

"*Catastroph, carastroph*," and as he saw us he said "you must come to the airport now, big *catastroph*." His level of insistence left us no option and he led us to the waiting bus.

As we turned left onto the airport road, the signs of a gale were evident but as we got closer to the airport the devastation became clear, reaching a climax as the whole airport came into view.

Looking along the road there was a clear path of severe destruction heading through the military side of the airport. It looked like some giant lawnmower had been driven through, leaving a path of devastation behind. Although there was obvious damage to the civil side it was much less dramatic. We drove down the road and saw that the 707 was no longer in the centre of the tarmac where it had been left. It had, as always, been chocked with the huge, rubber, Boeing chocks in the centre of each bogie. For the aircraft to move the wheels would have to climb over the chocks to move either back or forwards. We were astounded.

As the bus drove up to the gate we saw a huge piece of the concrete wall lying on the ground. Looking further along the wall there were other pieces of concrete wall on the yellow desert sand, leaving huge gaping holes in the almost three metre reinforced concrete wall. Once inside, fully-grown trees lay next to holes in the ground that, in the immediate past, had recently held them firmly in place. Huge military helicopters lay on their sides and some were fully inverted and lying on their smashed rotor blades. A Hercules was sitting on the desert sand where it had been deposited by the gale. A number of individuals were desperately trying to move the four-engined transport aircraft back onto the hard standing.

Moved up against the stairs

Our hearts nearly stopped when we approached our Boeing. She had been driven forward over the chocks and into the mobile stairs. Once out of the bus we looked at the damage trying to read all the telltale clues. The nosewheel had been lifted up, clear of the ground, and moved sideways more than two metres. The scuff marks showed the point where the nosewheel lifted clear of the tarmac. There were no other marks until the nose gear touched again leaving telltale scuffing. The aircraft's movement had been halted by the mobile staircase that had become wedged between the engine housing and the tarmac to such an extent that it had embedded itself in the tar.

Realising that the stairs had saved the day for us we set about rectifying the scene. Without them to stop it, the aircraft would have ended up in the soft sand. It would have been impossible to move it without special lifting equipment, and would probably have ended its days there just like others that I have heard about in Africa.

Once she had been given a thorough check over, the only concern was that of a small, sharp dent in the intake cowl. We all returned to the hotel with our thoughts to wile the night away.

The next morning we fuelled up and prepared to depart. Our takeoff was a bit apprehensive, as there was no way of determining what the effect of the dent would be on the airflow into the engine. I had visions of the disrupted airflow doing a multitude of nasty things to the flow through the engine, but time would tell. As we trundled down the runway our ears were fine-tuned to any hint of abnormality. In fact our concern was unfounded, she accelerated and leapt into the air without any problem. The flight back was otherwise uneventful, and we had a relaxed serene flight back to Pietersburg.

As the number of trips mounted up the over-flight clearances were becoming an increased financial burden and a matter of concern. Back at the office at Rand Airport I walked in on a discussion about the fees.

"If the fees are so high, why not fly up through Angola and across the ocean as far as possible and avoid some countries?" I suggested to Peter.

Nothing much happened and without much further comment I went about my chores. Soon I was called back in to explain my thoughts and discuss the question further. After plotting a route on the maps, in essence the ocean route should take 10 or 15 minutes more but would save some thousands of US Dollars in fees. The true test of whether the extra time would cover the saving in fees would only come out once we had tried out the new route.

I sat down with Paul, who had flown passenger 707's for South African Airways, and pushed around a few figures. Peter soon agreed that we would try the new route on the next trip to Algeria. He would apply for the clearances based on the new route, and the rest would be in the hands of fate. The crew waited impatiently for the next flight, we all wondered how it would work out.

The day arrived and at midnight, as usual, we braced ourselves for start-up clearance. As the glorious bird climbed into the black night above, carrying her precious ten tons of cargo, our individual thoughts and expectations kept us alert. Very soon the first benefit crept into our lives in the cockpit. We had underestimated the effect of the reduced traffic on the new route. As we steadily climbed up to our cruise height we were subjected almost no interruptions in our climb. In time this would turn the ability of the flight around significantly.

In the past our climbs had been regularly halted for periods to let the passenger aircraft through with their higher authority. Now, without those interruptions we were able to climb continuously to our cruising height. Another benefit emerged in the next few hours. In the early hours of the morning we had been accustomed to the turbulence advertising the Intertropical Convergence Zone where the Northern and Southern weather conditions combine. Using the new route there was almost no disturbance. I presumed that the ocean below was responsible for the clear air, but many authorities tell me that it is not the case. In any event each flight over the sea was characterised as being free of the dreadful lightning and turbulence that we had experienced in the past over the land mass. The ability to climb, and fly smoothly, without interruptions, soon showed its benefits. The route was proclaimed a great success.

Flight by flight we extended our capability, making the flight easier and enabling us to offer more to our client. By the time that we had run out of improvements we were climbing up to 41 000 feet as a matter of course. The extra altitude increased the efficiency of the jet and enabled us to achieve a fuel saving of 5 tons during each flight. Our initial consumption on the heavy climb of 10 tons per hour would reduce during the flight to just over 4 tons in the last hour, quite amazing.

We got into a routine, relying on the long flight each 3 to 4 weeks and gradually improving the condition of the aircraft. The client no longer wanted us to transport passengers due to the unrealistic clauses that insurance companies thrust on individuals regarding flying. Their place had been taken up with extra cargo in any event and we had a good business going and we looked forward to the next flight each time.

The next series of flights were very successful using the ocean route and I thoroughly enjoyed them. A vivid memory of the first flight on the new route comes to mind as I write this book. In the total blackness of night, just as we crossed the Angolan coast leaving the land behind us, some of the clouds began to take on a new hue. We became aware of a series of a number of places in the low cloud carpet under us that had transformed into a strange orange colour. We peered out the windows at the glowing patches passing far below us. Looking directly below it was clear that the light, seemingly radiating from the surface of the ocean, was being diffused in the clouds making the huge glowing areas. They were even larger than the illuminated areas around the towns we were used to seeing as we flew over. We soon discovered that they were in fact caused by the multitude of flames of oil wells burning off their waste gas.

Flying over the same area on the return journey the flames were barely discernible but almost invariably we would meet huge clouds as we crossed the coastline. At our cruising altitude of just over 40 thousand feet, the huge anvils of the storm clouds often towered above us. We were at the height where the tops of the fluffy storm clouds are pulled sideways to form the anvils that characterise the Cumulo Nimbus clouds. Peter used to refer to crocodiles in the sky and until I saw them I did not fully appreciate why. At our height we were at the level of the anvils, and sometimes they even towered above us. Looking straight at them, the anvils were drawn to one side of each cloud, making them often look like great white crocodiles suspended in the sky around us. I was amazed at the shapes in the sky around us and of course they were all basking in the bright sunlight undiluted by smog and cloud.

Those were really the last few recollections before things went a bit sour. Peter had been having on-going negotiations with the client who expressed an interested in his outfit. Only interested in the lion's share for himself, Peter dug in his heels and I could see disaster on the horizon. No amount of discussion and reasoning could persuade him otherwise and I sensed that we would lose the client.

In between flights I had been with him on the on-going quest for business. Even though we had the regular flights we needed to pick up another major client to spread the load and give us a loophole if the existing status changed. Try as we could we only gained the occasional single flights and I became a trifle concerned about the future.

Taking it all into account I was losing faith in the future that had been so bright in the past. There were a number of issues that added to my diminishing confidence in the organisation and I had to look at self-survival. My mind wandered back to the flights when we took up passengers. I recalled a particular discussion that I had had on an one of the first 707 flights. This chap had been enquiring about my career and we had been talking about my previous involvement with technical documentation. He said that if ever I was interested he could well do with someone to edit their manuals for them.

Suddenly it all made sense. I must contact them. I could not remember his name, and scarcely enough to describe him well. After a bit of application I remembered one of the passenger's names. Taking a shot in the dark I spoke to him and tried my best to describe the other chap. It was not long before I made direct contact and had an appointment set up.

I will not forget the meeting. He listened, asked a few questions and it all went quiet. He then offered me a cup of coffee and told me to wait there. he returned with an offer, asking me to start immediately. I went back to Peter, handed in my resignation with my reasons and he was somewhat disappointed to say the least.

I started at the new company, at a desk, a new experience once again. Much as I had feared, Tradewinds continued the downward slide and it was with extreme sadness and surprise that I heard that Peter had suffered a huge heart attack at a meeting and had succumbed later that night.

One of the middle-aged pilots took over command of the next 707 flight in preference to Paul who he argued was too old. Even though he was over 60 his licence was valid and he had buckets of 707 experience. On arrival at the destination they were warned of high cross winds and they presumably came in on a cautious approach. Despite Paul's experience he had to sit as a co-pilot while the self-appointed captain executed a really hard landing. So much so, that even the tower commented on it.

It transpired that he had damaged the so-called walking beam that moves the undercarriage leg. The large aluminium strut holds it in the locked down position and therefore takes care of the side loading on the leg.

They flew back and carried out another flight to Tanzania without mishap. On their return to Johannesburg however their luck ran out. The approach was going well until the engineer selected undercarriage down. Almost immediately he reported a loss of hydraulic pressure, and a sudden loss of hydraulic fluid. Luck was on their side as the gear was locked and they had some flap down. They landed and used the single shot emergency brake to stop the 'craft, and at least they were all safe.

The cracked walking beam had fractured as the gear was selected, and to their embarrassment had torn the accumulator loose so that it dropped into an industrial premises on the outskirts of the airport. The offending article was given to the Civil Aviation Authority who promptly grounded the aircraft, dramatically ending Tradewinds, the exploits of Peter's dream.

Ironically, the aircraft stood in the place where we had started the repairs until the damage was repaired. Subsequently she was sold and I was approached to spray on new registration over a weekend. I accepted, based on being paid when I started the job and not waiting forever as so often happened. My brother and my two sons were roped in to help and the four of us started work.

It was a strange feeling doing the job. Using the same equipment, on the same piece of grass, I painted on the new registration and I could not but reflect on the happy times spent since that time. The new registration signalled the end of it all and in fact the end of my commercial flying career.

Commercial flying had given me the most wonderful time that will always be cherished. I was very fortunate in having such a collection of wonderful, stimulating memories that will remain forever. I feel that I have been so very privileged to have experienced a number of the world's top aircraft.

I hope that my readers share the joy that flying has given me over all the years. My only regret is that I had not considered it seriously as a career all those years ago with Nick.

Chapter 43

Sitting on the edge of a plateau I looked over the most incredible vista some 2000 feet below me and I started thinking.

It is Father's day, 17th June 2001, and Jane has treated me to a peaceful weekend at a luxurious resort on the edge of the highveldt escarpment. Away from home, with nothing to do but relax in the peaceful surroundings. Far below the national road was visible winding its way past the dams of Millies Trout Farm, a regular stop on the way to the Kruger Park. The town of Machadadorp peeked out from behind a hill, asking not to be missed, as motorists do driving on the main road.

The view was unrivalled except to pilots who look at similar views each time they fly. Today, however was different. I was not moving, and so I did not have to concern myself over the usual factors like fuel status, weather, position, and other things that fill a pilot's head while they go about their tasks. Feeling as if I was in an aircraft, I looked down at the magnificent vista and my thoughts drifted back to the past week and then even further. The previous week had been frantically spent getting the last minor jobs done to complete Tiggy's rebuild. Only two days earlier I had witnessed her test flight, and with emotions welling up I watched her break ground in Bobby's capable hands.

2001 marked a number of important milestones. It was year number 1 in the new millennium. It had just been my eldest son Courtney's 21st birthday, it was 35 years earlier that I went solo in Tiggy for the first time and 60 years since her construction. A great year all round.

Looking down on the world below, thinking about those events gave me a huge feeling that the proverbial wheel had turned a full circle. The Strecker family had also been instrumental in that rebuild, helping out with advice and providing spares. Just like the car accident at the time of the first rebuild, I had been through a recent incident, having been thrown off a horse at full tilt. Also I was probably going to let my Commercial Licence lapse and revert to a Private Pilots Licence, just like I had all those years ago

Rather ironically the story started with me getting my PPL, progressed through the Tiger rebuild, through my subsequent car accident, my flying career, through another accident ending up at the second rebuild of Tiggy and back to a private pilot licence where it all started. I could not help wondering what was in store on the next turn of the wheel.

Getting her in the air again had gone well. Once she was ready and after much deliberation I asked my good friend Bob to do the test flight for me as I was not current on Tigers. Outside the Strecker hangar she greeted the sunshine proudly and waited for her test flight. As the Streckers got her going, I walked to a vantage point closer to the runway and she soon taxied past me with the characteristic Tiger exhaust note. What a wonderful feeling, standing under the wing of a DC4 with my family, looking towards the runway and seeing her take to the air again so gracefully. We watched Bob do some upper air work as he checked out her flying characteristics and came in for a landing. I could not believe that my baby was flying again. I felt a great feeling of warmth as we watched her taxi up in all her dignity.

A few days later the time came for me to take her home to Baragwanath. Again with my whole family around I settled into the once familiar cockpit and was amazed at how small and tight it was after all the other machines that I had flown. Being the middle of winter I was trussed up against the cold as I tried in vain to do up the seatbelts. I could not get them to fit with all the thick clothing and I got my boys to push me into the seat so that I could get the belts done up.

Courtney muttered something about middle age spread which was not particularly well received. It conjured up a vision of an old man trying to get into a suit too small for him. The only problem was that it was now an aircraft that was too small! Dismissing the images and with a final push from the lads, I was able to get the clip in place and was ready for action.

With my family cheering me on, and hardly able to breathe, I taxied out to the runway, lined up and took off. Flying her, again re-united, was a wonderful feeling and I progressed Westwards. As I approached Bara I reminded myself to exercise utmost care in a newly commissioned machine, and a little out of practice myself. I opted for the easy way and carried out a wheel landing and taxied off the runway. Surprised at how effortless it had been I breathed a sigh of relief as the seatbelts dropped off my shoulders, and taxied up to the hangar, bursting with pride.

Courtney had got his flying licence and was at home flying the syndicate Cessna 150, and Patrick was not far behind, progressing with his Private Pilots Licence. It was wonderful as the both drove up with Jane and we pushed her to bed in her new home.

The following weekend I took Patrick up in her for the first time. Courtney had been in her before she was stripped but being so much smaller, Pat had never had a go. By the end of the weekend the whole family was flown out and high on the emotions of it all and we had to resume the normality of the week. On the next weekend we organised a party for her, complete with a cake. Both the Stinson and the 150 were there, and we put up a bit of formation flying with the 150 and Bob's Tiger.

Suffice to say that earmarked the wheel nearing its full rotation. In the four years since then we have three competent Tiger pilots in the family. Both my sons absolutely love Tiggy and in fact I have to stand my place in the queue. My sons and I have have attended a few events and even got an EAA prize for the rebuild. Courtney is a competent teacher and a confirmed recreational pilot. Patrick on the other hand has been totally dedicated to flying as a career. I encouraged him to assist loading the aircraft on their flights to North Africa and as a result he gained a knowledge of the aircraft as well as knowing some of the personnel. Things have worked out well and over a period he has grown in ability and has been taken on by the company, initially to help their maintenance crew on a contractual basis. He then had a stab at Flight Operations and is now fully employed as co-pilot on the 20 seater Grumman Gulfstream. He is as happy as the proverbial tick and gets withdrawal symptoms when he has not flown for some time.

Jane and I are terribly proud of the two boys and their achievements. After all it is all up to the up and coming generations. They must add their memories and experiences to this saga to be able to turn the wheel the next rotation and write the next part of the story themselves.

www.ingramcontent.com/pod-product-compliance
Ingram Content Group UK Ltd.
Pitfield, Milton Keynes, MK11 3LW, UK
UKHW021317180426
11947UKWH00015B/1288